CONTENTS

C   Actions and states: verbs and their uses

Italian
Grammar

HANDBOOK

Derek Aust

Italian Grammar Handbook

The Author:

Derek Aust is an experienced teacher and examiner.

The Series Editor:

Christopher Wightwick is a former UK representative on the Council of Europe Modern Languages Project and principal Inspector of Modern Languages for England.

Other titles in the Berlitz Language Handbook Series:

French Grammar Handbook
German Grammar Handbook
Spanish Grammar Handbook
French Vocabulary Handbook
German Vocabulary Handbook
Spanish Vocabulary Handbook
Italian Vocabulary Handbook

French Verb Handbook
German Verb Handbook
Spanish Verb Handbook
Italian Verb Handbook

Author's acknowledgement
I would like to thank Daniela Becchio and colleagues at South Devon College for reading through a number of the chapters and for their comments and suggestions. A very big thankyou to my wife Vasilija for her help with the proof-reading and for her great patience, support and encouragement during the writing of this book.

Published by Berlitz Publishing Co., Ltd.,
Peterley Road, Oxford OX4 2TX

1st printing 1994

Printed in England by Clays Ltd, St Ives plc

D   People, things and ideas: nouns and noun phrases

How to use this handbook

This *Grammar Handbook* can be used in two ways.

• If you want to get a general picture of some aspects of Italian grammar, start with the introductory list of Contents. You can then read through the relevant sections of the text. The many cross-references will lead you to other, related topics.

• If you want to find out more about a specific grammatical point or about the use of particular Italian words or expressions, consult the extensive *Index* at the end of the book. The *Index* has many sub-headings, and in addition items are frequently referenced under more than one heading. The *Index* will point you to individual paragraph numbers.

The *Handbook* gives a great deal of information about grammatical forms and structures, but above all is designed to show how they fit in with what you want to say or write.

• Grammatical terms are treated as convenient labels and used whenever necessary, but the *Handbook* does not assume that you already know what they mean. All the sections of this book include explanations of grammatical terms.

• A key feature is the number of examples, drawn from a wide stock of Italian in current use. Wherever it makes sense to do so, these examples are linked together into a short dialogue, topic or narrative. If you do not understand a grammatical explanation, the example will help you to recognize the feature.

• This *Handbook* is intended for people who want to use their Italian. Where constructions are used only in formal contexts, this is made clear in the text.

 Finally, as a safety net, there are special warning sections wherever you see this sign, to help you avoid the more obvious traps and pitfalls.

A

PUTTING IDEAS INTO WORDS

1 Classes of words: parts of speech

1a What kind of word is it?

It is often impossible to say what class a word belongs to (what *part of speech* it is) until it is used in a sentence. On the other hand, understanding a sentence may well depend on knowing what part of speech a word is, so it is useful to be able to recognize grammatical classifications. In this *Handbook* we define each part of speech mainly by what it does - what it refers to and its function and position in a sentence. If you can also recognize it by its form, for example from its endings, then this is described as well.

The following paragraphs will refer briefly to the main classes of words, give their English and Italian names, some examples, and references to the paragraphs of the book where they are first defined.

1b Content words

Four classes of word (the *content words*) contain most of the meaning of the sentence.

(i) *Verbs* (**i verbi**)

Quest'estate *spero* di andare in Italia. *Penso* di andare a giugno. *Voglio* fare un giro della Toscana.	This summer I *hope* to go to Italy. I *am thinking* of going in June. I *want* to do a tour of Tuscany.

[For more on verbs ➤7-19.]

(ii) *Nouns* (**i sostantivi**)

Durante il mio *soggiorno* vorrei visitare molti *musei, castelli,* e *chiese*.	During my *stay* I would like to visit lots of *museums, castles* and *churches*.

[For more on nouns ➤20.]

(iii)   Adjectives (gli aggettivi)

Preferisco una vacanza *culturale* e mi piace visitare i monumenti *storici* e le chiese *antiche*. Per me, questa è la vacanza *ideale*.	I prefer a *cultural* holiday and I like to visit *historical* monuments and *ancient* churches. For me, this is the *ideal* holiday.

[For more on adjectives ➤22.]

(iv)   Adverbs (gli avverbi)

Alcuni miei amici vanno *spesso* in questa regione e mi dicono *sempre* che è *veramente* interessante.	Some of my friends *often* go to this area and they are *always* telling me that it is *very* interesting.

[For more on adverbs ➤26.]

1c   Structure words

Structure words do of course add to the meaning, but they do it mainly by the way they relate to the content words.

(i)   Auxiliary verbs (i verbi ausiliari)

The verbs **avere** and **essere** are used with other verbs to create a range of compound tenses.

***Sono* stato in Italia tre volte. L'ultima volta, a Pasqua, *ho* trascorso due giorni in Sardegna.**	I *have* been to Italy three times. The last time, at Easter, I spent two days in Sardinia.

[For more on auxiliary verbs ➤7c.]

(ii)   Pronouns (i pronomi)

Pronouns take the place of nouns, often to avoid unnecessary repetition.

Ho parecchi amici italiani. Purtroppo, non *li* **vedo molto spesso. Per restare in contatto, scrivo** *loro* **oppure telefono** *loro* **ogni tanto. Forse alcuni verranno a trovar***mi* **a Natale.**	I have several Italian friends. Unfortunately, I do not see *them* very often. To stay in touch, I write *to them* or telephone *them* every now and then. Perhaps some of them will come and see *me* at Christmas.

[For more on pronouns ➤23.]

(iii)   Determiners (i determinativi)

Determiners include some of the most common words in any language, such as the possessives (**il mio, la mia, i miei, le mie,** etc.), the demonstratives (**questo, quello**), and indefinites (**alcuni, pochi**).

I miei **amici di Cuneo verranno in Inghilterra per** *alcuni* **mesi per fare un corso d'inglese.**	*My* friends from Cuneo will be coming to England for *a few* months to do an English course.

[For more on determiners ➤21.]

(iv)   Prepositions (le preposizioni)

Prepositions are connecting words placed in front of nouns or their equivalent. They include words like **con** 'with'; **su** 'on'; **prima di** 'before'; **in** 'in'.

Verranno *in* **aereo. Purtroppo, non li potrò vedere** *prima della* **mia partenza per l'Italia.**	They will be coming *by* plane. Unfortunately, I shall not be able to see them *before* my departure for Italy.

[For more on prepositions ➤25.]

(v)   Conjunctions (le congiunzioni)

Conjunctions are used to join sentences, phrases or words. Some of the most frequently used conjunctions are **e** 'and'; **ma** 'but'; **quando** 'when'; **perché** 'because'.

Li potrò vedere *quando* tornerò dalle vacanze *perché* si fermano per due mesi.	I shall see them *when* I get back from holiday/vacation *because* they are staying for two months.

[For more on conjunctions ➤5a.]

(vi) *Exclamations* (gli esclamativi)

Exclamations express sudden emotions - surprise, relief, joy - in reaction to a situation. For example: **Che bello! Che peccato! Bravo!**

Che peccato che io non ci sia quando arrivano!	*What a pity* that I am not here when they arrive!

[For more on exclamations ➤24.]

Getting it down on paper: spelling and punctuation

This chapter describes the basic features of Italian spelling and punctuation. It does not deal directly with pronunciation, as attempts to describe sounds on paper are more likely to be a hindrance than a help.

2a   The Italian alphabet

(i)   There are 21 letters in the Italian alphabet. To these are added **J**, **K**, **W**, **X**, and **Y**, which appear in Italian in words of foreign origin. It is important to know the 26 letters and it is essential to be able to use the Italian alphabet when spelling names and addresses on the telephone, etc. Alongside each letter of the alphabet below is the name of the letter in Italian.

A a	**H** acca	**O** o	**V** vu
B bi	**I** i	**P** pi	**W** vu doppio
C ci	**J** i lungo	**Q** cu	**X** ics
D di	**K** cappa	**R** erre	**Y** ipsilon
E e	**L** elle	**S** esse	**Z** zeta
F effe	**M** emme	**T** ti	
G gi	**N** enne	**U** u	

Some examples of words commonly used in Italian that contain the letters **J**, **K**, **W**, **X**, **Y**:

scarpe da jogging, jazz, judo, kg, km (abbreviations for **chilogrammo** and **chilometro**), **karatè, bikini, walkman, whisky, windsurf, western** (film), **xenofobia, ex presidente, mixer, maxiprocesso** (the letter **x** is rarely used at the beginning of a word), **yacht, yoga, yogurt**.

•   When spelling aloud it is also useful to know the following words:

A maiuscola	capital A
b minuscola	small b

and the expression

Come si scrive?	How is it written?

H as an initial letter is rarely used in Italian. When it is used, for the most part in words of foreign origin, it is nearly always silent. Its use in certain words is to distinguish them from other words similarly pronounced but with entirely different meanings, such as: **ho** 'I have' and **o** 'or', **hai** 'you have' and **ai** 'to the', **ha** 'he/she has' and **a** 'to', **hanno** 'they have' and **anno** 'year'.

• Care should be taken in the pronunciation of double consonants. One should, for example, hear the double **m** in **mamma** (**mam-ma**) and the double **b** in **babbo** (**bab-bo**). This is particularly important in words where failure to stress the double consonant results in a change of meaning, as illustrated by the following examples:

nono	ninth	**sete**	thirst	**sera**	evening
nonno	grandfather	**sette**	seven	**serra**	greenhouse

(ii)   Capital letters

Capital letters are used less often in Italian than in English. Sentences always begin with a capital letter. They are not used in the following cases:

• Days of the week and months of the year [➤30a, 30b]:

giovedì 10 aprile	Thursday, April 10th

• Adjectives of nationality, including names of languages:

Un amico spagnolo.	A Spanish friend.
Mi piace scrivere in italiano.	I like writing in Italian.

It is common practice to use a small letter for nouns denoting nationality:

i tedeschi	the Germans

• Points of the compass:

il nord, **il sud**, **l'ovest**, **l'est**, **il sud-ovest**, etc.

But **il Settentrione** 'the North', **il Mezzogiorno** 'the South', **l'Oriente** 'the East', etc., when the reference is to a geographical area.

PUTTING IDEAS INTO WORDS

- Personal status and profession in titles:

la signora Martini	Mrs Martini
il dottor Gamberini	Doctor Gamberini
il colonnello Becchio	Colonel Becchio

(iii) Stress patterns

It would not be helpful to go into great detail about stress patterns in Italian. This is best acquired through experience of speaking and listening to native speakers of the language. As a general rule, however, the stress falls on the last but one vowel and on the end of the word if marked by an accent.

amico, banca, macelleria, università, benchè

As there are so many exceptions, it makes more sense to learn by using the language. Many dictionaries indicate stress and it would be wise to consult such a dictionary when in doubt. The importance of putting the stress in the right place, however, is best illustrated by the examples quoted below, where a misplaced stress gives rise to another meaning. The stress is underlined in the examples quoted.

l'ancora della nave	the ship's anchor
non è ancora arrivata	she still hasn't arrived
che cosa desideri?	what do you want?
questi sono i miei desideri	these are my wishes
un numero impari	an odd number
così impari	in this way you learn
i principi	the princes
i principi morali	moral principles
lo faccio subito	I'll do it straightaway
ha subito un'operazione	he underwent an operation
gli uccelli volano	birds fly
il gioco del volano	the game of badminton

(iv) Accents

In Italian there are two main accents: the acute accent - **accento acuto**, and the grave accent - **accento grave**. The circumflex is rarely used. Both accents are commonly placed on the final vowel, where they have three main functions:

- On words of two or more syllables, to show that the stress falls on the last syllable:

lunedì andrò, quaggiù, ventitré, cordialità, etc.

- On the following monosyllables:

ciò, già, giù, può, più.

- To distinguish between words that have the same spelling but different meaning:

è	'he/she/it is' (verb)
e	'and' (conjunction)
dà	'he/she/it gives' (verb)
da	'from, by', etc. (preposition)
là	'there' (adverb of place)
la	'the, her' (article, pronoun)
lì	'there' (adverb of place)
li	'them' (pronoun)
né	'nor' (conjunction)
ne	'of it' etc., 'from there' (pronoun, adverb)
sì	'yes' (adverb)
si	'himself, herself', etc., 'one' (pronoun)
sé	'himself, herself', etc., 'oneself' (pronoun)
se	'if, whether' (conjunction)
tè	'tea' (noun)
te	'you' (pronoun)

The acute and grave accents are used as follows:

- acute on closed **e**: **né, sé, perché, poiché, ventitré, vendé** (third person singular past definite of regular **-re** verbs)

- grave on open **e** and, usually, on the other vowels (**caffè, però, perciò, già, più, così**, etc.

If the rules regarding the use of accents were rigidly adhered to, then there should be an acute accent on closed vowels and a grave accent on open vowels. However, modern usage tends to prefer the grave accent, particularly on **à, ò, ù** and **ì**. The grave accent, therefore, will be used on these vowels throughout this Handbook.

2b   Punctuation

(i)   Punctuation marks

The main punctuation marks in Italian are:

.	**punto**	full stop, period
,	**virgola**	comma
;	**punto e virgola**	semi-colon
:	**due punti**	colon
?	**punto interrogativo**	question mark
!	**punto esclamativo**	exclamation mark
–	**trattino/lineetta**	hyphen, dash
<<...>> or "..." or '...'	**virgolette**	inverted commas, quotation marks
( )	**le parentesi tonde**	round brackets
[ ]	**le parentesi quadre**	square brackets
/	**la sbarretta**	bar-line
'	**apostrofo**	apostrophe

(ii)   Quotation marks

Quotation marks (**le virgolette**) are used to report what some-one else has said or to highlight a word or expression used in a particular way, for example metaphorical or ironic. Although three types of quotation marks exist in Italian **le virgolette basse** (<<...>>) are the ones most commonly used in newspapers and books, etc., whereas **le virgolette alte** ("...") are used in handwritten letters. The single inverted comma ('...') is normally used to highlight a particular word or phrase within a sentence.

Cosa intendi dire per la 'riforma' del sistema scolastico?	What do you mean by the 'reform' of the school system?

(iii)   The dash

The dash (**la lineetta/il trattino**) can be used to introduce direct speech. A common use is within the direct speech when reference is made to the speaker.

A differenza degli altri partiti – ha detto il deputato – il nostro ha preso provvedimenti per risolvere il problema.	"Unlike the other parties," said the member of Parliament/Deputy, "ours has taken steps to solve the problem."

(iv) *The hyphen*

The hyphen (**il trattino/la lineetta**) is used in the following cases:

- To separate two numbers:

Bisogna pagare intorno al 5-7 per cento.	You have to pay around 5 to 7 per cent.

- Between two nouns:

la linea Milano-Roma	the Milan-Rome line
il derby Juventus-Torino	the Juventus-Torino derby
i rapporti studenti-professori	student-teacher relationships

- When splitting a word at the end of a line:

simpa- **tico**	nice, pleasant

The word must end the line on a complete syllable. It would be wrong, therefore, to end the line with **simpat-**, as the **t** forms part of the next syllable **-ti**. Never end the line with a double consonant, for example, **intell-igente**. You should always split the double consonant thus: **intel-ligente**.

[For other uses of the hyphen ➤3a(ii).]

(v) *Brackets*

Round brackets (**le parentesi tonde**) are more frequently used than square brackets (**le parentesi quadre**). They serve to introduce into the sentence a comment made by the writer.

Il vantaggio (se qualche vantaggio c'è) sta nel fatto che...	The advantage - if there is some advantage - lies in the fact that ...

These brackets are often replaced by commas or hyphens.

(vi) *The apostrophe*

The main uses of the apostrophe are:

- For elision: *un'amica, l'aeroporto* [➤21e(ii), 21c(iv), (vi)].
- With the imperative forms *da', fa', sta', va', di'* [➤15b].
- With the abbreviated form *un po'* for *un poco* 'a little'.
- When the first two numbers are omitted from the year:

negli anni '80   in the 80s

(vii)   The comma

The use of the comma (**la virgola**) is for the most part the
same as in English. However, in presenting numbers, there
are important differences [►28a(G)].

In Italian a comma is used in decimals where in English there
would be a decimal point or a full stop/period:

L'inflazione è scesa al 4,7%.   Inflation has gone down to 4.7%.

A comma is used with large numbers in English. A full
stop/period (**il punto**) is used in Italian.

100.000 abitanti   100,000 inhabitants

Linking words together

3a *Compound words or phrases?*

All languages need ways of combining word meanings so as to express more complex ideas. This may be done either by joining two words together to form one (occasionally hyphenated) compound word, or by linking separate words to form phrases.

(i) *Compound words without a hyphen*

Italian has a large number of compound words. There are quite a few comprising verb + noun:

l'apribottiglie	bottle-opener
l'apriscatole	tin-opener
l'asciugamano	towel
l'aspirapolvere	vacuum cleaner
il cacciavite	screwdriver
il cavalcavia	fly-over/overpass
il grattacielo	skyscraper
la lavastoviglie	dishwasher
il parabrezza	windscreen/shield
il paraurti	bumper (on vehicle)
il portacenere	ashtray
il portachiavi	keyring
il portafoglio	wallet
il portavoce	spokesperson
il salvagente	lifebelt
lo stuzzicadenti	tooth-pick

• Other combinations include noun + noun, preposition + noun, noun + adjective:

la banconota	bank note	il sottopassaggio	
il capostazione	station master		underpass/subway
il cavolfiore	cauliflower	la cassaforte	safe
i senzatetto	the homeless	la terraferma	mainland

[For the formation of the plurals of compound nouns ➤20h(viii).]

(ii)   Compound words with a hyphen

The hyphen [►2b(iv)] is rarely used with compound words in Italian, but two places where it does occur are as follows:

• Where two nouns are linked together and the second one describes or defines the first:

le vacanze-studio	study holidays/vacation
una notizia-lampo	a news flash
la busta-paga	pay packet

It is difficult to give a hard-and-fast rule as you will certainly come across **busta paga** without the hyphen.

• In compound adjectives such as the following:

socio-economico	socio-economic [►22a(ii)]

3b   Phrases expressing a complex idea

In English the words 'tea' and 'cup' are both nouns, but in the expression 'tea-cup' the noun 'tea' describes 'cup'. The Italian language also makes use of nouns (and the infinitive form of verbs) in this way but the wordings are different. When one noun is used to describe another it generally requires a linking preposition such as **da** or **di**:

un bicchiere da vino*	a wine glass
una bottiglia da vino*	a wine bottle
la carta da lettere	writing paper
una tazza da tè*	a tea-cup
una sala da pranzo	dining-room
una sala da ballo	a dance-hall
una macchina da scrivere	a typewriter
una macchina da cucire	a sewing machine

The **da** in these examples is being used to convey the notion of purpose or function. Thus **un bicchiere da vino** is a glass for the purpose of drinking wine.

Note the distinction in meaning between the examples marked with an asterisk above and the following where the preposition **di** indicates the contents:

un bicchiere di vino	a glass of wine
una bottiglia di vino	a bottle of wine
una tazza di tè	a cup of tea

• **Di** is also generally used to indicate 'made of':

una giacca di cuoio	a leather jacket
un sacchetto di plastica	a plastic bag
un tavolo di legno	a wooden table

•   **Di** or **di** + the definite article [➤21c(vii)] is the most widely used link in noun phrases:

una partita di calcio	a football game/soccer match
una casa di campagna	a country house
una festa di compleanno	a birthday party
la fermata dell'autobus	bus-stop
l'orario dei treni	train timetable
le previsioni del tempo	weather forecast

There are many instances, however, where an adjectival structure is used instead of a noun phrase:

il bollettino meteorologico	weather report
un incidente stradale	a road accident
la stazione ferroviaria	railway/railroad station
la vita familiare	family life

This is only possible of course if the describing noun can be converted into an adjective. Even then, it is still current usage that determines whether the adjective is preferable, or whether **di** + the noun, or either can be used. To attempt, therefore, to provide a rule would in no way be helpful.

3c   *Suffixes*

Suffixes are endings that you add to a word to modify its meaning or sometimes to convert it to another part of speech. Italian uses a large number of them.

(i)   *Making adjectives from nouns*

A descriptive adjective is often formed by adding **-oso** to a noun. It often corresponds to the English suffixes '-y' and '-ous'.

la furia	fury	**sabbioso**	sandy
furioso	furious	**il rumore**	noise
lo spazio	space	**rumoroso**	noisy
spazioso	spacious	**la fama**	fame
la nuvola	cloud	**famoso**	famous
nuvoloso	cloudy	**l'avventura**	adventure
la sabbia	sand	**avventuroso**	adventurous

15

Abito in un quartiere molto rumoroso.	I live in a very noisy area.
Il mio appartamento è abbastanza spazioso.	My flat is quite spacious.

(ii) Making verbs from nouns or adjectives

A number of verbs are formed in Italian by adding the suffixes **-eggiare, -izzare** and **-ificare** to nouns and adjectives:

bianco	white	**nazionalizzare**	nationalize
biancheggiare	whiten	**moderno**	modern
la costa	coast	**modernizzare**	modernize
costeggiare	run along (the side of) the coast	**privato**	private
		privatizzare	privatize
la festa	party, celebration	**il nido**	nest
		nidificare	nest
festeggiare	celebrate	**elettrico**	electrical
l'analisi	analysis	**elettrificare**	electrify
analizzare	analyze	**identico**	identical
nazionale	national	**identificare**	identify

(iii) Diminutives and augmentatives

Italian has a great variety of suffixes which are added to nouns and adjectives to indicate smallness and largeness, but which often also contain other nuances. They normally take their gender according to that of the original noun or, in the case of adjectives, the noun they describe.

(A) One of the most widely used diminutives is **-ino** which indicates both smallness and endearment.

La tua *sorellina* è molto *carina*.	Your *little sister* is very *sweet*.
I miei parenti abitano in un *paesino* in piena campagna.	My relatives live in a *little village* in the heart of the countryside.

(B) Other diminutives are **-etto** and **-ello**.

Hanno una *casetta* vicino al mare.	They have a *little house* (*cottage*) near the sea.

Almeno si può respirare adesso con questo _venticello._	At least you can breathe now with this little breeze.

[For more detail on suffixes with nouns and adjectives ➤20k(i) and 22g(ii). Adverbs are occasionally modified by suffixes ➤26c.]

3d   Prefixes

Italian also uses a considerable number of prefixes, particularly before verbs, nouns and adjectives. Reference will be made to some of these prefixes in the relevant chapters. [For verbs ➤18e; for nouns ➤20k(ii); for adjectives ➤22g(i).]

3e   Side by side: words in apposition

Sometimes we add a phrase immediately after the names of people or things, giving further information about them. This explanatory phrase is said to be _in apposition_ to the name.
In Italian, a noun in apposition is not normally preceded by either the definite article [➤21c] or the indefinite article [➤21e].

Mia sorella, _infermiera_ all'ospedale da più di otto anni, ha deciso di dimettersi.	My sister, _a nurse_ at the hospital for more than eight years, has decided to resign.

B
PUTTING A SENTENCE TOGETHER: SYNTAX

Recognizing sentences

4a   What is a sentence?

A sentence is a spoken or written utterance which has a subject and a predicate. When talking, we often say things which are not sentences (for example exclamations [➤24] or isolated phrases which make perfect sense because we know the context), but in writing we usually try to use complete sentences. The way a sentence is put together is known as its *syntax*.

4b   The subject of a sentence

(i)   What is a subject?

Generally speaking the subject is the word or phrase whose action or state the sentence is describing:

L'*aereo* **parte da Londra alle otto.**	The *plane* leaves London at eight o'clock.

The subject of the sentence is **l'aereo**, and the main verb is **parte**.

In Italian, subject pronouns (**io, tu, lui, lei,** etc.- 'I', 'you', 'he', 'she', etc.) [➤23b(i)] are often not used, since the subject is expressed by the verb ending.

A che ora *devi* **partire di casa per prendere questo aereo?**	At what time *do you have to* leave home to catch this plane?

The impersonal subject 'it' is also often contained in the verb in Italian [➤8g].

Se *piove,* *è* **meglio stare a casa.**	If *it is raining, it is* better to stay at home.

(ii)   Passive sentences

The verb may be used in a form known as *passive* [➤17a], which means that the subject of the verb, instead of doing the action of the verb, becomes the receiver of the action:

La famiglia è stata accolta a braccia aperte dai miei amici italiani.	*The family* was welcomed with open arms by my Italian friends.

The subject of the sentence is **la famiglia** and the verb is **è stata accolta,** which is the passive form of **accogliere.** The welcoming is not done by the subject but by **i miei amici italiani.**

(iii)   Omission of the subject

In command forms [➤15] the subject is nearly always omitted but clearly understood because each form is distinct in itself.

Vieni a trovarmi stasera.	Come and see me this evening.
Stia tranquillo.	Keep calm.

In the first example the main verb is **vieni**, and the subject – understood but not stated – is **tu**. In the second example the verb is **stia**, and the subject – again not stated – is **Lei**.

4c   The predicate of a sentence

The predicate consists of the whole of the rest of the sentence, excluding the subject. It must have at least a main verb, that is, a verb in a tense, usually in the indicative [➤18c]. This verb *agrees* with its subject, that is, its form changes to match the subject. Chapter 7 describes the various types of verb and what they do.

L'aereo arrivò.	The plane arrived.

However, most predicates have more than this bare minimum. Other words and expressions are required to complete the information given about the subject.

L'aereo arrivò a Milano con dieci minuti di ritardo causa vento contrario.	The plane arrived in Milan ten minutes late because of a head wind.

In this case the predicate consists of the verb **arrivò** plus the remainder of the sentence, which is the adverbial expression of place **a Milano** [➤27b(iii)], the expression of time **con dieci minuti di ritardo** [➤27b(i)] and the causal phrase **causa vento contrario**.

Note that the compound preposition for 'because of' is **a causa di** [➤25c(xi)] but **causa** is perfectly acceptable in the above context.

4d   Types of sentence

There are three types of complete sentence:

- statements, which are the basic form;
- direct questions [➤6];
- commands [➤15].

All three must have a main clause; they may also have any number of subordinate clauses.

4e   Main clauses

A main clause is a sentence that can stand by itself, though of course it may not make sense unless you know what the speaker is talking about. The most common word order is subject + verb + object or complement, although other orders are possible in Italian [➤4g], and object pronouns [➤23b(ii), (iii)] precede the verb in most circumstances.

Mio fratello non capiva.	My brother didn't understand.

4f   Subordinate clauses

A subordinate clause is always dependent on a main clause, whose meaning it completes or expands. It is linked to the main clause by one of three types of word:

- a subordinating conjunction [➤5a(ii)];
- a question word [➤6d];
- a relative pronoun [➤23m].

In certain subordinate clauses in Italian, the verb will be in the subjunctive [➤16].
In the following example the main sentence is **Mio fratello non capiva** and the remaining clauses are subordinate to it.

Mio fratello non capiva perché volevo andare a vivere in un posto che dista cinquanta chilometri dalla città più vicina e dove non c'è niente da fare..	My brother didn't understand why I wanted to go and live in a place which is fifty kilometres/kilometers from the nearest town and where there is nothing to do.

4g The order of words

Word order is very fluid in Italian and is often varied according to the word or part of the sentence that the speaker wishes to emphasize. The following can therefore only be guidelines: there are no hard-and-fast rules.

(i) Subject + verb + object + adverbials

This order gives a neutral statement, with no particular emphasis on any element. Adverbials of time tend to come before those of place, although this may also depend on the emphasis the speaker intends.

Mio fratello ha un appartamento in città.	My brother has a flat/apartment in the town.

(ii) Verb + subject

However, the subject often follows the verb for reasons of emphasis.

È piccolo *il suo appartamento*. Ha detto *mio fratello* che è comodo per i negozi.	*His flat/apartment* is small. *My brother* said that it's convenient for the shops/stores.

(iii)

Any element of the sentence which needs to be highlighted may be brought forward to the beginning of the sentence, including the direct or indirect object, which then has to be duplicated by the redundant object pronoun [➤23b(vi)].

Questo appartamento l'ha comprato due anni fa. *L'anno scorso* pensava di vender*lo*.	He bought *this flat/apartment* two years ago. *Last year* he was thinking of selling it.

(iv)   *Adverbials*

Adverbials [➤27c] tend to be placed immediately before or after the verb they qualify, but the order may be changed to shift the emphasis.

***Due anni fa* mio fratello ha comprato questo appartamento.** **Mio fratello ha comprato questo appartamento *due anni fa*.** **Mio fratello ha comprato *due anni fa* questo appartamento.**	*Two years ago* my brother bought this flat/apartment.

It is particularly in the final example that more emphasis is being placed on **due anni fa** so that it was 'two years ago' and not 'three' for example. The importance of position is much more clearly highlighted in the spoken language through intonation and the tendency to pause at significant moments in the sentence.

(v)   *Questions*

In questions without a question word, the order is often verb + object + subject.

Ha comprato un appartamento tuo fratello?	Has your brother bought a flat/apartment?

Here again, no hard-and-fast rule applies and it would be perfectly acceptable to put the subject, **tuo fratello**, before the verb. As previously explained, however, the change in word order can result in a shift of emphasis. In questions where the subject is contained in the verb the word order is often the same as in English.

Perché ha deciso di comprare un appartamento in città?	Why did he decide to buy a flat/apartment in the town?

With **essere** 'to be', the complement – here **bello** – is often put before the subject.

È bello l'appartamento?	Is the flat/apartment nice?

The word order for both questions and statements can be the same:

È contento di abitare da solo?   Is he happy to live on his own?
È contento di abitare da solo.   He is happy to live on his own.

In speech the intonation indicates the difference between a question and a statement, whereas in writing the punctuation marks the difference.

[For word order with: adjectives ➤22b(i-iv); object pronouns ➤23b(v); exclamations ➤24a.]

Linking clauses together

5a   *Clauses with conjunctions*

Conjunction means 'joining'. There are two sorts of conjunction, *coordinating* and *subordinating*. Their names reflect their function in the sentence.

(i)   *Coordinating conjunctions*

Coordinating conjunctions link clauses of equal status: main with main, subordinate with subordinate. They tell us something about how the clauses' meanings relate to each other (reinforcing, contrasting, etc.), but they do not change the clause structure at all.

These are the common coordinating conjunctions:

e	and
anche	also, too
eppure	and yet
o/oppure	or
ma	but
però	however
infatti	in fact
dunque/perciò	so, therefore
sia ... sia	both ... and; whether ... or
o ... o	either ... or
non solo ... ma anche	not only ... but also
né ... né	neither ... nor

L'appartamento di mio fratello è bello *e* comodo.	My brother's flat/apartment is nice *and* convenient.
C'è *anche* una terrazza.	There's *also* a terrace.
Andrò a vederlo oggi *o* domani	I shall go and see it today *or* tomorrow.
Mi piace l'appartamento *ma* non mi piace il quartiere.	I like the flat/apartment *but* I don't like the area.

Infatti, non mi piace *né* il
quartiere *né* i suoi vicini.
È un quartiere *non solo* sporco
ma anche molto rumoroso.

In fact, I like *neither* the area *nor*
his neighbours/neighbors.
It's *not only* a dirty area *but also*
very noisy.

Ed is frequently used in place of **e** when the following word begins with a vowel.

Mio fratello *ed* io ci vediamo
ogni settimana.

My brother *and* I see each other
every week.

(ii) *Subordinating conjunctions*

Subordinating conjunctions here link subordinate clauses to the rest of the sentence. Usually the subordinate clause is the equivalent of an adverbial expression [►26]. Many subordinating conjunctions are followed by the subjunctive in Italian [►16], others by an indicative form of the verb [►12-14].

Quando vado a trovare mio
fratello preferisco prendere
l'autobus perché è sempre
difficile parcheggiare la
macchina in città.

When I go to see my brother I
prefer to take the bus because it's
always difficult to park the car in
town.

The subordinating conjunctions here are **quando** and **perché**, both followed by the present indicative **vado** and **è**.

Benché l'appartamento sia
piccolo, mio fratello invita
spesso i suoi amici a cena.

Although the flat/apartment is
small, my brother often invites his
friends to dinner.

The subordinating conjunction is **benché**, followed in present tense structures by the subjunctive, in this case **sia**.

(iii)

In the following list of frequently-used subordinating conjunctions, those which normally require a subjunctive are followed by (**S**):

a condizione che (S)   on condition that
affinché (S)   in order that

a meno che (S)	unless
anche se	even if
appena	as soon as
benché (S)	although
caso mai (S)	should
chiunque (S)	whoever
come	as
come se (S)	as if
comunque (S)	however, in whatever way
da quando	since
dato che	given that
dovunque (S)	wherever
dopo che	after
finché	until
in modo/maniera che (S)	so that
in modo/maniera che	with the result that
malgrado (che) (S)	despite the fact that
man mano che	(progressively) as
mentre	while
nel caso che (S)	in the event that
nonostante (che) (S)	despite the fact that
ogni volta che	every time that
ovunque (S)	wherever
perché	because
perché (S)	in order that
per quanto (S)	however
poiché	seeing as, since
prima che (S)	before
purché (S)	provided that
qualunque cosa (S)	whatever
che	that
quando	when
se	if
sebbene (S)	although
sempre che (S)	provided that, as long as
senza che (S)	without
siccome	as, since
sino a che	until
una volta che	once
visto che	seeing that

It is important to remember that some of these words also exist in similar forms as prepositions [➤25]. The essential difference is that a preposition is followed by a noun, or something which has the value of a noun, such as a pronoun, or an infinitive; a subordinating conjunction is followed by a complete clause. The following examples illustrate the difference:

senza il biglietto	without the ticket (preposition + noun)
senza di me	without me (preposition + pronoun)
senza sapere	without knowing (preposition + infinitive)
senza che lo sappiano	without them knowing (subordinating conjunction + subjunctive)

[For more details on prepositions ➤25; on subjunctives ➤16]

5b   *Relative clauses*

Relative clauses are introduced by relative pronouns [➤23m]. They describe or define a noun and thus do much the same job as an adjective [➤22]. The relative clause comes very soon (usually immediately) after the noun it refers to, for which reason the noun is known as the *antecedent*. When **che** is the object of the relative clause, the subject often follows the verb.

L'appartamento che ha comprato *mio fratello* **non era molto caro.**   The flat/apartment that *my brother* bought was not very expensive.

 When a preposition precedes a relative pronoun in Italian **che** cannot be used and must be replaced by **cui** or the appropriate form of **il quale, la quale,** etc. [➤23m(iv), (vi)].

L'appartamento *in cui* **abito io non mi è costato molto.**   The flat/apartment (*that*) I live *in* didn't cost me a lot.

 In Italian it is not possible to place the preposition at the end of the clause, as is frequently done in English. It is also fairly common practice to omit the relative pronoun in English whereas in Italian this is not done.

5c   *Direct and indirect speech*

There are two ways of reporting what people have said (or perhaps thought). Both are introduced by verbs like **dire** 'say', **rispondere** 'answer', **affermare** 'state', **pensare** 'think' and **credere** 'believe'. What is said is, in fact, the direct object of this verb [►8d] - it answers the question **Cos'ha detto X?** 'What did X say?'.

(i) *Direct speech*

The first way is simply to repeat word for word what was said or thought. This is called *direct speech*, and in English it is marked by the use of quotation marks or inverted commas. Italian punctuation is somewhat different [►2b]. The subject and 'reporting' verb are always inverted when they follow the words spoken.

- Ho sempre voluto comprare un appartamento in città - ha detto mio fratello.	"I've always wanted to buy a flat/apartment in the town," said my brother.

(ii) *Indirect speech*

The second way is known as *indirect speech* or *reported speech*. What was said is rephrased, usually in a clause introduced by **che** 'that' or a question word [►6d]. You cannot omit **che** in Italian as you can 'that' in English.

Mio fratello ha detto *che* aveva sempre voluto comprare un appartamento in città.	My brother said (*that*) he had always wanted to buy a flat/apartment in the town.

(iii) As you can see direct speech undergoes certain changes when it is reported in this way.

(**A**) The part of the verb and any pronouns present are changed so that they still refer to the right person (here from the first person - **io** - to the third person - **lui**).
(**B**) Verb tenses are changed, usually as in English, so that in the above example the perfect is changed to the pluperfect.
The following table shows how tenses change from direct to indirect speech, when the speech is subsequently reported:

Direct speech	*Indirect speech*
present tense	imperfect tense
perfect tense	pluperfect tense
future tense	conditional tense

- **Sono da Claudio. Ho lasciato qualcosa da mangiare nel frigorifero. Tornerò fra un'ora.**	"I am at Claudio's. I have left something to eat in the refrigerator. I shall be back in an hour."

becomes

Ha detto che era da Claudio. Aveva lasciato qualcosa da mangiare nel frigorifereo. Sarebbe tornato fra un'ora.	He said he was at Claudio's. He had left something to eat in the refrigerator. He would be back in an hour.

5d   Indirect questions

Indirect questions are a form of indirect speech [➤5c]. They obey the same rules and are introduced by the same types of verb, followed by the relevant question word. Indirect questions are used for various purposes:

(i)   To report a direct question that has been or will be asked

Ho domandato dove erano andati in vacanza. Domanderò dove vanno in vacanza.	I asked where they had gone on holiday/vacation. I shall ask where they are going on holiday/vacation.

(ii)   To ask more courteously

Potreste dirmi dove andate esattamente?	Could you tell me where you are going exactly?

(iii)   To say whether we know the answer to a question

Non so se porteranno con loro il cane.	I don't know whether they are going to take the dog with them.

[For the use of the subjunctive in indirect questions ➤16c(v).]

5e   *Reported requests and commands*

These can often be dealt with in Italian by a construction with the infinitive [➤8j(ii)C].

Gli ho detto di chiudere tutto a chiave.	I told him to lock everything up.

Asking for information: direct questions

6a *What is a direct question?*

A direct question is a form of direct speech. It tells us word for word what the person said or thought. The questions in the examples below are all direct questions – these are the actual words used, expecting a direct answer. But we often also talk about questions which have been or are going to be asked. These are indirect questions, which are discussed in paragraph 5d.

6b *True or false? Yes/No questions*

In this type of question we are asking whether something is true or not, so it is always possible to answer 'Yes' or 'No'. The subject and verb are often inverted in this type of question. See the section on word order [➤4g] for more detailed observations.

Abita in città *tuo fratello*? – Sì.	*Does your brother live* in town? – Yes.
È bello *il quartiere*? – **No.**	*Is the area* nice? – No.

6c *Checking up: tag questions*

Tag questions are statements with a question tag added to the end which asks for confirmation of the statement. English has a wide variety of tags such as 'isn't it?', 'didn't they?', 'aren't we?', etc. In Italian the usual all-purpose one is **vero?** In speech, **no** is often used after a positive statement.

Trovare un appartamento in città è difficile, *vero*?	To find a flat/apartment in the town is difficult, *isn't it*?
È stato fortunato, *no*?	He was lucky, *wasn't he*?

6d   Asking for details: question-word questions

We use these questions when we want to find out more about
something we already know. The questions always start with
a question-word, such as those listed below.

Many of the question words listed here are the same as or closely
related to relative pronouns [➤23m] or conjunctions [➤5a(ii), (iii)].
Do not confuse them!

(i)   People: **Chi? Di chi?** Who(m)? Whose?

Chi viene al cinema con me?	*Who* is coming to the cinema with me?
Di chi sono queste chiavi?	*Whose* keys are these?
Con chi vai al ristorante?	*With whom* are you going to the restaurant?

Con 'with' and other prepositions [➤25] must always precede the
question-word.

(ii)   Things: **Che? Cosa? Che cosa?** What?

Cosa facciamo stasera?	*What* are we doing this evening?
Che cosa vuoi fare?	*What* do you want to do?

(iii)   Selection: **Quale?** (plural **quali**) Which?

Quale dei due film preferisci vedere?	*Which* of the two films/movies do you prefer to see?
Dei famosi registi italiani *quali* conosci?	*Which* of the famous Italian film/movie directors do you know?

(iv)   Definition: **Che? Che tipo di?** What? What kind of?

Che film danno all'Astra?	*What* film/movie is on at the Astra?
Che tipo di film è?	*What kind of* film/movie is it?

(v) Description: **Come?** What ... like?

Com'era il film che hai visto sabato sera? – Molto comico.	*What* was the film/movie *like* that you saw on Saturday evening? – Very funny.

(vi) Time: **Quando? A che ora?** When? At what time?

Quando andiamo allora? – Domani sera. A che ora ci vediamo? – Alle otto davanti al cinema.	*When* are we going then? – Tomorrow evening. *At what time* shall we meet? – At eight o'clock outside the cinema/movie house.

(vii) Place: **Dove?** Where?

Dove si trova il cinema Astra? – È proprio in centro.	*Where* is the Astra cinema/movie house? – It's right in the centre/center.

(viii) Manner (methods and means): **Come?** How?

Come andiamo? In macchina?	*How* are we going? By car?

(ix) Quantity and degree: **Quanto, quanta, quanti, quante?** How much? How many?

Quanto tempo dura il film? – Non lo so. Quanti vengono al cinema?	*How* long (*how much* time) does the film/movie last? – I don't know. *How many* are coming to the cinema/movie house?

(x) Reasons: **Perché?** Why?

Perché non andiamo a mangiare una pizza dopo il film? – Che buon'idea!	*Why* don't we go and have a pizza after the film/movie? – What a good idea!

C

ACTIONS AND STATES:
VERBS AND THEIR USES

What verbs do

> For extensive treatment of the forms of Italian verbs, see the Berlitz *Italian Verb Handbook*.

7a Actions, feelings or states

Verbs are words that define *actions*:

Leggo molto.	I *read* a lot.

or which define *feelings* or *states*:

Mi *piace* leggere.	I *like* reading.
Sono studente.	I'*m* a student.

7b Simple and compound verbs

Italian verbs take the form either of single words (*simple* tense forms), as in the above examples, or *compound* forms which consist of the appropriate part of the verb **avere** or the verb **essere** and a past participle:

Ho sempre *avuto* una passione per la lettura.	I *have* always *had* a love for reading.

Verbs may have a compound form in one language but not in another:

Il mio primo insegnante di inglese *è stato* molto bravo e mi *ha aiutato* tanto.	My first English teacher *was* very good and *helped* me so much.

7c Auxiliary verbs

When **avere** and **essere** are used in this way to create com-

38

pound forms, they are known as *auxiliary* verbs, and are used in combination with a form of the main verb known as the *past participle* to produce a range of tenses [➤11b, 11c, 18]:

Mi *sarebbe piaciuto* imparare l'inglese alla scuola elementare.	I *would have liked* to learn English in elementary school.
Non *ho* mai *studiato* una lingua straniera.	I *have* never *studied* a foreign language.

Most verbs use **avere** to form compound tenses. [For those that use **essere**: ➤11c(ii)-(viii).]

What verbs govern

8a What does a verb govern?

(i) Transitive and intransitive verbs

All sentences must contain a subject and a predicate [➤4]. The predicate will consist of at least one main verb and, in the majority of cases, further information. In the example below, the predicate consists of the main verb only:

I miei amici *partono*.	My friends *are leaving*.

In the next example, the predicate consists of the verb plus further information:

I miei amici *hanno fatto le valigie ieri sera*.	My friends *packed their suitcases last night*.

Since subject pronouns [➤23b(i)] are often not expressed in Italian, it is possible for the subject and predicate, and therefore a complete sentence, to be contained in one word:

Partono.	They are leaving.

When a verb can stand in a sentence and be meaningful without the need to add further information (as with **partono** in the above examples), it is called intransitive. When a verb requires a direct object in order to complete its sense, it is known as transitive. In the second example, **hanno fatto** on its own would not make sense without the direct object **le valigie**.

(ii) In many cases, verbs can be used either transitively:

Gianni legge una rivista.	Gianni is reading a magazine.
Perché non mangi l'insalata?	Why don't you eat the salad?
Mi passi il pane per favore.	Can you pass me the bread, please.

or intransitively:

Gianni legge.	Gianni is reading.
Perché non mangi?	Why don't you eat?
Il tempo passa.	Time goes by.

These differences are usually indicated in a dictionary by the abbreviations 'v.i.' (verb intransitive) and 'v.t.' (verb transitive).

(iii) The predicate of a sentence may contain a great deal of additional information which, though useful to clarify or extend the meaning, is not necessary for the verb to perform its grammatical function.

I miei amici hanno fatto le valigie ieri sera prima di andare a letto.	My friends packed their suitcases last night before going to bed.

In the above example, the sentence would be meaningless if the verb **hanno fatto** was not followed by a direct object, in this case **le valigie**. If the remainder of the information were omitted, it would not affect the grammatical completeness of the sentence.

 Italian verbs may well be linked to their objects or other parts of the predicate in a different way from their English equivalents [➤8h]. For example, a transitive verb in English, taking a direct object, may require a preposition before its object in the equivalent Italian form:

Godono *di* buona salute.	They enjoy good health.

Some verbs which take a direct object in Italian need a preposition in English:

Aspetto l'autobus.	I am waiting *for* the bus.

Some take a preposition, but a different one in each language:

Dipende *dal* giorno.	It depends *on* the day.

[For more details on these differences ➤8h.]

8b Reflexive verbs

(i) Turning the action back on the subject

A reflexive verb is a verb whose action is turned back on the subject. The object is therefore the same person or thing as the subject.

Mi diverto sempre quando esco con i miei amici.	I always *enjoy myself* when I go out with my friends.
La mattina non *mi guardo* mai nello specchio per paura di svenire.	In the morning I never *look at myself* in the mirror for fear of fainting.
Si pesa ogni mattina.	He weighs himself every morning.

(ii)
There are many instances where reflexive verbs in Italian express an action whose reflexive nature is not stated (though it is perhaps understood) in English:

Durante la settimana *mi sveglio* alle sei, *mi alzo* quasi subito, *mi lavo* e *mi vesto*.	During the week, I wake up at six o'clock, I get up almost immediately, wash and get dressed.
Quando torno dal lavoro, *mi riposo*. Di solito *mi addormento* in una poltrona.	When I get back from work, I have a rest. Usually I fall asleep in the armchair.
Mi corico abbastanza presto.	I go to bed quite early.

(iii)
There are a number of instances where the reflexive meaning is absent altogether from the English equivalent:

Ho degli amici benestanti che *si lamentano* sempre del costo della vita ma non *si rendono* conto che c'è molta gente che ha difficoltà a sbarcare il lunario.	I have some well-off friends who are always complaining about the cost of living. but they don't realize that there are people who have difficulty in making ends meet.

Other similar examples include:

accorgersi	notice, realize	**affrettarsi**	hurry
affidarsi	rely on	**andarsene**	go away

avvicinarsi	approach	**pentirsi**	repent, regret
dimenticarsi	forget	**rammaricarsi**	regret
fidarsi	trust	**recarsi**	go
figurarsi	imagine	**ricordarsi**	remember
girarsi	turn around	**rivolgersi (a)**	speak , turn (to)
immaginarsi	imagine	**sbrigarsi**	hurry
infischiarsi	care nothing	**scusarsi**	apologize
	(about	**servirsi di**	use
	something)	**stupirsi**	be amazed
meravigliarsi	be amazed,	**trattenersi**	stay, remain
	wonder at	**tuffarsi**	dive
mettersi a	begin to	**vantarsi**	boast
opporsi	oppose, be	**vergognarsi**	be ashamed
	opposed to	**voltarsi**	turn around

 Many reflexive verbs can be used non-reflexively, as the following examples illustrate:

Mi sono svegliato.	I woke up.
Ci siamo girati per guardare.	We turned around to look.

but

Ho svegliato mio fratello.	I woke my brother up.
Abbiamo girato tutti i negozi.	We went around all the shops.

(iv) Actions done to each other

Verbs can be used in the reflexive form to express actions people do to each other. Because of this reciprocal action it is only possible to use the plural forms **noi**, **voi** and **loro**.

Purtroppo, non vedo spesso i miei amici italiani ma per restare in contatto o *ci scriviamo* **o** *ci telefoniamo.*	Unfortunately, I don't see my Italian friends often, but (in order) to stay in touch either *we write (to each other)* or *we telephone (each other).*

(v) Reflexive instead of English passive

Reflexive forms are frequently used where a passive form would be used in English [➤17e].

43

Non *si vendono* giornali qui.	Newspapers *are* not *sold* here.

(vi) There are a number of reflexive verbs that convey the meaning of 'becoming' or 'getting into a state', such as:

abituarsi	get accustomed	**raffreddarsi**	get/catch a cold
abbronzarsi	get tanned	**seccarsi**	get annoyed
annoiarsi	get bored	**stancarsi**	get tired
arrabbiarsi	get annoyed	**stabilirsi**	get settled
innervosirsi	get nervous	**ubriacarsi**	get drunk
preoccuparsi	get worried		

8c *The verbs* essere *and* stare

There are a number of occasions in Italian where the verb 'to be' is not conveyed by **essere** but by **stare** and attention should be paid to the following examples of its use:

• to inquire about someone's well-being

Come *stai*? – *Sto* molto bene grazie, e tu?	How *are* you? – I *am* very well, thank you, and you?

• to form the progressive tenses

Cosa *stai* facendo? – *Sto* scrivendo una lettera.	What *are* you doing? – I *am* writing a letter.

• in the phrase *stare per* 'be about to'

Il pullman *sta per* partire.	The (Pullman) coach *is about to* leave.

• in a number of idiomatic expressions such as:

stare attento	be careful
stare fresco	be in for it
stare sulle spine	be on tenterhooks
stare buono	be good
stare zitto	be/keep quiet
stare in pensiero	be worried

stare tranquillo	be quiet, calm
stare fermo	be/keep still
stare in piedi	stand
stare seduto	be seated
stare in ginocchio	kneel
stare fuori	be outside, be away from home

8d Verbs with one object: the direct object of transitive verbs

The majority of transitive verbs take one object, which is a direct object, the person or thing primarily affected by the action of the verb.

Marco scrive *una lettera*.	Marco is writing *a letter*.
Vedo *la mia amica* ogni sera.	I see *my friend* every evening.

The direct object of the verb can be determined by asking the question **Che cosa** 'What?' or **Chi** 'Whom?' In the first example, therefore, the answer to **Marco scrive che cosa?** is **una lettera**. In the second example, in response to the question **Vedo chi?**, the answer is **la mia amica**.

8e Verbs with two objects: direct and indirect objects

Some transitive verbs describe the transfer of the direct object to another person (or possibly thing). This person is then the indirect object of the verb. The main uses for indirect objects are described in the following paragraphs.

(i) Transferring something or someone

Verbs which describe the transfer of people, objects or information normally must have an indirect object if they are to make sense, though sometimes it may be assumed. There are a number of these verbs in Italian and they include the following:

chiedere	ask	**consigliare**	advise
consegnare	deliver	**dare**	give
dire	say, tell	**domandare**	ask
far sapere	let know	**far vedere**	show
insegnare	teach	**inviare**	send
mandare	send	**mostrare**	show
portare	bring	**presentare**	present, introduce

prestare	lend	**scrivere**	write
promettere	promise	**spiegare**	explain
regalare	give (as gift)	**suggerire**	suggest
restituire	give back		

Cos'hai regalato *a tua sorella* per il suo compleanno? – *Le* ho regalato un compact disc.	What did you give your sister for her birthday? – I gave *her* a compact disc/disk.

In Italian, as the above example shows, the indirect object - **tua sorella** - is introduced by the preposition **a**. In the reply the noun is replaced by the pronoun **le** 'to her'.

In English the indirect object is often not preceded by the preposition 'to' and it can be mistaken for a direct object i.e. 'I gave her'. English speakers need to pay particular attention to this. It is worth considering learning the above verbs in the following way to try and overcome this problem.

dare qualcosa a qualcuno give something to someone
spiegare qualcosa a qualcuno explain something to someone

English speakers have to take similar care when expressing passive constructions. In Italian, indirect objects cannot become the subject of a passive verb [➤17f] as they can in English.

(ii) Some verbs in Italian take an indirect object where the English equivalent has a direct object.

Assomiglia molto *a sua madre*.	She resembles *her mother* a lot.

[For other examples ➤8h(i).]

(iii) *Doing something for someone*

The indirect object form (generally in this case a personal pronoun) is frequently used in speech to express the idea of doing something for someone:

***Mi* puoi fare un piacere quando vai in città, *mi* compri un chilo di pane?**	Can you do (for) *me* a favour/favor when you go to town: can you buy (for) *me* a kilo of bread?

Gli ho trovato un bell'appartamento proprio in centro.	I have found (for) *him* a nice flat/apartment right in the centre/center of town.

The person or thing from which something is removed or taken is often expressed as the indirect object in Italian:

Mi ha strappato la lettera.	He snatched the letter away *from me.*
Il ladro *le* ha rubato la borsa.	The thief stole (*from her*) her handbag.

(iv)   Actions to the body or clothes

When an action is performed to a part of someone's body or clothing, the person is the indirect object and no possessive [►21c(viii)H, 21h(vi)] is used.

Il dottore *mi* ha fasciato il braccio.	The doctor bandaged my arm.
Quella macchia di caffè *le* ha rovinato il vestito.	That coffee stain has ruined her dress.

(v)   Order of objects

When both direct and indirect objects are nouns, the direct usually precedes the indirect if they are of similar length. If one object is significantly longer than the other, then this order is reversed:

Ho regalato *una giacca* a *mia madre.*	I gave *a jacket* to *my mother.*
Ho regalato a *mia madre una bellissima giacca verde.*	I gave *my mother a very beautiful green jacket.*

When both objects are pronouns, the indirect always precedes the direct.

Me l'ha prestato mio cugino.	My cousin lent *it* to *me.*

VERBS AND THEIR USES

[For the position of object pronouns in relation to the verb ➤23b(iv).]

8f   Objects and reflexive verbs

A great number of reflexive verbs are transitive verbs whose action is 'turned back' on the subject. The object, therefore, refers to the same person or thing as the subject [➤8b(i)]:

Giovanni *si lava*.	Giovanni *washes (himself)*.

In Italian, what is being said is **Giovanni lava Giovanni.**

(i)   Many Italian reflexive verbs are the equivalent of English intransitive verbs [➤8b(ii), (iii)].

Il treno *si è fermato* a tutte le stazioni.	The train *stopped* at every station.
Quanti giorni *ti fermi* a Venezia?	How many days *are* you *staying* in Venice?

(ii)   *The reflexive pronoun as indirect object*

The reflexive pronoun can also be the indirect object [➤8e], particularly when the subject is performing an action to a part of his or her own body or article of clothing [➤8e(iv)]:

Mentre riparavo la macchina *mi sono tagliato* il dito.	While I was repairing the car, I cut my finger.

In the above example the direct object is **il dito** and **mi** becomes the indirect object.

(iii)   The reflexive pronoun is also used in a reciprocal sense [➤8b(iv)], either as a direct or indirect object:

***Si salutano* ogni volta che *si vedono*.**	They greet *each other* every time they see *each other*.
***Vi scrivete* spesso? - No, ma *ci telefoniamo* una volta al mese.**	Do you write to *each other* often? – No, but we telephone *(to) each other* once a month.

8g *Impersonal and 'back-to-front' verbs*

An impersonal verb in English has the subject 'it', which has no real meaning by itself, but serves to introduce weather phrases and other verbs in sentences such as 'it is snowing', 'it is difficult to say', etc. In Italian the subject pronoun 'it' is contained in the verb and not expressed as a separate word. Impersonal verbs in Italian fall into the following categories:

(i) *Verbs referring to the weather and natural phenomena*

Apart from the verbs such as **nevicare** 'snow', **tuonare** 'thunder', **piovere** 'rain', etc. there are a number of expressions that use **fare**, and **c'è**.

iovere	rain	**fare bello**	be nice/fine
piovigginare	drizzle	**fare brutto**	be bad/awful
nevicare	snow	**fare notte**	get dark
gelare	freeze	**fare giorno**	get light
sgelare	thaw	**essere nuvoloso**	be cloudy
grandinare	hail	**essere umido**	be humid
lampeggiare	flash lightning	**essere afoso**	be heavy/sultry
tuonare	thunder	**essere mite**	be mild
fare caldo	be hot	**c'è il sole**	it's sunny
fare freddo	be cold	**c'è la nebbia**	it's foggy
fare fresco	be cool/fresh	**c'è la foschia**	it's misty

Note also

tirare vento	be windy

Durante questo periodo il tempo è molto variabile ma, purtroppo, fa sempre brutto: c'è la nebbia, fa molto freddo, nevica abbastanza, verso le quattro e mezzo fa già notte ... **D'estate, però, fa molto caldo, delle volte 32-34 gradi. Non piove quasi mai. Si sta meglio la sera quando comincia a fare più fresco.**	During this period of the year the weather is very changeable but, unfortunately, it's always awful: it's foggy, very cold, it snows a fair amount, it gets dark around 4:30 p.m. ... In summer, however. it's very hot, 32-34 degrees (centigrade). It almost never rains. You feel better in the evening when it begins to get cooler.

(ii) *C'è, ci sono: there is, there are*

These forms are used in the full range of tenses in the third person singular and plural:

Se questa nebbia non si dissipa, ci saranno molti incidenti stradali. Stamattina c'è stato un terribile incidente sul tratto di strada che passa davanti a casa nostra.	If this fog doesn't lift, there will be a lot of road accidents. This morning there was a terrible accident on the stretch of road that passes our house.

(iii)   The verb **essere** (third person singular) followed by an adjective, adverb or past participle.

Expressions such as **è facile** 'it's easy', **è possibile** 'it's possible', **è necessario** 'it's necessary', etc., **è bene** 'it's a good thing', **è male** 'it's a bad thing', **è meglio** 'it's better', **è vietato** 'it's forbidden', **è permesso** 'it's allowed' etc., are usually termed impersonal, because they are introduced by 'it'. However, they are not strictly so in Italian, as the following infinitive or clause is really the subject of the verb. In the examples below, the subject 'it' can be replaced by the following infinitive or clause in Italian (shown in italics).

È impossibile guidare con questa nebbia fitta. *Guidare* con questa nebbia fitta è impossibile. È bene che non dobbiamo uscire. *Che non dobbiamo uscire* è bene.	It's impossible to drive in this thick fog. To drive in this thick fog is impossible. It's a good thing that we don't have to go out. That we don't have to go out is a good thing.

(iv)   *Verbs expressing need, necessity, appearance, etc.*

There are a number of verbs that can be used impersonally in Italian which may be used personally in English. These verbs are either followed by a dependent clause whose verb is in the subjunctive [►16c(iii)] or by an infinitive [►8i]. The following verbs are used in this way:

accadere	happen	**bisognare**	be necessary
avvenire	happen	**convenire**	be fitting/a good
bastare	be enough/		idea
	sufficient	**costare**	cost

importare	matter, mind	sembrare	seem
interessare	be interested in	**servire**	be of use
occorrere	be necessary	**spettare**	be up to, be the
parere	seem, look like		duty of
riuscire	be	**succedere**	happen
	(+ adjective)	**toccare**	be up to

Pare che voglia piovere.	It looks like rain.
Non importa, non andiamo lontano, basta portare l'ombrello.	It doesn't matter, we aren't going far, we need only (it's enough to) take the umbrella.
Non serve a niente portare l'ombrello quando tira un vento così forte.	It's no use taking the umbrella when it's so windy.
Riesce difficile tenerlo aperto.	It's difficult to keep it open.
Non bisogna che tu venga con me.	You don't need to come with me. (It's not necessary for you to come with me.)

 These same verbs are (with the exception of **bisogna**), used always either in the third person singular or plural and often have an indirect object indicating the person to whom it matters, appears, etc.

Non *mi* interessa uscire quando fa così freddo.	I am not interested (it doesn't interest *me*) in going out when it is so cold.
Ci pare che le strade siano molto scivolose.	It seems *to us* that the roads are very slippery.
Gino, non *ti* conviene prendere la macchina. Per una volta *ti* tocca andare a piedi.	Gino, it's not a good idea (*for you*) to take the car. For once *you* must go on foot.
Prima di andare in macchina su queste strade scivolose, *ci* occorrono delle gomme nuove.	Before going on these slippery roads with the car, *we* need some new tyres/tires.

(v) ***Piacere*** *'like' and similar 'back-to-front' verbs*

There is a group of verbs in Italian which work the opposite way around to their English counterparts: the subject in English (usually a person) is the object in Italian. The verb is usually in the third person. If the object (a person) is a noun, it usually comes first preceded by the preposition **a**.

A mio fratello **piacciono i piatti vegetariani. Non gli piace affatto la carne.**	My brother likes vegetarian dishes. He doesn't like meat at all.

The main points about this construction are therefore:

• The Italian subject (**i piatti vegetariani**) usually follows the verb, which is plural if the subject is plural: i.e. if you like something plural, the verb is plural. You are saying 'Vegetarian dishes please my brother': 'they please him'.

• A pronoun object is often reinforced by **a** + the disjunctive pronoun [►23h(ii)], especially for emphasis.

A me **non mi piacciono i piatti vegetariani.**	I don't like vegetarian dishes.

• A number of verbs that can work in this way have already been mentioned in the previous section [►8(iv)].
Below are some others:

andare di	feel like	**mancare**	lack
capitare di	happen	**rimanere**	remain
dispiacere	be sorry	**rincrescere**	be sorry
dolere	hurt	**sfuggire**	escape (one's
far male	hurt		attention)

Anche se mi fa male la schiena, non mi va di andare dal medico. Per fortuna, mi sono rimasti degli antidolorifici. Se ti capita di andare in farmacia, ti dispiace comprarmi delle aspirine.	Even if I have a bad back, I don't feel like going to the doctor's. Fortunately, I have some painkillers left. If you happen to go into a chemist's/drugstore, would you mind buying me some aspirins?

• If the verb is influencing another person or thing to do something, the subjunctive is needed after **che** [►16c(i)].

Suggerisco che tu *stia* a casa.	I suggest that you *stay* at home.

8h   *Verb + preposition + noun*

Quite a number of verbs are linked to their object by a preposition - the most common being **a** or **di**. In most cases these verb-preposition combinations are fixed: it would not be possible to leave the preposition out or use a different one without at least changing the meaning and probably making no sense at all.

The following Italian verbs are either linked to their object by a preposition, which may not necessarily correspond to the English preposition, or are translated in English by a verb which takes a direct object.

Mia figlia *bada ai* bambini.	My daughter is taking care of the children.
Non ho potuto *resistere alla tentazione*.	I couldn't resist the temptation.
Assomiglia molto *a* sua sorella.	She looks a lot like her sister.
Dice che *ha bisogno di* soldi ma non *mi fido di* lui.	He says he needs money, but I don't trust him.

(i) Verbs linked with *a*

accennare a	refer to, mention
affacciarsi a	appear (at), look out (of)
affezionarsi a	become fond of, take a liking to
affidarsi a	trust in, rely on
aspirare a	aspire to
assistere a	witness, be present at
assomigliare a	resemble
avvicinarsi a	approach, get near
badare a	take care of
cedere a	give in to
concedere a	grant, allow
contribuire a	contribute to
credere a/in	believe in
dedicarsi a	devote oneself to
disubbidire a	disobey
giocare a	play (a game)
giungere a	reach, arrive at
interessarsi a/di	be interested in
mirare a	aim at
opporsi a	oppose, be opposed
partecipare a	take part in
pensare a	think about
prepararsi a	prepare, get ready for

provvedere a	provide for, see to
puntare a	aim at
resistere a	resist
ricorrere a	resort to
riferirsi a	refer to
rimediare a	put right, remedy
rinunciare a	give up
rispondere a	answer
rivolgersi a	turn to, speak to
sopravvivere a	survive
sottoporsi a	undergo
sovrintendere a	supervise
sparare a	shoot at
spettare a	be up to, be the responsibility of
telefonare a	telephone
tenerci a	care a lot about, attach importance to
toccare	be up to, be the responsibility of
ubbidire a	obey
voler bene a	be fond of, love

Mio figlio si dedica ai suoi studi. Al momento, pensa solo ai suoi esami. Non gioca più a tennis, che gli piace molto, non telefona ai suoi amici, che faceva quasi ogni sera, non ha risposto all'ultima lettera del suo corrispondente, non fa altro che studiare.

My son devotes himself to his studies. At the moment, he thinks only about his exams. He doesn't play tennis any more, which he likes a lot, he doesn't ring his friends, which he did almost every evening, he hasn't answered his pen pal's last letter; he does nothing but study.

(ii)   Verbs linked with **di**

accontentarsi di	make do with, be satisfied with
accorgersi di	notice, realize
approfittare di	take advantage of
diffidare di	mistrust
dimenticarsi di	forget
discutere di	talk about, discuss
fidarsi di	trust
godere di	enjoy
informarsi di/su	find out about
innamorarsi di	fall in love with

impadronirsi di	take hold of, master (a language)
intendersi di	know about, be an expert on
lagnarsi di	complain about
lamentarsi di	complain about
mancare di	lack
meravigliarsi di	be amazed at
occuparsi di	look after, take care of
pensare di	think of (opinion)
preoccuparsi di (per)	worry, care about
rendersi conto di	notice, realize
ricordarsi di	remember
ridere di	laugh at
riempire di	fill with
sapere di	taste, smack of
servirsi di	use, make use of
stancarsi di	get tired of
stupirsi di	be amazed at
trattarsi di	be a question of
vantarsi di	boast of, about
vergognarsi di	be ashamed of
vivere di	live on

> **Mio figlio si rende conto dell'importanza dei suoi studi. Io e mia moglie ci meravigliamo del suo impegno e della sua motivazione. Approfitta di ogni occasione per studiare. Non si lamenta mai della quantità del lavoro che deve fare.**
>
> My son realizes the importance of his studies. My wife and I are amazed at his commitment and motivation. He takes advantage of every opportunity to study. He never complains about the amount of work he has to do.

(iii) Verbs linked with **con**

arrabbiarsi con	be annoyed with
avercela con	have it in for
competere con	compete with
congratularsi con	congratulate
incontrarsi con	meet
prendersela con	be upset with
sposarsi con	get married to
trattare con	deal with

Mi congratulo con te.	I congratulate you.
Si è sposato con una ragazza francese.	He got married to a French girl.

(iv) Verbs linked with **per**

entusiasmarsi per	be enthusiastic about
lottare per	struggle, fight for
partire per	leave for
passare per	pass through
prendere per	mistake for
scambiare per	mistake for

L'ho preso per tuo cognato.	I mistook him for your brother-in-law.
Sono partiti per l'Italia due giorni fa.	They left for Italy two days ago.

(v) Verbs linked with **da**

allontanarsi da	go away
avere da	have to
dipendere da	depend on
fare da	act as
giudicare da	judge by/on
guardarsi da	beware of, avoid
provenire da	come from
scendere da	get out of (car, train, etc.)
servire da	serve for, be used as

Non è sempre possibile giudicare dalle apparenze.	It's not always possible to judge by appearances.
Durante il congresso ho fatto da interprete.	During the conference, I acted as interpreter.

(vi) Verbs linked with **in, su, verso** and **contro**

entrare in	enter
tradurre in	translate into
trasformare in	change, transform into

abbattersi su	hit
decidere su	decide on
incidere su	affect
indagare su	investigate
influire su	influence, affect
insistere su	insist on
riflettere su	reflect on, think about
salire su/in	board (bus, train)
avviarsi verso	head for
dirigersi verso	head for, make one's way towards
lottare contro	fight against

Siamo entrati in casa.	We entered the house.
La decisione, presa dal governo, inciderà sul costo della vita.	The decision taken by the government, will affect the cost of living.
L'uragano sta per abbattersi sulla costa.	The hurricane is about to hit the coast.

(vii) Conversely, the following verbs, which are linked to their object by a preposition in English, take a direct object in Italian.

approvare	approve of
ascoltare	listen to
aspettare	wait for
commentare	comment upon, talk about
cercare	look for
chiedere	ask for
domandare	ask for
guardare	look at
operare	operate on
pagare	pay for
sfiorare	touch on (a subject)
sfogliare	glance/skim through (book, newspaper)
sognare	dream about

A casa nostra preferiamo ascoltare i dischi o la radio che guardare sempre la televisione.	In our house we prefer listening to records or the radio to always watching television.

8i Verb + bare infinitive

The following are the main verbs which govern a bare infinitive, i.e. without any connecting preposition.

bastare	be enough, sufficient	**lasciare**	leave, allow
		occorrere	be necessary
bisognare	be necessary	**osare**	dare
convenire	be fitting/ worthwhile	**piacere**	please, like
		potere	be able
desiderare	want, wish	**preferire**	prefer
detestare	hate	**rincrescere**	be sorry
dispiacere	be sorry	**sapere**	know how to
dovere	have to, must	**sentire**	hear
importare	matter, be important	**servire**	serve, be of use
intendere	intend	**vedere**	see
interessare	interest	**volere**	want, wish

Quest'anno intendo trascorrere le vacanze estive in Italia. Desidero andarci per perfezionare il mio italiano. Naturalmente mi interesserebbe visitare i monumenti antichi.	This year I intend to spend the summer holidays/vacation in Italy. I want to go there to perfect my Italian. Naturally I am (would be) interested in visiting the ancient monuments.

 The infinitive construction after verbs expressing wish, preference, regret, etc., is possible only when the verb and the infinitive have the same subject. The verb + infinitive construction cannot be used in Italian to convey English sentences of the type 'want/prefer someone to'. To express this idea in Italian, a separate clause must be used with the subjunctive [➤16a,16c].

Quest'estate voglio *andare* in Italia.	This summer I want *to go* to Italy. (infinitive because subject is the same)
Non voglio *che* tu *vada* da solo.	I don't want *you to go* on your own. (separate clause introduced by **che** and the verb in the subjunctive because the subject is different)

8j   Verb + preposition + infinitive

A large number of verbs can be linked to a following infinitive by a preposition. As with verbs linked to nouns [➤ 8h], this is a fixed pairing that cannot be changed.

The most common linking prepositions are **a** and **di**, but some others are also used.

(i)   Verbs + a + infinitive

Verbs linked to an infinitive with **a** include many implying:

(A) Beginning

apprestarsi a	get ready to
cominciare a	begin to
iniziare a	begin to
mettersi a	start, set about -ing
prendere a	begin to
prepararsi a	get ready to
scoppiare a (ridere)	burst out (laughing)

(B) Motion

andare a	go to, go and, be going to
affrettarsi a	hasten, hurry to
correre a	run to
tornare a	return to
venire a	come to, come and, be coming to

(C) Encouraging, inviting, obliging

costringere a	force, compel to
forzare a	force to
incitare a	urge to
incoraggiare a	encourage to
invitare a	invite to
obbligare a	oblige to
persuadere a	persuade to
spingere a	urge, incite to
stimolare a	urge, encourage to

(D) The following verbs also use the linking preposition **a**:

abituarsi a	get used to	**autorizzare a**	authorize to
aiutare a	help to	**azzardarsi a**	dare to
apprendere a	learn to	**continuare a**	continue to

VERBS AND THEIR USES

convincere a	convince to	**provare a**	try to
decidersi a	make up one's mind to	**rassegnarsi a**	resign oneself to
divertirsi a	enjoy (doing)	**riuscire a**	succeed in, manage to
esitare a	hesitate to		
imparare a	learn to	**sfidare a**	challenge to, defy to
impegnarsi a	undertake to		
insegnare a	teach to	**tardare a**	delay in -ing
limitarsi a	limit oneself to	**tendere a**	tend to
portare a	lead to	**tenere a**	be eager to

Ieri sera ho provato ad imparare questi verbi. Ho cominciato a studiare intorno alle sette. Dopo un'ora, ero riuscito ad impararne una trentina. A quel punto, volevo smettere ma un amico mi ha incoraggiato ad andare avanti.	Last night I tried to learn these verbs. I started studying around seven o'clock. After an hour, I had managed to learn about thirty. At that point, I wanted to stop, but a friend encouraged me to go on.

(ii) Verbs + **di** + infinitive

Verbs linked to an infinitive with **di** include:

(A) Those which indicate the ending or stopping of an action or separation from it:

cessare di	stop, cease
finire di	finish
smettere di	stop
stancarsi di	tire of
stufarsi di	get fed up of/with

(B) Those where the **di** conveys literally 'of':

accusare di	accuse of
pentirsi di	repent of
rammaricarsi di	repent of, feel sorry for
trattarsi di	be a question of
vantarsi di	boast of
vergognarsi di	be ashamed of

(C) The following verbs also use the linking preposition **di**:

accettare di	accept	**ammettere di**	admit
accorgersi di	notice, realize	**aspettarsi di**	expect

avere bisogno di	need	**parlare di**	talk (of doing)
avere intenzione di	intend	**pensare di**	plan, think of
avere paura di	be afraid	**permettere di***	allow
avere vergogna di	be ashamed	**pregare di**	beg, ask
avere voglia di	feel like	**pretendere di**	profess,
badare di	take care to		claim
cercare di	try	**proibire di***	prohibit
chiedere di*	ask	**promettere di***	promise
consigliare di*	advise	**proporre di***	propose
credere di	believe	**rendersi conto di**	realize
decidere di	decide	**ricordare/si di**	remember
dichiarare di	declare	**rifiutare/si di**	refuse
dimenticare/si di	forget	**rischiare di**	risk, be in
dire di*	say, tell		danger of
domandare di*	ask	**risolvere di**	resolve,
fare finta di	pretend		decide
fingere di	pretend	**ritenere di**	consider
giurare di	swear to	**sapere di**	know
immaginare di	imagine	**scegliere di**	choose
impedire di	prevent	**sembrare di**	seem
mancare di	fail to	**sentirsi di**	feel
meravigliarsi di	be surprised at	**sforzarsi di**	try hard to
meritare di	deserve	**sognare di**	dream
minacciare di	threaten	**sperare di**	hope
non vedere l'ora di	look forward to	**suggerire di**	suggest
offrire di	offer	**temere di**	fear
ordinare di*	order	**tentare di**	try, attempt
parere di	seem	**vietare di**	forbid, prohibit

Note: The above list includes some *verbal phrases*, such as **avere bisogno di**, which is in fact a verb + noun + preposition. However, they function in the same way as the other verbs listed.

Abbiamo deciso di vendere la macchina perché consuma troppa benzina. Un amico ha offerto di comprarla e ci ha chiesto di tenerla per qualche settimana mentre cerca di vendere la sua. Abbiamo promesso di aspettare un po'. Ad ogni modo, non pensiamo di comprare un'altra macchina.

We have decided to sell the car because it uses too much petrol/gasoline. A friend has offered to buy it and he has asked us to keep it for a few weeks while he tries to sell his. We have promised to wait a while. In any case, we are not thinking of buying another car.

• The verbs in the list marked with an asterisk have a particular structure, i.e. verb + indirect object + **di** + infinitive.

Abbiamo promesso ai nostri amici *di* aspettare un po'.	We have promised (to) our friends to wait a while.

It might be helpful to learn this particular structure in the following way:

promettere a qualcuno di fare qualcosa	promise (to) someone to do something

The **a qualcuno** will help to remind you to use the indirect object and the **di fare** serves as a reminder that you always have to put the preposition **di** before the following infinitive.

[For indirect object pronouns ➤23b(iii).]

(iii)   *Verbs +* ***per*** *+ infinitive*

finire per	end by, finish by	**servire per**	be used for
lottare per	fight for	**stare per**	be about to

Abbiamo finito *per* accettare la sua offerta.	We ended up by accepting his offer.

8k   *Verb + the present participle or 'gerund'* [➤10b, 10d]

This is a very common construction in English, but its use in Italian is limited to the following circumstances.

(i)   ***Stare*** *+ gerund*

Stare + gerund is used to form the progressive or continuous tenses [➤10e(ii)], usually the present or imperfect, and occasionally the future. These correspond closely with the English progressive tenses, but care must be taken that the action being referred to is/was actually in progress at the time.

Cosa stai facendo?	What are you doing? (at this very moment)
Sto scrivendo una lettera alla mia corrispondente italiana.	I am writing a letter to my Italian penfriend/pen pal.

Stavo scrivendo una lettera quando ho sentito bussare alla porta.	I was writing a letter when I heard a knock at the door.

In the following example, the present tense is used because the action is not actually in progress at the point of reference.

Non esco stasera perché devo scrivere alcune lettere.	I'm not going out this evening because I have to write some letters.

(ii)   *Andare* + *gerund*

Andare is sometimes used to form the progressive tenses when a cumulative progression is indicated.

Andava **parlando di questa corrispondente per ore e ore.**	She went on talking about this penfriend/pen pal for hours and

[For the use of the gerund standing on its own (= by/while doing) ➤10e(i). For other translations of the English '-ing' ending ➤10e(iii).]

8l   *Verb + past participle*

The verbs which most frequently combine with past participles in Italian are **avere** and **essere** when used as auxiliaries to form compound tenses [➤11c].

The verb **essere** is also used with past participles to form passive constructions, such as:

La lettera *è scritta.*	The letter *is written.*

[For verbs other than **essere** to express the passive ➤17d. To express in Italian the idea conveyed by the English expression, 'to have/get something done', ➤9e.]

⑨ Attitudes to action: modal verbs

A modal verb seldom carries a full meaning by itself. Instead, as the examples in this chapter will show, a modal verb says something about the relationship between the subject and the full verb, which is in the infinitive [➤10a]. It creates a *mood* for the verb which follows.

Note: Object pronouns may precede the modal verb or be attached to the end of the infinitive [➤23b(iv)].

***Ci* devo andare. /Devo andar*ci*.**	I have to go *there*.
***Te lo* possiamo comprare/possiamo comprar*telo*.**	We can buy *it for you*.

The most frequently used modal verbs in Italian are:

dovere	have to, must
potere	be able, can
sapere	know how to
volere	wish, want

The precise use and variations of meaning of the modal verbs are explained in the sections which follow.

9a Dovere

The verb **dovere** expresses obligation, the idea of having to do something, adding nuance and variation to this central meaning by the use of different tenses. It corresponds to a range of English equivalents, such as 'have to …', 'must …', 'should …', 'ought to …', 'should have …', etc. It is also used (as in English) to express strong supposition such as 'He must be at least forty'.

(i) In the present tense

As the most *immediate* tense, the message conveyed by the present tense of **dovere** is usually fairly strong.

Prima di uscire *devi* mettere in ordine la tua camera.	Before going out you *must* tidy up your room.
***Devo* andare a comprare qualcosa in città. Quando torno tutto *deve* essere al suo posto, altrimenti guai!**	I *have to* go and buy something in town. When I get back, everything *must* be in its place; otherwise look out!

It also expresses strong supposition.

***Devi* arrabbiarti quando i figli lasciano la roba dappertutto.** ***Dev'*essere molto difficile tenere la casa sempre in ordine.**	You *must* get annoyed when the children leave things everywhere. It *must* be very difficult to always keep the house tidy.

(ii) In the perfect tense

Mia moglie *ha dovuto* comprare qualcosa per la cena.	My wife *had to* (*has had to*) buy something for dinner. (obligation)

Note the following construction:

Mia moglie *dev'essere andata* in città.	My wife *must have gone* to town. (supposition)

(iii) In the imperfect tense

Mia moglie *doveva* andare in città per fare la spesa.	My wife *had to* (= *was going to have to*) go to town to do the shopping. (obligation)
Mia moglie *doveva* andare in città per fare la spesa.	My wife *was supposed to* go to town to do the shopping. (supposition)

(iv) In the conditional

The conditional of **dovere** is widely used and its equivalent meaning in English is 'ought' or 'should'.

La mia mamma ha ragione. *Dovrei* mettere la mia camera in ordine prima di uscire.	My mother is right. I *should* (ought to) tidy up my room before going out. (obligation)

There are occasions where the idea of compulsion or obligation is expressed by the appropriate tense of **essere** and the past participle of **costringere** or **obbligare**.

Se non mettessi la mia camera in ordine *sarei costretto* a stare a casa.	If I didn't tidy up my room I *would have to* stay at home.
Sono obbligato a mettere in ordine la mia camera prima di uscire.	I *have to* (*am obliged to*) tidy up my room before going out.

(v)   In the conditional perfect

The conditional perfect conveys the equivalent of the English 'ought to have … '/'should have …'.

Avrei dovuto mettere la mia camera in ordine ieri sera.	I *should have (ought to have)* tidied up my room last night. (obligation)

It is occasionally used to convey 'would have had to …'.

Se non avessi messo in ordine la mia camera prima di uscire, l'*avrei dovuto* fare al mio ritorno.	If I hadn't tidied up my room before going out, I *would have had to* do it on my return.

(vi)   In the pluperfect tense

Aveva dovuto mettere in ordine la sua camera prima di uscire.	He *had had to* tidy up his room before going out.

 Dovere also exists as an ordinary non-modal verb, with the meaning 'to owe'.

Quanto ti *devo*?	How much do I *owe* you?

9b Potere

(i) *Be able to, can*

Potere conveys the idea of 'being able to ...', 'being physically capable of ...', 'being allowed to ...', 'having permission to ...', and is expressed in English in a variety of ways, such as 'can', 'could', 'may' and 'might'.

Posso entrare?	*May* I (*Can* I) come in? (permission)
Non *possiamo* venire domani sera.	We *cannot* come tomorrow evening. (unable to)
Non *posso* chiudere questa finestra.	I *can't* close this window. (incapable)

In the third example above, it is possible to use **riuscire a** in place of **potere.**

Non *riesco a* chiudere questa finestra.	I *can't* close this window.

Riuscire expresses 'succeed in ...', 'manage to ...' or 'be able to ...'.

Quando parli in fretta non *riesco a* capire tutto.	When you speak quickly, I *can't* (*don't manage to/don't succeed in*) understand everything.

Note that it is common practice to omit **potere** with verbs of perception, such as **sentire** 'hear,' 'feel' and **vedere** 'see'. This possibility also applies to **trovare** 'find'.

Parla più forte per favore perché non ti *sento*.	Speak more loudly please because I *can't hear* you.
Ho tolto i miei occhiali per fare la doccia e adesso non li *trovo*.	I took off my glasses to have a shower and now I *can't find* them.
Senza gli occhiali, non *vedo* niente.	Without my glasses, I *can't see* anything.

A more formal way of expressing permission is to use **permet-tere** with the infinitive [➤8j(ii)C].

Mi *permette* di dire una parola?	*May I (Will you allow me to)* say a word?

The impersonal phrase **si può** [➤17e(ii)] is often used when seeking permission, particularly when the action (the infinitive) is not expressed.

***Si può* (fumare)?**	*May I/May we* (smoke)?

Fumare need not be expressed because in a real life situation the gesture would make it obvious what one is seeking permission to do.

(ii)   *Possibility*

Potere also expresses possibility, especially when used in the conditional mood:

***Potrei* telefonare più tardi.**	I *could* (= could possibly) telephone later.
Avresti *potuto* telefonare ieri sera.	You *could have* called last night.

 Great care has to be taken when conveying the English 'could', which may be a past tense or a conditional. It is important to consider the underlying message and the function of 'could', i.e. does it mean *possibility* or *inability?* The two examples below illustrate the point.

***Potrei* uscire domani sera ma stasera non posso perché sono troppo impegnato.**	I *could* go out tomorrow evening, but this evening I can't because I am too busy.
Non *potevo* uscire perché ero troppo impegnato.	I *could*n't go out because I was too busy.

In the first example the meaning is 'I *could possibly* go out tomorrow evening ...' (= conditional) whereas the second example means 'I *was not able* to go out ...' (= past tense, in this case the imperfect). It is often a good guide to rephrase the English using 'be able'. If this is done for the first example the meaning becomes nonsense. In the second example, however, 'could' and 'was able' are interchangeable.

Potere can also be used to express indignation.

Avrebbero potuto dirci che non venivano.	They *could have* told us that they weren't coming.

(iii) *Può darsi*

Possibility can also be expressed by using the impersonal reflexive form **può darsi** [➤16c(iii)].

Può darsi che siano malati.	*Maybe (It's possible that)* they're ill/sick.

9c Sapere

(i) *Sapere* vs *potere*

Sapere has only limited use as a modal verb, with the meaning 'know how to'. However, since this idea is frequently expressed in English by the word 'can', English speakers have to be careful not to confuse the use of **sapere** and **potere**.

Mi *puoi* dare una mano a tradurre questa lettera visto che *sai* parlare italiano, vero? – Va bene, ma non *posso* farlo adesso.	*Can* you give me a hand to translate this letter seeing as you *can (know how to)* speak Italian, can't you? – Very well, but I *can't* do it now.

Sapere is also used in the sense of 'be in a position to ...' or 'be capable of ...'.

Quando il professore di storia mi ha interrogato sulla lezione precedente *ho saputo* rispondere a quasi tutte le sue domande.	When the history teacher questioned me about the preceding lesson, I *could* answer almost all his questions.
Sapresti riconoscere quella ragazza se la vedessi un'altra volta?	*Would* you (*Would you be able to*) recognize that girl if you saw her again?

(ii) *Sapere* to know

Sapere is used much more frequently as a non-modal verb, meaning 'know a fact'.

Sai a che ora chiudono le banche?	Do you *know* at what time the banks close?

 Conoscere must be used when the meaning is 'be acquainted with a person or place'.

Non *conosco* molto bene questa regione.	I don't *know* this region very well.
Nella nostra strada *conosciamo* due famiglie.	In/On our street we *know* two families.

9d Volere

(i) Expressing wish

As with other modal verbs [➤9a-c], **volere** has a variety of equivalents in English. It is the basic verb in Italian for expressing wish:

Non *voglio* andare al cinema. – Cosa *vuoi* fare allora?	I *don*'t *want* to go to the cinema/movies. – What do you *want* to do then?

(ii) Expressing willingness and polite requests

Volere is also widely used to express willingness and polite requests:

Non so proprio cosa fare perché mio figlio non *vuole* studiare.	I really *don*'t know what to do because my son *will* not study.
Vuoi qualcosa da bere?	*Would you like* something to drink?
Volete stare zitti per favore?	*Will you* be quiet, please?

(iii) Expressing intention

Volere can convey the idea of 'be going to ...', 'want to ...', 'intend to ...'.

– Cosa *vuoi* fare quando finisci i tuoi studi universitari? – A dire il vero, non ho la più pallida idea. Quando ero a scuola, *volevo* fare il medico ma poi ho cambiato idea.

– What do you *want* to do when you finish your university studies? – To tell you the truth, I haven't got the faintest idea. When I was at school, I *wanted* to become a doctor but then I changed my mind.

(iv)   Should/would like

To say you *would like* to do something is most frequently expressed by the conditional form of **volere**.

Quando finisco i miei studi *vorrei* diventare insegnante.

When I finish my studies, I *would like* to become a teacher.

It is also possible to use the conditional [➤14d] of **piacere**.

Quando finisco i miei studi *mi piacerebbe* diventare insegnante.

When I finish my studies, I *would like* to become a teacher.

Forms of politeness can also be conveyed in Italian by **gradire**.

Gradirei un bicchiere di acqua minerale.
Gradiresti una tazza di caffè?

I *should like* a glass of mineral water.
Would you *like* a cup of coffee?

(v)   Should have/would have liked

To say you would like to have done something, use the conditional perfect [➤14e] of either **volere** or **piacere**.

A scuola *avrei voluto* (*mi sarebbe piaciuto*) imparare il tedesco.

At school I *would have liked* to have learnt German.

 When you want or would like someone else to do something, you must use **volere** or **piacere** + the subjunctive [➤16c(i)].

| I miei genitori volevano che (io) imparassi il francese. | My parents *wanted me to learn* French. |

Note the use of **volere** in the following expressions:

Voglio bene **ai miei genitori.** Tutti gli *vogliono bene*.	I *love* my parents. They *are* all *fond of* him.
Sembra che *voglia* **piovere.**	It looks as if it *might* rain.
Quanto *ci vuole* **per arrivare all'aeroporto? – Con la macchina** *ci vogliono* **due ore.**	How long *does it take* to get to the airport? – By car *it takes* two hours.
Cosa *vuol dire* **questa parola?**	What *does* this word *mean*?
Al giorno d'oggi, conoscere le lingue *vuol dire* **molto.**	Nowadays, a knowledge of languages *means (counts for)* a lot.
Ho sempre dei brutti voti in matematica. – Ma cosa *vuoi* **se non studi mai?**	I always get bad marks in maths. – But what *do* you *expect* if you never study?

[For the use of the auxiliary **essere** or **avere** with modal verbs ►11c(vii).]

9e   Fare, lasciare *+ infinitive*

The verbs covered in this section are not modal verbs [►9a-d], but can be used with infinitives in similar ways, to create new or modified meanings.

(i)   Fare

(A) To say you are having or getting something done, you use **fare** followed *immediately* by the infinitive.

| **Ho** *fatto aggiustare* **la lavastoviglie.** | I *have had* the dishwasher *repaired*. |
| **Quando l'***hai fatta* **aggiustare?** | When *did* you *have* it *repaired*? |

With **fare** + infinitive constructions, any object pronoun (*l'* in the above example) is placed before **fare**, not attached to the following infinitve as in the majority of verb + infinitive forms.

(B) Fare + infinitive also means 'to get someone to do something'.

Ho *fatto tradurre* la lettera dalla mia amica.	I *got* my friend *to translate* the letter.

Notice that the word order in Italian is different from that of the English. The Italian word order does not allow you to put either **la lettera** nor **dalla mia amica** between **fatto** and **tradurre**.

When both **fare** and the following infinitive have an object, the one relating to **fare** becomes the indirect object.

Ho fatto assaggiare questo formaggio *al mio amico*. Fa*gli* assaggiare questo formaggio.	I got *my friend* to taste this cheese. Get *him* to try this cheese.

Both these sentences imply that you are inviting or asking someone to do something whereas in the previous example you are getting the job done *by* someone.

(C) Fare + reflexive verb in infinitive: if the infinitive following **fare** is reflexive, the reflexive pronoun is omitted.

Quello che mi fa *arrabbiare* è che ho appena comprato questa lavastoviglie.	What makes me *angry* is that I have just bought this dishwasher.

(D) Note also:

far aspettare	keep (someone) waiting
far capire	give (someone) to understand
far entrare	show (someone) in
far passare	let (someone) through/by
far vedere	show (to someone)
fare venire	send for (someone)

Scusami se ti *ho fatto aspettare*. Mi *hanno fatto capire* che non potevano venire. La *faccio entrare*?	Sorry if I *have kept* you *waiting*. They *gave* me *to understand* that they were not able to come. Shall I *show* her *in*?

Mi *ha fatto vedere* la lettera che aveva ricevuto.	He *showed* me the letter he had received.

(ii) *Lasciare*

With a following infinitive, **lasciare** means 'let someone do something', or 'let something happen'.

Se vuole andare all'estero con i suoi amici, *lascialo andare*.	If he wants to go abroad with his friends, *let* him *go*.

The special rules relating to pronouns and to reflexive verbs when **fare** is used with an infinitive [➤9e(i) above] also apply to **lasciare** when used in this way.

Note also the following idiomatic uses:

Lasciamo perdere/andare!	*Let's forget about it!*
Lascia stare quella radio.	*Leave* that radio *alone* (*Hands off* that radio!).

10 Verb forms not related to time: non-finite forms

10a The infinitive

The infinitive is the part of the verb most commonly listed in dictionaries. It names a certain activity or state without saying when it happens (a *non-finite* verb form). It often completes the meaning of the main verb.

(i) Infinitive endings

The majority of infinitives in Italian end in **-are (trovare), -ere (vedere)** or **-ire (aprire)**. There are a small number of verbs that have irregular infinitives, such as **porre** 'put', **tradurre** 'translate' and **trarre** 'draw, pull'.

(ii) Uses of the infinitive

The main uses of the infinitive are described in these paragraphs:

➤8i 'bare' infinitives;
➤8j verbs + prepositions + infinitives;
➤9 modal verbs + infinitives;
➤15b(i) negative imperative with **tu**;
➤15d(i) as an alternative to the imperative.

(iii) The infinitive as a noun

An infinitive often functions like a noun and can serve as either subject, object or predicate. The infinitive used as a subject or object can be preceded by the masculine form of the definite article.

(*Il*) *viaggiare* mi piace molto.	I like *travelling*.
Preferisco *andare* in aereo.	I prefer *going* by plane.
Questo è *domandare* troppo alla mia amica che detesta (*il*) *viaggiare* in aereo.	This is *asking* too much of my friend, who hates *travelling* by plane.

Some infinitves have become nouns in their own right, such as:

il dispiacere	displeasure, regret	**il dovere**	duty
l'essere	being	**il piacere**	pleasure

(iv)   Prepositions + infinitive

The infinitive is the only part of the verb that can be used after prepositions [▶25b(iii)]. In addition to the prepositions that link the infinitive to a preceding verb, there are certain prepositions which may be followed by an infinitive:

al fine di	with a view to, in order to
al posto di	instead of
allo scopo di	for the purpose of, with the aim of
con	with
dopo	after
invece di	instead of
per	(in order) to
senza	without
tra	between, what with

Quest'anno la mia amica ed io abbiamo intenzione di iscriverci a un corso estivo a Firenze *allo scopo di migliorare* il nostro italiano. *Invece di andare* in aereo la mia amica preferisce andare in macchina *per poter* andare in giro alla fine del corso. *Tra il viaggiare, il dormire, il mangiare* ecc. ci costerà un occhio della testa.

This year my friend and I intend enrolling on a summer course in Florence *with the aim of improving* our Italian. *Instead of going* by plane, my friend prefers to go by car *in order to be able* to travel around at the end of the course. *What with the travelling, accommodation and food,* etc., it will cost us the earth.

 Dopo is always followed by the past infinitive, the only permissible exception to this rule being **dopo mangiato** 'after eating'.

Dopo aver parlato a lungo dei vari corsi, abbiamo deciso di fare quello a Firenze.

After talking at length about the various courses, we have decided to do the one in Florence.

10b What are the present participle and the gerund?

In Italian the *present participle* (**il participio presente**) is distinguished both by its ending and function from the *gerund* (**il gerundio**). The present participle of the majority of verbs is formed by adding **-ante** or **-ente** to the stem of the verb [▶10c(i) below]. The gerund is formed by adding the endings **-ando** or **-endo** to the stem [▶10d(i) below]. Although the present participle and gerund both convey the English form '-ing', they have quite separate functions in Italian and particular care will have to be taken not to confuse them. The functions of both will be explained in the following paragraphs.

10c The present participle

(i) Formation

The present participle is formed by adding **-ante** to the stem of **-are** verbs and **-ente** to the stem of **-ere** and **-ire** verbs.

parlare	**parl*ante***	speaking
contenere	**conten*ente***	containing
servire	**serv*ente***	serving

The plural is formed by replacing **-e** with **-i**.

There are a few participles that have irregular formations, such as:

nutriente	nourishing
proveniente	deriving, coming from
ubbidiente	obeying

(ii) Use of the present participle as a verb

The present participle is seldom used with a verbal function in Italian and it would be advisable to use only the examples you have come across. The present participles listed below are among those that can be used with a verbal function.

appartenente	belonging to
attestante	testifying
concernente	concerning
contenente	containing
indicante	indicating
proveniente	deriving, coming from
rappresentante	representing
riguardante	concerning, regarding

| Il treno *proveniente* da Genova è in arrivo sul binario sette. Durante il viaggio ho letto un articolo *riguardante* il vertice dei paesi *appartenenti* all'ONU (Organizzazione delle Nazioni Unite). | The train *coming* from Genova is arriving on platform 7. During the journey, I read an article *regarding* the summit meeting of the countries *belonging to* the United Nations. |

Whenever you are in any doubt about the use of a present participle, the best solution would be to replace it with a *relative clause*.

| Il treno *che proviene* da Genova ... Ho letto un articolo *che riguarda* ... I paesi *che appartengono* all'ONU ... | The train *(that is) coming* from Genova ... I read an article concerning (*which concerns*) ... The countries *that belong* to the United Nations ... |

(iii) Use of the present participle as an adjective

One of the most frequent uses of the present participle is as an adjective.

acqua *corrente*	*running* water
la lezione *seguente*	the *following* lesson
un bambino *ubbidiente*	an *obedient* child

When it functions as an adjective the participle must agree with the noun it describes.

| una borsa *pesante* | a *heavy* bag |

but

| delle borse *pesanti* | *heavy* bags |

[For agreement of adjectives ending in -e ➤22a(i)B.]

(iv) Present participle as a noun

There are a number of instances where the present participle has acquired the function of a noun, as shown by the following examples:

il cantante	singer
il conoscente	acquaintance
la corrente	stream, draught/draft
l'insegnante	teacher
il passante	passerby
il rappresentante	agent, representative

Note, however, that many '-ing' nouns in English have equivalents in Italian which do not derive from the present participle, for example:

la caccia	hunting	**la lettura**	reading
la dattilografia	typing	**il nuoto**	swimming
l'equitazione	horse riding	**la pesca**	fishing
il giardinaggio	gardening	**la scherma**	fencing

10d *The gerund*

(i) *Formation*

The gerund is formed in the same way as the present participle, except that the endings are **-ando** for **-are** verbs and **-endo** for **-ere** and **-ire** verbs. Italian has two forms of the gerund, the present and the past.

arrivare	**arriv***ando*	arriving (present)
arrivare	**ess***endo* **arrivato**	having arrived (past)
vedere	**ved***endo*	seeing (present)
vedere	**av***endo* **visto**	having seen (past)
finire	**fin***endo*	finishing (present)
finire	**av***endo* **finito**	having finished (past)

 Unlike the present participle, the gerund never changes.

It is worth noting the irregular forms of the following verbs:

bere	**bevendo**	drinking
dire	**dicendo**	saying
fare	**facendo**	doing, making
tradurre	**traducendo**	translating
porre	**ponendo**	putting
trarre	**traendo**	pulling, drawing

Should the need arise to use the present participle of the above verbs, then replace **-endo** with **-ente**.

10e   Main uses of the gerund

(i)   'By doing', 'on doing', 'while doing', 'because of doing'

The gerund has a verbal function and is often used to convey the English 'by -ing', 'on -ing', 'while -ing', and 'because of -ing'.

Facendo il corso a Firenze, spero di migliorare molto il mio italiano.	*By doing* the course in Florence, I hope to improve my Italian a lot.
Passando per la Francia, io e la mia amica coglieremo l'occasione per visitare altri luoghi.	*While going* through France, my friend and I will take the opportunity to visit other places.
Arrivando a Firenze, dobbiamo trovare una sistemazione.	*On arriving* in Florence, we have to find accommodation.
Non avendo molti soldi, cercheremo di prenotare due posti in un ostello della gioventù.	*Not having (because we don't have)* much money, we shall try and reserve two places in a youth hostel.

When the meaning being conveyed is 'although -ing', then the gerund in Italian is preceded by **pur:**

Pur avendo una conoscenza elementare della lingua italiana preferiamo iscriverci al corso per principianti.	*Although having (Although we have)* an elementary knowledge of the language, we prefer to enrol on a beginners' course.

The present form of the gerund can be used to indicate a simultaneous action.

Sfogliando un giornale italiano ho visto l'annuncio per questo corso a Firenze.	*While looking through* an Italian newspaper, I saw the advertisement for this course in Florence.

The past gerund tends to be used less frequently. When it is used, the action described occurs prior to the action of the verb in the main sentence.

Avendo visto l'annuncio, ho deciso di scrivere subito per chiedere informazioni relative al corso.	*Having seen* the advertisement, I decided to write immediately to ask for information about the course.

Note that the past gerund is formed from the present gerund of the auxiliary **essere** or **avere** and the past participle of the verb.

[For which auxiliary to use ►11c; for position of pronouns with the gerund ►23b(iv).]

The gerund nearly always refers to the subject of the main sentence. This is true for all the examples quoted above. When the gerund does not refer to the subject of the main sentence, then it is advisable to use a subordinate sentence introduced by the appropriate conjunction.

Sfogliando il giornale ho visto l'annuncio.	*While looking through* the newspaper, I saw the advertisement. (same subject = *I*)
Ho visto la mia amica *che sfogliava* il giornale.	I saw my friend *looking through* the newspaper. (different subject, i.e. *the friend* was looking, not *I*).

(ii) Progressive tenses

The gerund is also used after **stare, andare** and occasionally **venire** to form the *progressive tenses* [►8k(i)-(ii)].

Perché *stai sfogliando* il giornale italiano?	Why *are you looking through* the Italian newspaper?
La mia amica *andava leggendo* le riviste e i giornali italiani per migliorare la sua comprensione della lingua.	My friend *kept on reading* Italian magazines and newspapers to improve her understanding of the language.

(iii) Translating the English '-ing'

In other circumstances, the English verb ending '-ing' is usually rendered by the infinitive in Italian, either dependent upon another verb (with or without a linking preposition [►8i,j]) or used as a verbal noun [►10a(iii)]. If the subjects of the two verbs are different, a subjunctive may be needed.

Smetti di *guardare* la televisione un attimo. Come faccio a parlarti del corso se continui a *fissare* quel televisore?	Stop *watching* television a moment. How can I speak to you about the course if you continue *staring at* that television set?

Leggere mi aiuta a migliorare la comprensione della lingua. Prima di *andare* a fare il corso in Italia, intendo *leggere* molto in italiano.	*Reading* helps me to improve my understanding of the language. Before *going* to do the course in Italy, I intend *reading* a lot in Italian.

10f   The past participle

(i)   Formation

The past participle of regular verbs is formed as follows:

infinitive	**past participle**
trovare	trov*ato*
vendere	vend*uto*
finire	fin*ito*

[For verbs that have irregular past participles ➤18d(i), 19g(ii),19h.]

(ii)   The uses of the past participle

(**A**) In the formation of compound tenses [➤11c]:

Ho *mandato* la lettera.	I have *sent* the letter.
Saranno già *partiti*.	They will already have *left*.

[For agreement of the past participle in compound tenses ➤11d.]

(**B**) To form the passive with **essere, andare** and **venire**:

La lettera è stata *imbucata*.	The letter has been *posted/mailed*.
Questa lettera va *imbucata* oggi.	This letter must be *posted/mailed* today.
Ulteriori dettagli verranno *mandati* domani.	Further details will be *sent* tomorrow.

Note that the past participle agrees in gender and number with the subject of **essere, andare** and **venire**. [For full details of the passive ➤17.]

(**C**) As an adjective, in which case it agrees with the noun in the usual way ➤ 22a(i):

un'occasione *mancata*	a *missed* opportunity
le finestre *chiuse*	the *closed* windows

• Some past participles have become an adjective in their own right and may be used with **essere** with no hint of a passive:

Nella mia famiglia, siamo tutti *appassionati* dello sport.	In my family, we are all *enthusiastic about* sport.

(**D**) As a noun:

i *sopravvissuti* della tragedia	the *survivors* of the tragedy
la *scomparsa* della ragazza	the *disappearance* of the girl

(**E**) In *participle* clauses, where English may need a relative or other construction:

Il bambino, *investito* dalla macchina, è stato ricoverato all'ospedale.	The child, (who was) *knocked down* by the car, has been admitted to the hospital.

The past participle can also be used in absolute clauses meaning 'something having been done' or 'when something has/had been done'.

Scritta la lettera, sono andato ad imbucarla.	*When I had written the letter* (*the letter written*), I went to post/mail it.

When the verb in the absolute clause is transitive, then it must agree in gender and number with the object (**la lettera**) it governs. When the verb in the absolute clause is intransitive and it refers to the subject of the main clause, then the past participle agrees in gender and number with that subject.

Partiti di casa, siamo andati subito alla stazione.	*Having left* the house, we went straight to the station.

The *past* participle is sometimes used in Italian, particularly when describing positions, where in English the *present* participle is used:

appoggiato	leaning
seduto	sitting
sdraiato	lying (down)

Il ragazzo era *sdraiato* per terra.	The boy was *lying* on the ground.

The passage of time and the use of tenses

11a   What do tenses tell us?

Tense is not the same thing as *time*, though the same words are often used to refer to both. Time is a fact of life, in which there are only three time zones (past, present and future). Tenses, on the other hand, are grammatical structures which often reflect a way of looking at an event as well as recording when it happened. Both the number of tenses, the names given to them and their uses vary greatly from one language to another.

11b   One word or two? Simple and compound tenses

In the language of grammar, a *simple* tense is a one word form, while a *compound* tense uses two or more words (an auxiliary verb + one or more past participles or a gerund, depending on the tense).

Italian verbs have two series of tenses: the *simple* and the *progressive* (or *continuous*). The latter type [➤10e(ii)] will be referred to as *progressive* tenses throughout this book. In theory, any tense can have a progressive form, though it is most frequently used in the present and imperfect.

Cosa *stai facendo* in cucina?	What *are you doing* in the kitchen?
Sto lavando i piatti.	*I am washing* the dishes.
Stavo mangiando quando hai telefonato.	*I was eating* when you rang/called.

11c   Auxiliary verbs used to form compound tenses
(i)   Avere

Most verbs in Italian - all transitive verbs and a certain number of intransitive verbs - form their compound tenses using **avere** as the auxiliary.

aver trovato	to have found	perfect infinitive
ho trovato	I have found, I found	perfect
avevo trovato	I had found	pluperfect
avrò trovato	I shall have found	future perfect
avrei trovato	I would have found	conditional perfect
ebbi trovato	I had found	past anterior
abbia trovato	I have found, I found	perfect subjunctive
avessi trovato	I had found	pluperfect subjunctive

(ii)   Essere

A considerable number of Italian verbs form their compound tenses with **essere:**

essere andato	to have gone	perfect infinitive
sono andato	I have gone, I went	perfect
ero andato	I had gone	pluperfect
sarò andato	I shall have gone	future perfect
sarei andato	I would have gone	conditional perfect
fui andato	I had gone	past anterior
sia andato	I have gone, I went	perfect subjunctive
fossi andato	I had gone	pluperfect subjunctive

Which verbs form their compound tenses with **essere**?
The MAJORITY of intransitive verbs;
MOST impersonal verbs;
ALL reflexive verbs.
[For a definition of transitive and intransitive ➤8a(i).]

(iii)   *Intransitive verbs*

It is possible to categorize a number of verbs used intransitively under certain headings:

(**A**) Verbs that indicate movement and, in some instances, lack of movement:

andare	go
arrivare	arrive
cadere	fall
emigrare	emigrate
entrare	enter
essere	be
fuggire	escape
giungere	arrive, reach
partire	leave

passare	go through, drop in
restare	stay, remain
rimanere	stay, remain
salire	go/come up
scappare	run away
scendere	go/come down
sorgere	rise
stare	be, stay
tornare	return
uscire	go out
venire	come

Ieri *siamo stati* a casa tutto il giorno.	Yesterday *we were* at home all day.
Sabato sera *sono andato* al cinema. *Sono uscito* verso le sette e *sono tornato* a casa a mezzanotte.	On Saturday evening *I went* to the cinema/movies. *I went out* about seven o'clock and *got back* home at midnight.

(**B**) Verbs that indicate some process of change, often of a physical or psychological nature:

apparire	appear
arrossire	blush
comparire	appear
crescere	grow up
dimagrire	lose weight
divenire	become
diventare	become
fiorire	flower, blossom
guarire	recover
impallidire	turn pale
impazzire	go mad
ingrassare	put on weight
invecchiare	age, grow old
morire	die
nascere	be born
scomparire	disappear
scoppiare	blow up, burst out
sparire	disappear
svanire	vanish, disappear
svenire	faint

Sono cresciuto in campagna.	*I grew up* in the country.
È nata nel 1978.	*She was born* in 1978.
Sono scoppiati a ridere.	*They burst out* laughing.
Sono ingrassato di cinque chili.	*I have put on* five kilos.

(C) Other verbs used intransitively that take **essere** include:

dipendere	depend
durare	last
emergere	emerge, come out
esistere	exist
intervenire	intervene
prevalere	prevail
ricorrere	turn to, resort to
risultare	turn out to be
riuscire	succeed, manage

Sono riuscito a capire tutto.	*I managed* to understand everything.
Lo spettacolo *è durato* due ore e mezza.	The show *lasted* two and a half hours.

(iv)   Impersonal verbs

(A) Verbs referring to the weather [➤8g(i)], such as **piovere, nevicare, gelare, grandinare, lampeggiare, tuonare** etc., traditionally took the auxiliary **essere** but modern usage tends to accept either **essere** or **avere**, for example:

è nevicato or **ha nevicato**	it has snowed/it snowed

(B) There are a number of verbs that are, or can be, used impersonally which take **essere**. They include the following:

accadere	happen
avvenire	happen
bastare	be sufficient
capitare	happen
convenire	be fitting, be advisable
costare	cost
bisognare	be necessary
dispiacere	be sorry
importare	matter

mancare	lack, miss
occorrere	be necessary
parere	seem, appear
rincrescere	be sorry
sembrare	seem, appear
servire	be of use
spettare	be up to, be the duty of
succedere	happen
toccare	be up to
valere	be worth
volerci	take, require

Cos'è *successo*?	What *has happened*?
Ci *è voluta* più di un'ora per arrivare alla stazione.	It *took* more than an hour to get to the station.
Mi *è piaciuto* molto il libro.	I *liked* the book a lot.
Però, mi *è costato* parecchio.	However, *it cost* me a lot.

Note that **voluta** agrees with the feminine singular subject **un'ora**.

(v) *Reflexive verbs*

All verbs used reflexively take **essere**:

***Mi sono svegliato* alle sette, *mi sono alzato* subito, *mi sono lavato* e *mi sono vestito*.**	I *woke up* at seven o'clock, *got up* immediately, *washed* and *got dressed*.

Many verbs used reflexively also have non-reflexive forms, in which case they take **avere**:

***Ho svegliato* mio fratello.**	I *woke up* my brother.
***Ho alzato* la mano.**	I *raised* my hand.
***Ho lavato* i piatti.**	I *washed* the dishes.
***Ho vestito* il bambino.**	I *dressed* the child.

(vi) *Verbs that can take either **essere** or **avere***

There are some verbs that take **essere** when they are used intransitively and **avere** when they are not. Some of the most common ones include:

aumentare	increase
cambiare	change
cominciare	start
correre	run
diminuire	decrease, go down
finire	finish
guarire	cure, recover
migliorare	improve
passare	pass, spend (time)
peggiorare	worsen
salire	go up, get in
saltare	jump, skip
scendere	go down, get out of
suonare	ring
vivere	live
volare	fly

La mia vita *è cambiata*.	My life *has changed*. (intransitive)
Ho cambiato idea.	*I have changed* my mind. (transitive)
È saltato in acqua.	He jumped into the water. (intransitive)
Ha saltato il pranzo.	*He skipped* lunch. (transitive)
Siamo scesi dal treno.	*We got off* the train. (intransitive)
Abbiamo sceso le scale.	*We went down* the stairs. (transitive)
Il mio italiano *è migliorato*.	My Italian *has improved*. (intransitive)
Ho migliorato il mio italiano.	*I have improved* my Italian. (transitive)

Note that some of the verbs mentioned in the above list take either **avere** or **essere** when used intransitively. In such cases, there is a difference in meaning according to the auxiliary used.

Correre, saltare and **volare** take **essere** when they indicate 'movement to a place', and **avere** in other intransitive expressions.

Siamo volati alla stazione.	We flew (rushed) to the station.
Dopo la lezione *sono corso* a casa.	After the lesson, *I ran* home.
Sono saltato dalla macchina.	*I jumped* from the car.

but

Abbiamo corso **per un'ora.**	*We ran* for an hour.
Ho saltato **per dieci minuti.**	I *jumped* for ten minutes.
Non *ho* **mai** *volato* **in un elicottero.**	I *have* never *flown* in a helicopter.

Note also that **vivere** can take either **avere** or **essere** when used intransitively.

Sono vissuti (Hanno vissuto) **in quell'appartamento per quasi dieci anni.**	They *lived* in that flat/apartment for almost ten years.

(vii) The modals *dovere, potere* and *volere* [➤9a, 9b, 9d]

Although it was considered more correct to use **essere** with the above modals when their accompanying infinitive required **essere**, modern usage accepts either **essere** or **avere**. In fact, the tendency is to use **avere** relatively frequently these days when one wishes to emphasize the value of the modal verb.

Non *siamo potuti* **venire al matrimonio.**	*We could* not *come* to the wedding.
Sono voluto **partire di buon'ora.**	I *wanted* to leave early.
La mia amica *è dovuta* **rimanere a casa.**	My friend *had* to stay at home.

These three modals take **avere** when the infinitive that follows would use **avere** to form its compound tense.

Non *abbiamo voluto* **prendere il treno delle sette.**	*We did* not *want* to catch the seven o'clock train.
Alla fine *ho dovuto* **mandare un telegramma.**	In the end, I *had* to send a telegram(me).
Non *ha potuto* **prestarmi il libro.**	*She could* not lend me the book.

If **dovere, volere** or **potere** is used with a reflexive verb, then there are two possible constructions. The auxiliary is **essere** when the reflexive pronoun precedes the modal and **avere** when the reflexive pronoun remains attached to the infinitive.

Mi sono dovuto alzare presto.	I had to get up early.
but	
Ho dovuto alzar*mi* presto.	I had to get up early.

(viii)   The passive [➤17]

Essere is used to form all tenses of the passive.

La macchina *è riparata*.	The car *is repaired*.
Non *saranno* tutti *invitati*.	They *will* not all *be invited*.
Molte case *sono state danneggiate*.	Many houses *have been damaged*.

[For verbs other than **essere** to express the passive ➤17d.]

11d   Past participle agreement in compound tenses

The following rules for agreement of past participles apply across all compound tenses.

(i)   Compound tenses formed with *avere*

The past participle of a verb conjugated with **avere** *never* agrees:

• with the subject:

Maria ha *comprato* la gonna.	*Maria has bought the skirt.*

• nor with a preceding indirect object pronoun [➤23b(iii)]:

Le ho *dato* il giornale.	I *gave her (= to her)* the newspaper.

Agreement is *optional*:

• when the direct object precedes the verb:

La gonna che Maria ha *comprato* è molto cara. or *La gonna che* Maria ha *comprata* è molto cara.	*The skirt* that Maria has *bought* is very expensive.

The direct object is the relative pronoun [►23m(ii)] **che**, which stands for **la gonna**, thus the agreement. In this type of relative construction it is much more common to leave the past participle unchanged, i.e. **la gonna che Maria ha** *comprato*.

• when the direct object pronouns are **mi, ti, ci, vi** [►23b(ii)]:

Maria, *ti* ho *vista* (*ti* ho *visto*) in città.	Mary, I *saw you* in town.

• when the pronoun **ne** [►23f] refers to a specific quantity. In this case, the **ne** can agree with the noun it refers to or the quantity:

Quanto vino hai bevuto? – Ne ho *bevuto/bevuti* due bicchieri.	How much wine did you drink? – I drank two glasses.
Quante sigarette hai comprato? – Ne ho *comprate/comprati* tre pacchetti.	How many cigarettes did you buy? – I bought three packs.
Quanti spaghetti hai mangiato? – Ne ho *mangiati/mangiato* mezzo chilo.	How much spaghetti did you eat? – I ate half a kilogram(me).

The past participle *must* agree:

• when it is preceded by the direct object pronouns **lo, la, li, le** [►23b(ii)]:

Maria *l'(la)* ha *comprata* stamattina.	Maria *bought it* this morning.

• when the pronoun is **ne** and the meaning being conveyed is 'some' or 'part of' something:

Hai bevuto del vino? – Sì, *ne* ho *bevuto*.	Have you drunk some wine? – Yes, I have *drunk some (of it)*.
Hai comprato delle sigarette? – Sì, *ne* ho *comprate*.	Have you bought some cigarettes? – Yes, I have *bought some (of them)*.
Hai mangiato degli spaghetti? – Sì, *ne* ho *mangiati*.	Have you eaten some spaghetti? – Yes, I have *eaten some*.

(ii)   *Compound tenses formed with **essere***

The past participles of compound tenses formed with **essere** agree in number and gender with the subject of the verb:

Ieri sera sono *andato* al concerto con mio fratello. *I miei genitori* sono *rimasti* a casa e *mia sorella* è *uscita* con il suo ragazzo.	Last night *I went* to the concert with my brother. *My parents stayed* at home and *my sister went out* with her boyfriend.

In the case of reflexive verbs, the past participle can agree either with the subject:

La ragazza si è *lavata* i capelli.	*The girl washed* her hair.

or the direct object:

La ragazza si è *lavati i capelli*.	The girl *washed her hair*.

12 **The present tenses**

The *indicative* tenses explained in chapters 12 to 14 (as opposed to *subjunctive* tenses explained in chapter 16), are used to assert that something is true or certain.

12a *The simple present [➤18c(i)]*

This has a variety of functions. It can describe the following:

(i) *What the situation is now*

Cosa *fai*? – *Leggo* il giornale.	What *are* you *doing*? – I'm *reading* the newspaper.

[See also the present progressive ➤12b.]

(ii) *What happens sometimes or usually*

***Leggo* il giornale ogni sera.**	I *read* the newspaper every evening.
Di solito *guardo* il telegiornale prima di cenare.	I usually *watch* the TV news before having dinner.

(iii) *What is going to happen soon or in the future*

In such expressions the future is specified by a *time expression*.

Marco, apparecchia per favore, fra poco *mangiamo*.	Marco, lay/set the table please; *we shall be eating* shortly.

Note: In Italian it is fairly common to express immediate future tense ideas using the present tense.

Ci *vediamo* l'anno prossimo.	*We shall see each other* next year.

La settimana prossima *andiamo* in vacanza.	Next week *we are going* on holiday/vacation.

(iv) What has been happening up to now and may be going to continue

***Abito* in questa casa da cinque anni, cioè dal 1988.**	*I have been living* in this house for five years, that is, since 1988.

This is an occasion where different tenses are used in Italian and English. Note also that the English words 'since' or 'for' are conveyed in Italian by ***da***.

The above construction can also be expressed in the following ways:

È da cinque anni che abito in questa casa. or **Sono cinque anni che abito in questa casa.**	I have been living in this house for five years.

Note that in the first example the verb **è** is *always* singular, whereas in the second type of construction the verb has to agree in number with the noun that follows, for example, **è un anno** but **sono cinque anni**.

To ask 'how long someone/something has been -ing', it is possible to use either **da quanto tempo** or **quanto tempo è che?**

***Da quanto tempo* abiti in questa casa? – Da cinque anni.** ***Quanto tempo è che* piove? – Da tre ore.**	*How long* have you been living in this house? – For five years. *How long* has it been raining? – For three hours.

(v) Narrative present

The present tense in Italian can be used in both speech and writing to describe recent or distant past events. This is called the *historic* or *narrative* present and it has the effect of bringing to life or of dramatizing the action or event. Its use is more widespread in Italian than in English, where it tends to be limited to newspaper headlines of the type 'Tennis star signs new contract'.

Ti *chiedo* di darmi una mano a spostare i mobili, *dici* che *vieni* subito e mezz'ora dopo *stai* sempre *seduto* davanti al televisore.	I *ask(ed)* you to give me a hand to move the furniture; you *say (said)* you *will come (would come)* right away and half an hour later you *are (were)* still *sitting* in front of the television set.
Cinquant'anni fa il regista di questo film *muore* in un incidente stradale.	Fifty years ago, the director of this film/movie *died* in a road accident.

12b   The present progressive

The present progressive is formed with the present tense of **stare** + the gerund [➤10e(ii)]. In some circumstances it may also be formed using **andare** or **venire** as the auxiliary. It is used as an alternative to the simple present [➤12a(i)] but the action *must* be in progress at the time referred to.

Cosa *stai facendo*? – *Sto leggendo* il giornale.	What *are you doing*? – I am *reading* the newspaper.

You cannot use this tense to say what *is happening shortly*, as in 12a(iii).

The past tenses

Italian has the following past tenses: the perfect (**passato prossimo**), the imperfect (**imperfetto**), the past definite (**passato remoto**), the pluperfect (**trapassato prossimo**) and the past anterior (**trapassato remoto**).

13a *The perfect*

This is a compound tense formed with the present tense of **avere** or **essere** and the past participle [➤11c(i), 11c(ii)]. [For complete conjugation of the perfect tense ➤19; for past participle agreements ➤11d.]

In Italian the perfect tense, sometimes called the *present perfect*, has two uses. One corresponds almost exactly to the English perfect tense 'I have written'. The other replaces the simple past or past definite tense [➤18c(vi)] 'I wrote'.

The perfect tense can be used:

(i) To convey the idea of something that started in the past but is still connected to the here and now:

Mi è sempre piaciuto **l'italiano.**	*I've always liked* Italian. (and I *still* like it)
Ma *non sono mai andato* **in Italia.**	But *I've never been* to Italy. (up to *now*)

(ii) To talk about a series of repeated actions that have happened up to the present:

Ho spesso pensato **di andare in Italia con una mia amica**	*I've often thought* of going to Italy with a friend of mine.

(iii) To talk about a past action or event that is completely finished but whose effects are still felt now:

Purtroppo, questa mia amica *ha* ***perso*** **il suo lavoro.**	Unfortunately, this friend of mine *has lost* her job. (and *now* she cannot afford to come to Italy with me even if she wanted to)

(iv)   To talk about a recent event:

Hai visto **la tua amica? – Sì, l'***ho* *vista* **stamattina**.	*Have you seen* your friend? – Yes, *I saw (have seen) her this morning.*

Note: In the North and some parts of Central Italy, it is common to use the perfect tense, rather than the past definite, to talk about completed past actions and events even though they happened some time ago.

Due anni fa *ho pensato* **di andare in Italia ma alla fine** *ho deciso* **di andare in Francia**.	Two years ago *I thought* of going to Italy, but then *I decided* to go to France.

13b   *The imperfect [➤18c(v)]*

One of the most frequent uses of the imperfect tense is to convey the English 'was/were -ing', 'used to'. The tense often denotes an unfinished or repeated action in the past. It is used in the following situations:

(i)   *To indicate something which was unfinished or continuing, often interrupted by another event:*

Guardavo **un film alla televisione quando la mia amica mi ha telefonato.**	*I was watching* a film/movie on television when my friend rang/called me.

Note: There is also a progressive form of the imperfect which may be used in examples such as the one above [➤8k(i)].

Stavo guardando **un film alla televisione quando la mia amica ha telefonato.**	*I was watching* a film/movie on television when my friend rang/called.

(ii) *To indicate something repeated or habitual in the past:*

Quando la mia amica *lavorava*, *uscivamo* insieme almeno due volte alla settimana.	When my friend *was working, we went out (we would go out/we used to go out)* together at least twice a week.

 As the above examples show, the imperfect is expressed in English in a number of forms. When the English is 'was/were doing' or 'used to do', the decision to use the imperfect is straightforward. Care is needed, however, on the many occasions where the English form suggests another tense, as in 'went out/would go out' above. Note also that a repeated past action, which is not a habit, is conveyed by the perfect tense [➤13a] and not the imperfect:

La mia amica mi *ha telefonato* due volte.	My friend *rang/called* me twice. (i.e. on *two separate occasions*, each one *complete* in itself)

(iii) *To indicate two simultaneous actions:*

Mentre *guardavo* la televisione, *sbrigavo* le faccende domestiche.	While *I was watching* television, *I did* the housework.

(iv) *To give a descriptive background in the past:*

La mia amica *lavorava* in un'agenzia di viaggi. Le *piaceva* molto il suo lavoro anche se la paga non *era* molto buona. Siccome l'agenzia *si trovava* a un chilometro da casa sua, *andava* sempre a piedi. Quando *pioveva*, *prendeva* l'autobus.	My friend *worked* in a travel agency. She *liked* her work a lot even if the pay *wasn't* very good. As the agency *was situated* a kilometre/kilometer from her home, she always *went* on foot. When it *rained*, she *caught* the bus.

(v) To express an intention or wish that remains unfulfilled or unrealized. In spoken Italian, the imperfect is often used instead of the conditional perfect [➤14e], and especially with **dovere, potere** and **volere**:

La mia amica *poteva* (*avrebbe potuto*) trasferirsi a un'altra agenzia e poi non *perdeva* (*avrebbe perduto*) il lavoro ma ha respinto l'offerta.	My friend *could have* transferred to another agency and then she *would*n't *have lost* her job, but she rejected the offer.

(vi) Instead of the present tense or present conditional to express polite requests:

***Vuoi* (*Volevi*) uscire stasera?**	*Did you want (Were you wanting) to go out this evening?*
Ti ho telefonato perché *vorrei* (*volevo*) chiederti un piacere.	I rang/called you because I *would like* (*was wanting*) to ask you a favour/favor.

(vii) Instead of the pluperfect subjunctive and conditional perfect in constructions introduced by **si** [➤16j(iii)]:

Se *ti trasferivi* (*ti fossi trasferita*) a quell'altra agenzia, non *perdevi* (*avresti perduto*) il	**lavoro.** If you *had transferred* to that other agency, you *would*n't *have* lost the

(viii) In expressions of time, introduced by *da*, to indicate that something *had been going on* a certain time, and might well have continued:

***Lavoravo* da tre anni presso quell'agenzia di viaggi quando mi hanno chiesto di trasferirmi.**	I *had been working* at that travel agency for three years when they asked me to transfer.

Note: The same construction can also be expressed as follows:

Erano tre anni che lavoravo presso quell'agenzia... or **Era da tre anni che lavoravo presso quell'agenzia...**	I had been working at that agency for three years...

13c The past definite [➤18c(vi)]

The past definite is used to describe past events that have completely finished. It tells you what *happened* on a particular occasion.

La mia amica *lasciò* la scuola all'età di 16 anni e *trovò* subito un lavoro presso un'agenzia di viaggi.	My friend *left* school at the age of 16 and immediately *found* a job with a travel agency.

The past definite can refer to short, quickly finished actions or to events that ended after a longer period of time, which could be weeks, months, years or even centuries.

Lavorò presso questa agenzia per tre anni.	She *worked* at this agency for three years.

The use of the past definite is now mainly limited to the written language. However, this tense is used in spoken Italian in some parts of Central Italy and particularly in the South, even when the actions or events referred to are *recent*.

Ieri sera io e la mia amica *andammo* al cinema.	Yesterday evening my friend and I *went* to the cinema/movies.

In Northern Italy, the tendency would be to use the perfect instead of the past definite in all of the above examples, both in speech and informal writing.

13d The pluperfect

This is a compound tense formed with the imperfect of the auxiliary **avere** or **essere** [➤11c(i), 11c(ii)] and the past participle. It corresponds in most cases to the English pluperfect, indicating what *had happened before* a subsequent event in the past. Its name means 'more than perfect, further back in the past'.

Ero appena *arrivato* a casa quando *telefonò* la mia amica.	I *had* just *arrived* home when my friend rang/called.

Voleva dirmi che *aveva deciso* **di lasciare il suo posto presso l'agenzia di viaggi.** *Aveva lavorato* **lì per tre anni.**	She wanted to tell me that she *had decided* to leave her job at the travel agent's. She *had worked* there for three years.

 When you want to say that something had been going on for a certain time, and was likely to continue, you use the imperfect with **da** + time expression [➤13b(viii)], not the pluperfect.

13e The past anterior [➤19]

This is a compound tense formed with the past definite of **avere** or **essere** and the past participle. This tense is not used in spoken Italian. It can be found in literary and other printed texts. It has the same meaning as the pluperfect [➤13d] and is used after conjunctions of time (**dopo che** 'after', **quando** 'when', **appena** 'as soon as') when the past definite is used in the main clause:

Appena la mia amica *ebbe lasciato* **la scuola, trovò un lavoro.**	As soon as my friend *had left* school, she found a job.

In speech, and often in writing, the past anterior would be replaced by the pluperfect.

Appena la mia amica *aveva lasciato* **la scuola...**	As soon as my friend *had left* school...

14 The future and conditional tenses

14a The simple future [▶18c(iii)]

The simple future (**il futuro semplice**) is the literal equivalent of the English future tense, i.e. it tells you what will happen at a point in the future, although it is not the only, or even necessarily the most common way of expressing this concept [▶12a(iii)]. It is used for the following:

(i) To state simply what will happen

Prima di uscire *mi laverò* i capelli.	Before going out, *I shall wash* my hair.

(ii) To express definite convictions and plans

Domani sera *resterò* a casa e non *farò* niente.	Tomorrow evening *I shall stay* at home and *do* nothing.

(iii) To give emphatic, often rather condescending instructions, as in English

Non *starai seduto* tutta la sera a fare niente, *risponderai* a quella lettera.	*You will* not *sit down* all evening doing nothing; *you will answer* that letter.

(iv) To express supposition or approximation. In English such expressions are often conveyed by 'must', 'may be', 'could'.

Saranno le undici passate e non è ancora tornato a casa. Dove *sarà*? – *Sarà* con il suo amico Roberto.	*It must be* after eleven o'clock. Where *could he be*? – *He may be* with his friend Roberto.

(v)   *In sentences introduced by* **se**

Se non *tornerà* fra poco, *telefonerò* al suo amico.	If *he is* not *back* soon, *I shall ring/call* his friend.

Note that English uses the present tense after 'if' whereas Italian has a future tense. However, it is also possible and fairly common to use the present tense in Italian after **se**.

Se non *torna* fra poco, *telefonerò* al suo amico.	If *he is* not *back* soon, *I shall ring/call* his friend.

(vi)   *After conjunctions of time*

The future is normally required after a range of time words such as **quando** 'when', **appena** 'as soon as' and **finché** 'as long as' when the verb in the main sentence is also future. After the conjunction of time, a present tense would be used in English.

Quando *arriverà* a casa, *sarà* stanco morto. Finché *vivrò*, non *capirò* mai perché deve sempre tornare a casa tardi.	When *he arrives* home, *he will be* dead tired. As long as *I live*, *I shall* never *understand* why he always comes home late.

14b   *The future perfect*

The future perfect (**il futuro anteriore**) is a compound tense using the auxiliary **essere** or **avere** in the future tense [➤11c(i), 11c(ii)] + the past participle. It tells you what *will have happened* and is used:

(i)   *To say what will have happened, often by the time something else happens*

Saranno preoccupati i tuoi genitori? – No, *saranno andati* a letto.	Will your parents be worried? – No, *they will have gone* to bed.

(ii)   To indicate supposition and approximation, similarly to paragraph 14a(iv), where the English verb would usually be in the perfect.

Ma dove *sarà andato? Avrà perduto* l'ultima corriera.	But where *can he have gone?* He *must have missed* the last bus.

(iii)   *After conjunctions of time*

The rule governing the use of the future perfect after the conjunctions of time **quando** 'when', **appena** 'as soon as' and **dopo che** 'after' is the same as for the use of the simple future tense referred to in 14a(vi) above.

Quando *avremo finito* di guardare questo programma, andremo a letto.	When *we have finished* watching this program(me), we shall go to bed.

Notice that such sentences do not use a future or future perfect in English after the conjunction of time, but a perfect tense. Particular care is therefore needed when expressing this idea in Italian.

14c   *Alternatives to the future*

The simple future tense is not the most frequent way of expressing future time in Italian, especially in everyday speech. Other forms are often used and these include:

(i)   *The present tense [➤12a(iii)]*

The present tense is frequently used, as in English, to refer to the immediate future, especially for prearranged events.

A che ora *ci vediamo* domani sera? – Alle otto in piazza. – E cosa *facciamo?* – Prima, *facciamo* una bella passeggiata lungo il fiume, poi *andiamo* a mangiare una pizza. – E dopo? – Dopo, *torniamo* a casa.	At what time *are we seeing (shall we see) each other* tomorrow evening? – At eight o'clock in the square. – And what *are we doing?* – First, *we are going* for a nice walk along the river, then *we are going* to have a pizza. – And then? – Then, *we are going* home.

Italian uses the simple present here, *never* the present progressive.

(ii) **Pensare di**, *etc*

Future plans and intentions are also conveyed by **pensare di, avere intenzione di, avere in mente di** and **avere in programma**.

Cosa *pensi di* fare quest'estate? – Ho *in mente di* andare negli Stati Uniti. *Hai* qualcosa *in programma* per questo finesettimana? – No, *ho intenzione di* rimanere a casa.	What *are you thinking of* doing this summer? – *I intend* going to the United States. *Have you* something *planned* for this weekend? – No, *I intend* staying at home.

 Care must be taken with English expressions such as 'Will you close the door?', where the English auxiliary 'will' does not express futurity but willingness [➤9d(ii)].

Vuoi chiudere la porta, per favore?	*Will* you close the door, please?

14d **The present conditional** *[➤18c(iv)]*

The present conditional (**il condizionale presente**) has a number of uses, including:

(i) *Polite requests and preference*

Vorrei un chilo di pomodori. *Potrei* assaggiare un po' di questo formaggio? *Preferirei* pagare con un assegno.	*I would like* a kilo of tomatoes. *Could I* try a bit of this cheese? *I would rather* pay by cheque/check.

(ii) *Making suggestions and giving advice*

Dovrebbero prendere il treno delle nove e quindici. Io non *prenderei* quello che parte mezz'ora prima perché è sempre affollato.	*They should* catch the 9:15 train. *I would*n't catch the one that leaves half an hour before because it's always crowded.

(iii) *In reported speech*

To report what someone else is saying:

Anche gli altri dicono che sarebbe meglio partire più tardi.	Even the others say that *it would be* better to leave later.

 Great care has to be taken over the use of the conditional in reported speech. When the verb of reporting is in the past tense, then the conditional perfect must be used in the dependent clause [➤14e(iv)].

(iv) *To say what would happen under certain conditions, often after a clause with* **se** *[➤16j]*

Che cosa *faresti* tu Maria? **Se io fossi in te, *accetterei* il consiglio degli altri.**	What *would you do*, Maria? If I were you, *I would accept* the advice of the others.

(v) *To express a doubt*

È meglio partire più tardi? – Non *saprei*.	Is it better to leave later? – *I do*n't *know* (*I would*n't *know*).

The use of the conditional tense conveys a mood of *uncertainty,* which would not be the case if the present tense were used.

(vi) *To quote someone else's opinion or to report unconfirmed news*

Secondo un mio amico, i macchinisti *farebbero* sciopero domani.	According to a friend of mine, the train drivers *are going on* strike tomorrow.

14e   *The conditional perfect*

The conditional perfect tense (**il condizionale passato**) is a compound tense formed with the conditional of the auxiliary **avere** or **essere** [➤11c(i), 11c(ii)] and the past participle. It tells you what *could have happened*. The uses are much the same as those explained under paragraph 14d, only now the actions and events referred to are in the *past*. It is used in the following situations:

(i)   *To express an unfulfilled wish or preference*

Avrei *voluto* un chilo di pomodori.	*I would have liked* a kilo of tomatoes.
Avrei *preferito* pagare con un assegno.	*I would have preferred* to pay by cheque/check.

(ii)   *To make suggestions and give advice*

Avresti *dovuto* prendere il treno delle nove e quindici come avevo detto io.	*You should have* caught the 9:15 train as I told you.

(iii)   *When used negatively, to convey a sense of surprise or disbelief*

Io non *avrei* mai *preso* il treno che parte mezz'ora prima perché è sempre affollato.	*I would* never *have taken* the train that leaves half an hour before because it's always crowded.

(iv)   *In reported speech*

Gli altri hanno detto che *sarebbe stato* meglio partire più tardi.	The others said that *it would be* better to leave later.

 In reported (indirect) speech, when the verb in the main sentence is in the *past tense*, then the *conditional perfect* must be used in the subordinate clause introduced by **che**, unlike English which uses the present conditional. This rule applies in similar constructions when the main sentence contains the past tense of verbs such as **pensare, credere, sperare, immaginare, promettere**, etc.

| Sapevo che *avresti preso* il treno delle nove e quindici. | I knew that *you would take* the 9:15 train. |

However, the present conditional may be used when the action is to be realized at some point in the future.

| Speravo che *partiresti* domani mattina. | I was hoping that *you would leave* tomorrow morning. |

(v) *To say what would have happened under certain conditions, after a clause with* **se** *[►16j]*

| Che cosa *avresti fatto* tu Maria? | What *would you have done,* Maria? |
| Se fossi stata in te, *avrei accettato* il consiglio degli altri. | If I had been you, *I would have accepted* the advice of the others. |

Note: Past hypotheses after **se** can be expressed by using an imperfect tense in both sentences [►16j(iii)]:

| Se *ero* in te, *accettavo* il consiglio degli altri. | If *I had been* you, *I would have accepted* the advice of the others. |

(vi) *To express a personal opinion about a past action*

| Penso che *avresti dovuto* accettare il loro consiglio. | I think *you should have* accepted their advice. |

Note: To express 'should' or 'ought to' use **dovere**. To express 'could' or 'might' use **potere**.

| *Avresti potuto* prendere il pullman. | *You could have* taken the coach/bus. |

 Would' in English does not necessarily imply condition and may denote willingness [►9d(ii)], in which case the imperfect or past definite of **volere** is used.

| Non *voleva/volle* dare retta a nessuno. | He *would*n't listen to anyone. |

It may also describe an habitual action in the past, when the imperfect of the verb is used [►13b(ii)].

| Ogni mattina *si alzavano* alla stessa ora. | Every morning *they would get up* at the same time. |

It is possible to convey the same meaning by using **solere** 'be accustomed/used to' + the infinitive.

| Ogni mattina *solevano* alzarsi alla stessa ora. | Every morning *they would (used to) get up* at the same time. |

Requests and commands: the imperative

15a What does the imperative express?

The *imperative* is used for a variety of purposes, including requests, commands, warnings, instructions, invitations and advice.

15b Formation of the imperative

In Italian, because there are four ways of saying 'you' – informal singular and plural, formal singular and plural [➤23b(i)] – there are four imperative forms, both positive and negative. They all say DO something or DON'T do it. The informal **tu** and **voi** forms are the same as those of the present indicative [➤18c(i)], with the exception of the **tu** form of regular -are verbs. The formal **Lei** and **Loro** take the corresponding forms of the *present subjunctive* [➤18c(ii)]. The first person plural **noi** 'let's' is also expressed by the corresponding form of the subjunctive, which is identical to that of the present indicative. The imperative forms of regular verbs are as follows:

	Parlare	Prendere	Aprire	Finire
(tu)	parla	prendi	apri	finisci
(Lei)	parli	prenda	apra	finisca
(noi)	parliamo	prendiamo	apriamo	finiamo
(voi)	parlate	prendete	aprite	finite
(Loro)	parlino	prendano	aprano	finiscano

Parla più piano per favore.	*Speak* more slowly, please.
Prendiamo il treno delle sei.	*Let's take* the six o'clock train.
Apra la finestra per cortesia.	*Open* the window, please.
Finite di parlare delle vacanze.	*Stop* talking about the holidays/vacation.

Note also the following verbs that have some irregular **tu** and occasionally **voi** forms (marked with an asterisk):

	Essere	**Avere**	**Andare**	**Dare**
(tu)	sii*	abbi*	va'* (vai)	da'* (dai)
(Lei)	sia	abbia	vada	dia
(noi)	siamo	abbiamo	andiamo	diamo
(voi)	siate*	abbiate*	andate	date
(Loro)	siano	abbiano	vadano	diano

	Dire	**Fare**	**Stare**
(tu)	di'*	fa'* (fai)	sta'* (stai)
(Lei)	dica	faccia	stia
(noi)	diciamo	facciamo	stiamo
(voi)	dite	fate	state
(Loro)	dicano	facciano	stiano

(i) *Negative imperatives*

Negative imperatives are formed by putting **non** before the verb form. The exception to the rule is the second person singular **tu** where **non** is followed by the infinitive:

Apri la porta.	Open the door.
but	
Non aprire **la porta.**	*Don't open* the door.

otherwise

Andiamo. Non andiamo.	Let's go. Let's not go.
Guardi. Non guardi.	Look. Don't look.

(ii) *Position of pronouns with the imperative*

Pronouns are attached to the **tu, noi** and **voi** forms so that they form one word:

Guarda*lo*.	Look at *him*.
Andiamo*ci*.	Let's go *there*.
Vendete*la*.	Sell *it*.
Comprate*ne* due.	Buy two *of them*.

However, they are placed in front of the **Lei** and **Loro** forms:

Le dica di aspettare.	Tell *her* to wait.
Lo vendano.	Sell *it*.

The one exception to this rule is **loro** 'to them' which always comes after an imperative form and can never be attached to it.

Di' *loro* di aspettare.	Tell *them* (= to them) to wait.

When **va'**, **da'**, **di'**, **fa'** and **sta'** are followed by an object pronoun – with the exception of **gli** – the initial consonant of the pronoun is doubled.

Di*mm*i tutto.	Tell *me* everything.
Va*cc*i subito.	Go *there* straightaway.
Di*ll*e la verità.	Tell *her* the truth.
Fa*ll*o per domani.	Do *it* by tomorrow.
but	
Di*gli* di telefonarmi.	Tell *him* to ring/call me.
Da*gli* qualcosa da bere.	Give *him* something to drink.

(iii)   Position of pronouns with the negative imperative

With the **tu** form the pronoun can precede the infinitive or be attached to it:

Non *lo* fare or Non far*lo*.	Don't do *it*.

Although this option is open to the **noi** and **voi** forms, normal practice is to attach the object pronouns to the imperative.

Non compriamo*lo* adesso.	Let's not buy *it* now.
Non guardate*mi*.	Don't look at *me*.

With **Lei** and **Loro** the pronouns remain in front of the imperative:

Non *la* mangi.	Don't eat *it*.
Non *ci* vadano.	Don't go *there*.

Note: These same rules, as well as those described under ➤15(ii) above, apply to the position of the reflexive pronouns [➤23c] of reflexive verbs.

Non *ti* preoccupare or Non preoccupar*ti*.	Don't worry.
Non preoccupate*vi*.	Don't worry.
Non *si* alzi.	Don't get up.
Sbriga*ti*.	Hurry up.
Sediamo*ci*.	Let's sit down.
Sveglia*te*vi.	Wake up.

[For more detailed information on the uses and position of pronouns ➤23b(ii-v).]

15c   *Some common uses of the imperative*

The imperative may indicate:

- A request

Telefonami quando hai più informazioni.	*Ring/call* me when you have more information.

- A command or order

Vai a lavarti le mani prima di mangiare.	*Go* and wash your hands before eating.

- A warning

Non toccare la frutta.	*Don't touch* the fruit.

- An instruction

Rispondete alle seguenti domande.	*Answer* the following questions.

- An invitation

Se non ti piace la birra, *prendi* qualcos'altro.	If you don't like beer, *have* something else.

• A piece of advice

Ripassate l'imperativo prima dell'esame.	*Revise/review* the imperative before the exam.

15d   *Other ways of expressing imperatives*

(i)   *Infinitive*

The infinitive [➤10a] is frequently used as an imperative in notices, instructions, recipes, etc., for reasons of clarity and brevity.

Non sporgersi dal finestrino. *Leggere* attentamente il testo.	*Don't lean out* of the window. *Read* the text carefully.

(ii)   *divieto di* + noun, *è vietato* + infinitive

Divieto di accesso. È vietato fumare.	No access. No smoking.

(iii)   *Present indicative*

In colloquial speech, the present indicative with question intonation is sometimes used to soften the command into a request. The same effect can be created by a modal verb [➤9] + infinitive, similar to the English device.

Mi *porta/può portare* un'altra bottiglia di acqua minerale, per favore?	*Can* you *bring* me another bottle of mineral water, please?
Mi *spiega/vuole spiegare* la differenza?	*Will* you *explain* the difference to me?

16 Areas of uncertainty: the subjunctive

16a What does the subjunctive do?

The subjunctive (**il congiuntivo**) is widely used in Italian both in speech and in writing. It tends to refer to events or actions that are not certain to happen. The expressions used to convey such actions or events reflect uncertainty, wish, preference, fear, doubt, vagueness, unreality, etc. This is in direct contrast with the *indicative*, which describes with a greater degree of *certainty* what has happened, is happening or will happen. Compare the following sentences:

Sono sicuro che *vengono*.	I am sure that they *are coming*. (indicative, states certainty)
È possibile che *vengano*.	It's possible that they *are coming*. (subjunctive, expresses uncertainty)

As in the above example, the subjunctive is mainly used in subordinate clauses, in many cases introduced by **che,** but it can occur in main clauses in certain forms of the imperative [➤15 and 16h(i)] and in a few other cases [➤16h(ii)]. The subjunctive is an important part of the Italian language and one which requires close study.

The following paragraphs aim to set out general principles and guidelines relating to the use of the subjunctive in Italian. It would be unwise to to think that *all* the following rules are strictly applied, particulary in the spoken language, where you will come across variations in its use. Reference will be made to such variations whenever possible.

As a *general rule* the subjunctive is not used unless there is a change of subject in the sentence. If the subject remains the same, other constructions such as the infinitive are usually preferred:

Stasera *voglio uscire*.	This evening *I want to go out*.
Non *voglio che tu esca* stasera.	*I* don't *want you to go out* this evening.

In the first example there is no change of subject and therefore the infinitive has to be used after **voglio**. In the second example the subjunctive must be used because there is a change of subject.

16b   The tenses of the subjunctive

[For the formation of the present and imperfect subjunctive ►18c(ii), 18c(vii); for perfect and pluperfect subjunctive ►16b, 19; for auxiliary **avere** or **essere** to form compound tenses ►11c.]

The subjunctive has four tenses: present, imperfect, perfect and pluperfect. All four tenses are used in Italian and the tense of the subjunctive will be determined by the tense of the verb in the clause on which the subjunctive depends. [For sequence of tenses ►16i.]

Penso che *capiscano* tutto.	I think they *understand* everything. (present)
Penso che *abbiano capito* tutto.	I think they *have understood* everything. (perfect)
Pensavo che *capissero* tutto.	I thought they *understood* everything. (imperfect)
Pensavo che *avessero capito* tutto.	I thought they *had understood* everything. (pluperfect)

16c   The subjunctive after certain verbs

The subjunctive is used with the following categories of verbs, of which the most common examples are listed:

(i)   *Verbs of wishing, wanting, liking, preferring, ordering, permitting, forbidding, insisting, expecting, etc.*, when followed by *che*:

aspettare che...	await...
aspettarsi che...	expect...

attendere che...	await...
augurarsi che...	wish, hope...
desiderare che...	want...
impedire che...	prevent...
insistere che...	insist...
lasciare che...	let...
ordinare che...	order...
permettere che...	permit, allow...
piacere che (mi piace etc.)...	like...
preferire che...	prefer...
proibire che...	forbid, prohibit...
sperare che...	hope...
suggerire che...	suggest...
volere che...	wish, want...

Ai miei genitori *non piace che io esca* **ogni sera.** *Preferiscono che stia* **a casa almeno due o tre sere alla settimana.** *Insistono* **sempre** *che faccia* **più lavoro scolastico perché, naturalmente,** *vogliono che superi* **a pieni voti gli esami di fine anno.** *Si aspettano che vada* **all'università.**	My parents do not *like me going out* every evening. They *prefer me to stay* at home at least two or three evenings a week. They always *insist on me doing* more school work because, naturally, they *want me to pass* my end-of-year exams with flying colours/colors. They *are expecting me to go* to university.

- Of the verbs listed above, **impedire, ordinare, permettere, proibire, suggerire** and **lasciare** may be used with the infinitive [▶8i(ii)C, 9e(ii)], even when the subject of the main verb and the infinitive would be different. In fact, this construction is preferable particularly when the object of the main verb is a pronoun.

I miei genitori non *proibiscono che io esca.* but the preferred translation is **I miei genitori non** *mi proibiscono di uscire.*	My parents *don't forbid me to go out.*

After **aspettarsi, augurarsi, desiderare, piacere, preferire, sperare** and **volere**, the infinitive construction should be used only if the subject is the same in both halves of the sentence.

Mi piace *uscire*. Non voglio *stare* sempre a casa a studiare. Spero di *passare* gli esami ma non mi aspetto di *passarli* a pieni voti.	I like *to go out*. I don't want always *to be* at home studying. I hope *to pass* the exams, but I don't expect *to pass* them with flying colours/colors.

[For verbs that require a preposition before a following infinitive ►8j.]

(ii) *Verb constructions expressing emotions such as pleasure, surprise, disbelief, disappointment, regret, anger, fear, etc., when followed by* **che***:*

avere paura che...	be afraid that...
dispiacere (mi dispiace, etc.) che...	be sorry, regret that...
essere arrabbiato che...	be annoyed that...
essere contento/felice che...	be pleased/happy that...
essere deluso che...	be disappointed that...
essere infelice/scontento che...	be unhappy/displeased that...
essere sconvolto che...	be upset that...
essere sorpreso/stupito che...	be surprised that...
essere spiacente che...	be sorry that...
essere triste che...	be sad that...
meravigliarsi che...	be amazed that...
rincrescere che...	regret that...
stupirsi che...	be surprised that...
temere che...	fear that...

Sono contento che i tuoi esami *siano andati* bene. *Mi meraviglio*, però, *che tu sia riuscito* a passarli con dei voti così alti dato che uscivi quasi ogni sera.	*I am happy that* your exams *went* well. *I am amazed*, however, *that you managed* to pass them with such high marks given that you went out almost every evening.

 As with many of the verbs in these lists, if the subject is the same in both halves of the sentence, an infinitive construction is preferred to the subjunctive:

Sono molto contento *di aver superato* tutti i miei esami.	I am very pleased *that I have passed* all my exams.

Siamo spiacenti *di non poter* venire al ristorante per festeggiare la buona notizia.	We are sorry *(that) we are unable* to come to the restaurant to celebrate the good news.

(iii) *Impersonal constructions expressing necessity, possibility, probability, importance, urgency etc., when followed by* ***che****:*

accade che...	it happens that...
basta che...	it is enough that...
è bene che...	it is a good thing that...
bisogna che...	it is necessary that...
capita che...	it happens that...
conviene che...	it is better/advisable that...
è difficile che...	it is difficult for/unlikely that...
è facile che...	it is easy/likely that...
importa che...	it matters/is important that...
è impossibile che...	it is impossible that...
è improbabile che...	it is unlikely that...
è inutile che...	it's no use/pointless ...
è male che...	it is a bad thing that...
è meglio che...	it is better that...
è naturale che...	it is natural that...
è necessario che...	it is necessary that...
occorre che...	it is necessary that...
pare che...	it seems that...
è peggio che...	it is worse that...
è un peccato che...	it is a pity that...
è possibile che...	it is possible that...
è preferibile che...	it is preferable that...
è probabile che...	it is probable/likely that...
può darsi che...	it may be that...
sembra che...	it seems that...
è strano che...	it is strange/odd that...
succede che...	it happens that...
è utile che...	it is useful that...
vale (la pena) che...	it is worth (the trouble) that...

***È meglio che* si *faccia* qualcosa al più presto possibile..**	*It is better that* we *do* something as quickly as possible.

Bisogna che il governo *prenda* questi provvedimenti per ridurre il tasso di inflazione.	*It is necessary that* the government *takes* these steps to reduce the rate of inflation.
Sembra che le cose *vadano* di male in peggio.	*It seems that* things *are going* from bad to worse.

 Many of these impersonal constructions will be followed by the infinitive in Italian if they are followed immediately by the infinitive in English.

Bisogna *prendere* questi provvedimenti.	It is necessary *to take* these steps.
È meglio *fare* qualcosa al più presto possibile.	It is better *to do* something as quickly as possible.
Mi sembra *di aver letto* un articolo sul giornale di ieri riguardo agli ultimi provvedimenti presi dal governo.	I seem *to have read* an article in yesterday's newspaper regarding the latest measures taken by the government.

(iv) *Verb constructions expressing personal opinion, doubt, uncertainty, denial:*

credere che...	believe that...
(non) dire che...	(not) say that...
dubitare che...	doubt that/whether...
negare che...	deny that...
pensare che...	think that...
(non) sapere che...	(not) know that...
ritenere che...	consider, think that...

Dubito che questi provvedimenti *possano* risolvere l'attuale crisi economica.	*I doubt whether* these measures *can* solve the present economic crisis.
Non *credo che* il governo *abbia fatto* abbastanza per rimediare alla situazione.	*I don't believe that* the government *has done* enough to remedy the situation.

Note that some of the above expressions are used negatively and this contributes to the idea of doubt and uncertainty.

Positive statements of certainty take the indicative.

So che il governo non *ha fatto* abbastanza.	*I know that* the government *hasn't done* enough.

This also applies where plain statements of fact are made, such as **è vero/certo che ...** 'it's true/certain that', **sono sicuro che ...** 'I am sure that...', without an emotional reaction or value judgement.

È vero che il governo non *ha fatto* abbastanza.	*It is true that* the government *hasn't done* enough.

(v) *The subjunctive is used in indirect questions introduced by* **se, come, quando, quanto, perché, dove,** *etc.:*

Mi domando *perché* il governo non *abbia fatto* di più.	I wonder *why* the government *hasn't done* more.
Non capisci forse *quanto sia* delicata l'attuale situazione.	Perhaps you don't understand *how* delicate the present situation *is*.

Whilst it is more correct to use the subjunctive in indirect questions, there is a growing tendency to use the indicative in the spoken language.

Non capisco *perché* non *hanno fatto* qualcosa.	I don't understand *why* they *haven't done* something.

(vi) The subjunctive is used after **il fatto che**... 'the fact that...' when its clause begins a sentence in which the main verb represents an emotional reaction or value judgement. Sometimes **il fatto** is omitted but the subjunctive is still used.

Il fatto che ci sia tanta disoccupazione è inaccettabile. *Che ci sia* tanta disoccupazione è inaccettabile.	*(The fact) that there is* so much unemployment is unacceptable.

È un fatto che ... ('it is a fact that...') would not take a subjunctive because it is stating a *reality*.

È un fatto che *c'è* tanta disoccupazione.	It's a fact that *there is* so much unemployment.

16d   The subjunctive in adverbial clauses

The subjunctive is used in subordinate adverbial clauses when the action *was not a reality* at the time of the action of the main verb. Some subordinating conjunctions [➤5a(ii)] will always take the subjunctive; others do sometimes, depending on the 'reality' of the action they refer to.

(i)   Clauses of time

The subjunctive is required after **prima che** 'before' and **finché non** 'until'.

Devo preparare la loro camera *prima che arrivino*. Però, non voglio buttare giù la pasta *finché non siano arrivati*.	I have to prepare their room *before they arrive*. However, I don't want to put the pasta on to cook *until they have arrived*.

 The indicative is used after **finché** 'as long as' and also with other conjunctions and adverbial expressions of time [➤14a(vi)], such as:

appena	as soon as
dopo che	after
mentre	while
quando	when
una volta che	once

***Appena saranno arrivati*, preparerò da mangiare.**	*As soon as they have arrived*, I shall prepare the meal.

(ii)   Clauses of purpose

The following conjunctions and phrases, all containing the basic idea 'in order that something shall happen', need the subjunctive since the action is clearly not yet a reality, i.e. it has not yet happened.

affinché...	so that, in order that...
in maniera che...	so that...
in/di modo che...	so that...
perché...	so that, in order that...

> **Vi faccio tutti questi esempi** *perché impariate* **a usare correttamente il congiuntivo. Cerco di spiegare un po' alla volta** *in modo che* **tutto** *sia* **chiaro.**
>
> I am giving you all these examples *so that you learn* to use the subjunctive correctly. I am trying to explain a little at a time *so that* everything *is* clear.

 When **in/di modo che**... and **in maniera che**... mean 'with the result that...' (i.e. when the action has or had clearly happened) then they take the indicative and not the subjunctive.

> **Il professore ha spiegato un po' alla volta il congiuntivo** *in modo che* **la maggior parte degli studenti lo** *sa* **usare correttamente.**
>
> The teacher explained the subjunctive a bit at a time *with the result that (so that)* the majority of the students *can* use it correctly.

Note also that **perché** takes the indicative when it means 'because'.

> **La maggior parte degli studenti usa correttamente il congiuntivo** *perché* **il professore l'***ha spiegato* **un po' alla volta.**
>
> The majority of the students use the subjunctive correctly *because* the teacher *explained* it a little at a time.

(iii)   Clauses of concession

The subjunctive is used after the following conjunctions:

benché...	although, even though, even if...
malgrado (che)...	in spite of the fact that...
nonostante (che)...	in spite of the fact that...
sebbene...	although, even though, even if...
seppure...	even if, even though...

These conjunctions normally refer to a hypothesis rather than an actual fact, hence the need for the subjunctive.

Che is usually omitted after **malgrado** and **nonostante**.

Benché sia difficile, farò del mio meglio per spiegare l'uso del congiuntivo.	*Although it is difficult,* I shall do my best to explain the use of the subjunctive.

The following expressions are always followed by the subjunctive because they always introduce a hypothesis:

ammettiamo che...	let's assume that...
mettiamo che...	let's suppose that...
poniamo che...	let's suppose that...
supponiamo che...	let's suppose that...

Ammettiamo che il professore non *riesca* a spiegare tutto in una volta.	*Let's assume that* the teacher *does*n't *manage* to explain everything in one go.

(iv)   Clauses of condition

The subjunctive is always used after the following conjunctions:

a condizione che...	on condition that, provided that...
a meno che (non)...	unless...
a patto che...	on condition that...
purché...	provided that, on condition that...
salvo che (non)...	unless, provided that...

A meno che non piova preferisco partire di buon'ora. Sono disposto ad andare con la mia macchina *a condizione che paghiate* la benzina.	*Unless it is raining* I prefer to leave early. I am willing to go in my car *on condition that you pay* for the petrol/gasoline.

(v)   Other conjunctions requiring the subjunctive

caso mai...	should, in the event that...
nel caso che...	in the event that...
per paura che (non)...	for fear that...
qualora...	in case, if...
senza che...	without...

Caso mai faccia **brutto tempo domani, possiamo sempre fare qualcos'altro.**
Ho deciso di prendere la macchina *senza che* i miei genitori lo *sapessero.*

Should the weather *be* bad tomorrow, we can always do something else.
I decided to take the car *without* my parents *knowing.*

(vi) Uses of the infinitive when the subjects are the same

When the subjects of the main and subordinate verbs are the same, the following prepositional forms are used with the infinitive [▶10a(iv)]:

per	in order to	**prima di**	before -ing
per paura di	for fear of -ing	**senza**	without -ing

Prima di partire, **ascolterò il bollettino meteorologico alla radio.**

Ho deciso di prendere la macchina *senza dire* niente ai miei genitori.

Before leaving, I shall listen to the weather report on the radio.

I have decided to take the car *without saying* anything to my parents.

'I' is the subject of both 'leave' and 'listen' in the first example and 'decide' and 'say' in the second. It is natural in such cases to avoid the use of the subjunctive.

16e The subjunctive after indefinite pronouns and adjectives

The subjunctive is used in clauses introduced by the following indefinite pronouns and adjectives:

chiunque	whoever
comunque	however, no matter how
dovunque	wherever
qualunque	whichever
qualunque cosa	whatever
qualsiasi cosa	whatever

Chiunque venga **con noi deve contribuire al costo della benzina.**

Whoever comes with us must contribute to the cost of the petrol/gasoline.

Dovunque vogliate andare sono disposto a guidare.	*Wherever you want* to go I am willing to drive.
Qualunque decisione *prendiate* sull'itinerario, fammela sapere entro stasera.	*Whatever* decision *you take* about the route, let me know it by this evening.
Comunque decidano i miei amici, io andrò lo stesso.	*However* my friends *decide*, I shall go all the same.

None of the statements made after **chiunque, dovunque, qualunque** and **comunque** is a reality and that is the reason for using the subjunctive.

Note that another way of expressing 'however' is **per quanto** followed by an adjective + verb:

Per quanto brutto sia il tempo domani, preferisco fare qualcosa che stare a casa.	*However bad* the weather *may be* tomorrow, I prefer to do something than to stay at home.

(i) *Whether... or not*

This type of construction also requires a subjunctive.

Che piova o che faccia bello, non mi importa.	*Whether it's raining or nice* doesn't matter to me.

16f   *The subjunctive in relative clauses [➤23m]*

(i) *The subjunctive after the indefinite antecedent*

The subjunctive is used in relative clauses which imply 'anyone who..'/'anything which..', i.e. when the antecedent [➤23m(i)] is not exactly defined. Compare the following examples:

La ditta vuole assumere *una segretaria che abbia* una ottima conoscenza di inglese e di spagnolo.	The firm wants to employ *a secretary who has* a very good knowledge of English and Spanish.

i.e. any secretary who meets that requirement, therefore the subordinate verb is in the subjunctive.

L'amministratore delegato della ditta ha già *una segretaria che parla* perfettamente queste due lingue.	The general manager of the firm already has *a secretary who speaks* these two languages perfectly.

This secretary is already employed by the firm and it is a known fact that she speaks these languages, therefore the verb is in the indicative.

Quando l'amministratore delegato va a Torino per motivi di affari, la sua segretaria gli deve sempre trovare *un albergo che sia* proprio in centro città.	When the general manager goes to Turin on business, his secretary always has to find him *a hotel that is* right in the city centre/downtown.

i.e any hotel which is in the city centre/downtown: subjunctive.

Non gli piace *quell'albergo che si trova* a tre chilometri dall'aeroporto perché è troppo lontano dallo stabilimento che deve visitare.	He doesn't like *that hotel which is* three kilometres/kilometers from the airport because it's too far from the factory that he has to visit.

i.e. the (known) hotel that he stayed in before: indicative.

• Sometimes, especially when used with **cercare, volere** and similar verbs, this construction also carries the idea of purpose [►16d(ii)], and translates the English 'somebody to do something'.

Cerco *qualcuno che faccia* da interprete quando vengono i rappresentanti da Madrid.	I am looking for *someone to act* as interpreter when the representatives from Madrid come.

(ii) *The subjunctive after a negative antecedent*

The subjunctive is used in relative clauses that depend on a negative, such as **niente/nulla** 'nothing' or **nessuno** 'no one'/'no'.

Non c'è *nessuno* in ufficio *che sappia* parlare spagnolo. Non c'è *nessuna probabilità che si possa* trovare un interprete prima di domani.	There is *no one* in the office *who can* speak Spanish. There is *no likelihood of finding* an interpreter before tomorrow.

(iii)   The subjunctive after a superlative

The subjunctive is used in a relative clause following a superlative:

Questa è una delle mansioni segretariali *più esigenti che io abbia* mai *dovuto* compiere.	This is one of the *most demanding* secretarial tasks that *I have* ever *had to* carry out.

Note that the words **primo** 'first', **ultimo** 'last', **unico** and **solo** 'only' are treated as superlatives for this purpose:

È *l'unica* persona in ufficio *che sia* in grado di compiere questa mansione.	She's *the only* person in the office *who is* able to carry out this task.

The use of the subjunctive after a superlative is not always strictly adhered to in contemporary spoken Italian.

The subjunctive is not required after 'the only... to...'/'the first ... to', etc. In constructions of this type use **a** + the infinitive.

Era la *prima* segretaria *ad essere* assunta da questa ditta.	She was the *first* secretary to *be* taken on by this firm.

Note the optional but often preferable use of **ad** before an infinitive that begins with a vowel.

16g   The subjunctive after a comparative

The subjunctive is used in clauses following a comparative:

Questa segretaria è *più dotata di quanto pensassimo*. È *più dotata che non sembri*.	This secretary is *more talented than we thought*. She is *more talented than she seems*.

In the second type of construction **non** must precede the verb. It is also possible to express this type of comparison with **di quel che** + the indicative.

È più dotata di quel che sembra.	She is *more talented than she seems.*

16h The subjunctive in main clauses

(i) As an imperative [➤15]

The subjunctive is used to convey the **Lei/Loro** forms of the imperative, i.e. the polite forms.

Si accomodino.	*Please take a seat.*
Parli più piano per cortesia.	*Speak* more slowly, please.

(ii) To express a wish

Che tu sia sempre felice!	*May you always be happy!*

A strong wish that something should or should not happen can be expressed in Italian by **magari** + the imperfect or pluperfect subjunctive, the imperfect perhaps suggesting that the likelihood of the wish being granted is very remote, and the pluperfect a regret that the wish hasn't been fulfilled.

Magari fosse possibile!	*If only it were possible!*
Magari fosse stato possibile!	*If only it had been possible!*

Note: **Magari** can also stand by itself to endorse a previous statement or question.

Sarebbe bello avere più tempo libero. *Magari!*	It would be nice to have more free time. *I should say so/If only/Of course!*
Ti piacerebbe avere più tempo libero? *Magari!*	Would you like to have more free time? *I should say so!*

16i   The sequence of tenses with the subjunctive

The most usual combinations of tenses are as follows:

(i)   *Main clause* in present, imperative, future, or perfect indicative.*Subordinate clause* in present or perfect subjunctive [➤18c].

Spero **che tutto** *vada* **bene.**	*I hope* that everything *goes* well.
Sono contento **che** *abbiano*	*I am pleased* that *they have*
deciso **di venire a trovarci.**	*decided* to come and see us.
Spolvera **i mobili** *prima che*	*Dust* the furniture *before* the
arrivino **gli ospiti!**	guests *arrive!*
Non *ho pensato* **che** *arrivino*	*I didn't think* that *they were*
oggi.	*arriving* today.

It is possible to have a present tense in the main clause and the imperfect subjunctive in the subordinate clause if the sense requires it.

Mi dispiace **che non** *potessero*	*I am sorry* that everyone *couldn't*
venire tutti quanti.	come.

(ii)   *Main clause* in imperfect, perfect, past definite, pluperfect, present conditional, conditional perfect indicative.*Subordinate clause* in imperfect or pluperfect subjunctive [➤18c].

Pensavo **che** *venissero* **alla fine**	*I thought* that *they were coming* at
del mese.	the end of the month.
Sarebbe **difficile che**	*It would be* difficult for them *to*
cambiassero **i loro progetti.**	*change* (= *that they change*) their
	plans.
Mi *sembrò* **che** *si fossero riferiti*	*It seemed* to me that *they had*
alla data del loro arrivo	*referred* to the date of their arrival
nell'ultima lettera.	in their last letter.

It is important to bear in mind that where the future or conditional is used in the subordinate clause in English, then the appropriate future or conditional tense can be used after many constructions in Italian, i.e. there is no need to use the subjunctive.

Spero che *arriveranno* fra poco.	I hope that *they will arrive* soon. (future indicative)
or	
Spero che *arrivino* fra poco.	I hope that *they will arrive* soon. (present subjunctive).
Speravo che *sarebbero venuti* alla fine del mese.	I was hoping that *they would come* at the end of the month. (conditional perfect)
or	
Speravo che *venissero* alla fine del mese.	I was hoping that *they would come* at the end of the month. (imperfect subjunctive)

Note that the past conditional is used in Italian when the verb in the main clause is a past tense [➤14e(iv)].

16j *'If' clauses*

[See also paragraph 14d on the present conditional and 14e on the conditional perfect.]

Whether the subjunctive is used or not in the 'if' clause after **se** depends on the type of condition: is it open, remote, fulfilled or unfulfilled? The following are the most common structures.

(i) *Open condition*

The condition is entirely open, it may or may not be fulfilled: **se** is followed by the present or future *indicative* [➤18c] (*never* the present subjunctive), and the main verb will usually be in the present, imperative or future [➤18c], just as in English.

Se non *arrivano/arriveranno* fra poco, *dovrò* uscire.	If *they do*n't *arrive* soon, *I shall have to* go out.
Se non *vengono* prima dell'una, *possiamo* mangiare.	If *they do*n't *come* before one o'clock, *we can* eat.

It is also possible to use the perfect tense after **se** to convey this idea of an open condition.

Se non *sono arrivati* prima dell'una, possiamo mangiare.	If *they have* not *arrived* before one o'clock, we can eat. (i.e. they may or may not have arrived before one o'clock)

(ii) Remote condition

The condition is remote or contrary to fact: **se** is followed by the imperfect subjunctive [➤18c(vii)] and the main clause is in the conditional [➤18c(iv)].

Se *arrivassero* prima dell'una, *potremmo* mangiare tutti insieme.	If *they arrived* (*were to arrive*) before one o'clock, *we could* eat all together. (i.e. they are unlikely to arrive before one)

(iii) Unfulfilled condition

The condition is unfulfilled, contrary to fact: **se** is followed by the pluperfect subjunctive [➤16b, 19] and the main clause is in the conditional perfect [➤14e].

Se *fossero arrivati* prima dell'una, *avremmo potuto* mangiare tutti insieme.	If *they had arrived* before one o'clock, *we could have* eaten all together. (but they didn't arrive before one, so we couldn't all eat together – *condition unfulfilled*)

It is possibile to have a present conditional in the main clause, if the situation requires it.

Se *fossero arrivati* in orario, non *sarei* così preoccupato.	If *they had arrived* on time, *I would* not *be* so worried.

Note: It is fairly common, particularly in spoken Italian, to replace the pluperfect subjunctive after **se** and the conditional perfect in the main clause with the imperfect indicative in both clauses.

Se *arrivavano* prima dell'una, *potevamo* mangiare tutti insieme.	If *they had arrived* before one o'clock, *we could* all *have* eaten together.

(iv) *Fulfilled condition*

The condition can be considered as fulfilled if the action/event has taken place. In these cases, the most suitable tense of the indicative is used after **se**.

Se non *sono arrivati*, **è perché c'è molto traffico sull'autostrada.**	If *they haven't arrived*, it's because there is a lot of traffic on the motorway/highway.

(v) *What if...?*

'What if...?' is expressed by **e se** ... + present indicative, imperfect or pluperfect subjunctive as in the following examples:

E se non *vengono?*	What if they don't come?
E se non *venissero?*	What if they didn't come?
E se non *fossero venuti?*	What if they hadn't come?

(vi) *As if...*

'As if...' is expressed by **come se**... with the imperfect or pluperfect subjunctive.

Parli *come se* **non** *venissero*.	You are talking *as if they weren't coming.*
Parli *come se fosse successo* **qualcosa.**	You are talking *as if something had happened.*

17 Things done to you: the passive

17a What does the passive express?

(i) Receivers and doers of action

In the passive, the subject of the verb is the receiver of the action of the verb, rather than the doer. Compare these two examples:

Il meccanico *ha riparato* la macchina.	The mechanic *has repaired* the car. (active)
but	
La macchina *è stata riparata* dal meccanico.	The car *has been repaired* by the mechanic. (passive)

In the passive, the *direct object* (**la macchina**) of the transitive verb becomes the subject. That is why it is only transitive verbs that can be used in the passive [▶8a(i), 8d]. All the same, the passive is not just another way of saying the same thing as the active form. It emphasizes different things, especially what happens to the subject. The passive construction also enables us to omit the doer of the action because it is not necessarily important to know who (or what) did it.

La macchina è stata riparata.	The car has been repaired.

17b Formation of the passive

The passive is formed with the appropriate tense of **essere** + the past participle. The past participle must agree with the subject. This rule applies also when two past participles are used.

La portiera della macchina *è stata ammaccata* ma *sarà riparata* fra un paio di settimane.	The car door *has been dented*, but *it will be repaired* within a couple of weeks.

17c   Expressing the agent or instrument

The person or thing the action is done *by* is called the *agent* or *instrument* respectively. These would have been the subject of the transitive verb. In Italian both the agent and the instrument are preceded by **da**, meaning 'by'.

La portiera della macchina sarà riparata *da un carrozziere.*	The car door will be repaired *by a panel beater.*
La portiera è stata ammacccata *da una motocicletta.*	The car door has been dented *by a motorcycle.*

17d   Verbs other than essere *to express the passive*

(i)   Venire

Venire can be used in place of **essere** but *only* in simple tenses [➤11b]. Although **venire** underlines the *carrying out* of the action whereas **essere** puts emphasis on the *state*, the difference in meaning is often minimal.

La macchina *viene* **riparata**.	The car *is being* repaired.

(ii)   Andare

Andare can replace **essere** with verbs such as **perdere** 'lose', **disperdere** 'lose, waste', **sprecare** 'waste', etc.

La mia polizza d'assicurazione **è** *andata persa*.	My insurance policy *has been lost.*

Andare can also be used, in the simple tenses only, to convey the meaning of *obligation*.

La riparazione *va fatta* **entro la fine di questa settimana.**	The repair *must be done* by the end of this week.
La fattura *andrà inviata* **alla compagnia di assicurazioni.**	The bill *will have to be sent* to the insurance company.

In this type of structure **andare** is taking the place of the relevant tense of **dovere** + **essere**.

La riparazione *deve essere*
fatta...
La fattura *dovrà essere*
inviata....

(iii)   Restare *and* rimanere

Restare and **rimanere** can replace **essere** when the following past participle describes a state, such as **sconvolto** 'upset', **deluso** 'disappointed', **stupito** 'amazed', **chiuso** 'closed', **aperto** 'open', etc.

In seguito all'incidente stradale *sono rimasto* molto depresso. Questa officina *resterà* chiusa per le prime due settimane di agosto.	Following the road accident, *I was* very depressed. This garage *will remain* closed for the first two weeks of August.

 As in English, the modal verbs [➤9] do not have a passive form. The accompanying infinitive must therefore be put into the passive.

La compagnia d'assicurazioni *deve* pagare la fattura. La fattura deve *essere pagata* dalla compagnia di assicurazioni.	The insurance company *must* pay the bill. (active) The bill must *be paid* by the insurance company. (passive)

17e   Alternatives to passive constructions

The passive is used far more widely in Italian in the written language, newspaper reporting, for example, than it is in the spoken language, where the constructions outlined below tend to be preferred.

(i)   The si passivante

A widely used construction in Italian is the pronoun **si** - known as the **si passivante** - with the third person singular or plural of the verb. The verb after **si** will be in the *active* form. In this type of construction **da** cannot be used to introduce an agent or instrument, i.e. you cannot express who or what the action is done by.

Dove *si faranno* le riparazioni?	Where *will* the repairs *be done*?
Non *si fa* la carrozzeria in questa officina.	The bodywork *is* not *done* in this garage.

(ii) *The impersonal **si***

The impersonal **si**, with the third person singular of the verb, performs the same general function in Italian as the English 'one' and can, therefore, be expressed in a variety of ways, such as 'we', 'you', 'they', 'people'.

Non *si* sa mai quello che succederà.	*You* never know what will happen.
Cosa *si* fa adesso senza la macchina?	What do *we* do now without the car?

• **Si** is used in a range of impersonal expressions [➤8g]. It is an extremely useful way of avoiding an English passive construction.

si crede	it is believed
si dice	it is said
si pensa	it is thought
si prega	it is requested, you are asked
si prevede	it is envisaged
si può	one may
si sa	it is known
si spera	it is hoped

***Si prevede* che finiranno il più del lavoro entro la fine di questa settimana.**	*It is envisaged* that they will finish most of the work by the end of this week.

Great care has to be taken when the verb following **si** has a *plural direct object*. In this case, the **si passivante** [➤17e(i) above] must be used and the verb agrees with the following plural.

Dove *si comprano i pezzi di ricambio*?	Where *do you buy the spare parts?*

17f   *Passive constructions: limitations of use in Italian*

Passive constructions can be used in Italian *only* where the verb in the active form would take a *direct object*. In the passive, the direct object of the transitive verb becomes the subject [➤17a above].

It is important to remember, therefore, that English constructions such as 'I was given...', 'I was taught...', I was told...', cannot be translated literally into Italian since each of the corresponding verbs in Italian, **dare, insegnare** and **dire** takes an *indirect* object [➤8e(i)]. It is possible therefore to translate a sentence such as 'I was given a book' in the following ways:

Mi è stato dato un libro.	A book has been given to me.
or	
Mi hanno dato un libro.	They gave me a book.

The second type of construction is the one that Italians are more likely to use.

Types of Italian Verb

18a Predictability: conjugating a verb

The whole set of a verb's stems and endings is known as its *conjugation*. The various parts of this set are predictable at several levels.

(i) Regular verbs

Regular verbs are verbs for which you can predict any part of any tense from the spelling of the infinitive [➤10a], plus of course a knowledge of the rules! In Italian, there are three conjugations of regular verbs, each with a distinct infinitive ending:

parlare	speak	(first conjugation)
vendere	sell	(second conjugation)
dormire	sleep	(third conjugation)

By far the majority of Italian verbs are of the **-are** type. Moreover, virtually all newly coined verbs are automatically **-are** verbs, for example **fotocopiare** 'photocopy'.

(ii) Irregular verbs

Verbs in which some parts cannot be predicted in this way are known as *irregular*. Some of the most frequently used verbs in Italian are irregular. [For tables of irregular verbs ➤19g, 19h; for a more extensive treatment ➤Berlitz *Italian Verb Handbook*.] Some irregular verbs form groups, so if you know one you can predict the forms of any of the others. For example **togliere** 'remove', **cogliere** 'pick, gather' and **sciogliere** 'dissolve' all behave in the same way [➤19h].

(iii) Compound verbs

A compound verb is a verb where a prefix is added to the *base* verb. With very few exceptions, compound verbs [➤18e] conjugate in the same way as their base verb. So, for example, **contenere** 'contain', **mantenere** 'maintain' and **sostenere** 'support' all follow the model of **tenere** 'hold'.

18b   Major groups of verbs: how are they conjugated?

(i)   The three major conjugations

In the formation of tenses in Italian, there are many features which are common to all conjugations, and to both regular and irregular verbs. These will be evident from the descriptions of the rules for the formation of each tense. Frequent reference will be made to the *stem* of the infinitive. For the three regular conjugations, this is obtained by removing the **-are, -ere** or **-ire** ending from the infinitive:

Infinitive	*Stem*
parlare	**parl-**
vendere	**vend-**
dormire	**dorm-**

There are two types of verbs that belong to the second conjugation; verbs like **leggere**, where the stress falls on the third to last syllable, and verbs like **vedere**, where the stress falls on the penultimate syllable. Verbs belonging to the third conjugation also fall into two categories; those which follow the **dormire** model, and a substantial number of others that insert **-isc** between the stem and the ending in the **io, tu, lui/lei** and **loro** forms of the present indicative and present subjunctive and the **tu, Lei** and **Loro** forms of the imperative. An example of this type of verb is **capire** [▶19f].

18c   Formation of tenses

In all verbs there are some tenses whose stems and endings can be predicted if you know one of the other parts of the verb. Parts which cannot be predicted in this way have to be learned, but once these principal parts are known, it is usually possible to predict other parts.

It is helpful to know how to get the stem on to which to put the endings for each tense, and any spelling adjustments that may need to be made. The following sections give a breakdown of the stem endings for each tense, and any pitfalls to watch out for.

The term *indicative* is used to describe the 'ordinary' tenses, as opposed to the *subjunctive* forms [▶16].
The model regular verbs used in chapters 18 and 19 are **parlare** 'speak', **vendere** 'sell' and **dormire** 'sleep'.

(i)   Present indicative [▶12a]

Regular forms of the present indicative are produced by adding the following endings to the stem of the infinitive:

parl(are)	-o	-i	-a	-iamo	-ate	-ano
vend(ere)	-o	-i	-e	-iamo	-ete	-ono
dorm(ire)	-o	-i	-e	-iamo	-ite	-ono

[For subject pronouns **io** 'I', **tu** 'you', etc. ➤ 23b(i).]

Remember that verbs like **capire** insert **-isc-** between the stem and the endings for the first three persons of the singular and the third person plural. The endings are the same as for **dormire**.

It is worth noting that the endings for the first and second person singular and the first person plural are identical for the three conjugations. The second person plural retains the characteristic vowel of the infinitive ending; **-a, -e, -i**.

Attention needs to be paid to the following groups of verbs that undergo modifications or spelling changes, usually in order to maintain the same pronunciation.

(A) First conjugation verbs

• Verbs whose stem ends in **-g** or **-c**, for example **pagare** 'pay' and **cercare** 'look for', have an **h** before the vowel **i**: **paghi, paghiamo, cerchi, cerchiamo**. (This same rule is applied when the following vowel is **e** [➤18c(iii) below].)

• Verbs in **-iare** have only one **-i** in the second person singular if the **-i** of **-iare** is unstressed, for example **studi** (**studiare** 'study') because the stress falls on the first syllable.

• Verbs in **-iare** have a double **i** in the second person singular if the **-i-** of the stem is stressed, for example **scii** (**sciare** 'ski').

(B) Second conjugation verbs

• Although verbs in **-gliere**, for example **scegliere** 'to choose' will be listed under irregular verbs, they do not have that many irregular forms. In the present tense, the consonants **-gl-** are reversed in the first person singular and third person plural, **scelgo** and **scelgono**, but the endings are those for regular second conjugation verbs. As the stress does not fall on the final **-i** of the stem, the second person singular of this verb, and others like it, has only one **-i**: **scegli**.

• Verbs ending in **-durre**, such as **produrre** 'produce', **tradurre** 'translate', **ridurre** 'reduce', etc., are straightforward once the first person singular is known. For example, **produrre** changes to **produco**, and the endings are then the same as those of any other regular second conjugation verb.

- Similarly, verbs like **trarre** 'pull, draw' have a pattern that, once acquired, can be applied to other verbs based on it. To form the stem remove **-rre**. The endings are those for regular second conjugation verbs. The first person singular and third person plural have a **-gg-** between the stem and the ending, i.e. **traggo, traggono.**

(ii) *Present subjunctive [➤16]*

The present subjunctive of regular verbs is formed by adding the following endings to the stem of the infinitive:

parl(are)	-i	-i	-i	-iamo	-iate	-ino
vend(ere)	-a	-a	-a	-iamo	-iate	-ano
dorm(ire)	-a	-a	-a	-iamo	-iate	-ano

Verbs of the **capire** type have the same endings as **dormire** and the formation is the same as for the present indicative.

As you can see, the endings of the singular are the same, -**i** for the first conjugation and -**a** for the second and third conjugations. The endings of the first and second persons plural are identical for all three conjugations. The third person plural retains the characteristic vowel of the singular form.

As the first three persons of the present subjunctive are the same, the subject pronouns - **io, tu,** etc. - are often used to avoid any ambiguity.

Refer to the explanations in 18c(i) above for rules governing the following:

- Verbs whose stem ends in **-c** or **-g**
- Verbs in **-iare** with unstressed **i**
- Verbs ending in **-iare** with stressed **i**
- Verbs ending in **-durre**
- Verbs based on **trarre**

(iii) *Future [➤14a]*

The stem of the future tense of regular verbs is obtained by removing the final -**e** of the infinitive. The characteristic vowel -**a**- of first conjugation verbs changes to -**e**-. The stems, therefore are:

parler-   **vender-**   **dormir-**

The future endings are the same for both regular and irregular verbs.

Note the grave accent on the first and third person singular, indicating that the ending is stressed.

| -ò | -ai | -à | -emo | -ete | -anno |

Attention needs to be paid to the following groups of verbs that undergo modifications or spelling changes:

(A) Verbs ending in **-care** and **-gare** will have an **h** after the **c** or **g** throughout the future tense to retain the hard sound, for example:

cercare 'look for' **cerc*h*erò, cerc*h*erai,** etc.
pagare 'pay for' **pag*h*erò, pag*h*erai, etc.**

(B) Verbs ending in **-ciare**, **-giare** and **-sciare** drop the **i** throughout the future tense:

cominciare 'begin'	**comincerò, comincerai,** etc.
viaggiare 'travel'	**viaggerò, viaggerai,** etc.
lasciare 'leave, let'	**lascerò, lascerai,** etc.

(C) Some verbs, and also their compounds [➤18e], have contracted stems, i.e. they lose the characteristic vowel of the infinitive ending:

andare	andrò	go
avere	avrò	have(auxiliary)
cadere	cadrò	fall
dovere	dovrò	have to, must
potere	potrò	be able
sapere	saprò	know
vedere	vedrò	see
vivere	vivrò	live

(D) Some verbs, and also their compounds, modify their spelling, so that the stem has a double **r**:

bere	berrò	drink
parere	parrò	seem
rimanere	rimarrò	remain
tenere	terrò	hold, keep
valere	varrò	be worth
venire	verrò	come
volere	vorrò	want

(E) A few two-syllable verbs in **-are** retain the vowel of the infinitive ending:

dare	darò	give
fare	farò	do, make
stare	starò	be, stay, remain

(iv)   *Conditional [➤14d]*

The stem of the conditional is formed in exactly the same way as the future [➤18c(iii)].
The conditional endings are:

-ei   -esti   -ebbe   -emmo   -este   -ebbero

Note: Any modifications to the future stem referred to in 18c(iii) above will also apply to the conditional.

 Do not confuse the first person plural ending of the future tense **-emo** with that of the conditional **-emmo**.

(v)   *Imperfect indicative [➤13b]*

To obtain the stem remove the infinitive ending. The imperfect indicative endings are as follows:

-are verbs
-avo   -avi   -ava   -avamo   -avate   -avano

-ere verbs
-evo   -evi   -eva   -evamo   -evate   -evano

-ire verbs
-ivo   -ivi   -iva   ivamo   -ivate   -ivano

Thus the first person singular of each of the model verbs is:
parlavo, vendevo, dormivo.

 Essere is the only verb in this tense that has a completely irregular form:

ero   eri   era   eravamo   eravate   erano

Note also the following:

bere	**bevevo**	drink
dire	**dicevo**	say, tell
fare	**facevo**	do, make

Verbs ending in **-durre**:

produrre	**producevo**	produce
tradurre	**traducevo**	translate

Verbs ending in **-arre**:

attrarre	**attraevo**	attract
distrarre	**distraevo**	distract

(vi) Past definite [➤13c]

To obtain the stem remove the infinitive ending. The past definite endings are as follows:

-are verbs

-ai	-asti	-ò	-ammo	-aste	-arono

-ere verbs

-ei	-esti	-é	-emmo	-este	-erono
(-etti)		(-ette)			(-ettero)

-ire verbs

-ii	-isti	-ì	-immo	-iste	-irono

Note: • **-ere** verbs have an alternative form for the first and third person
singular and the third person plural. It is acceptable to use either form.

As a general rule, verbs whose stem ends in **t**, for example, **battere**
(**batt-**) 'beat' do not have this alternative form.

• With the exception of the third person singular of **-are**
verbs, which have -o instead of -a, the past definite endings
are identical but for the characteristic vowel of the infinitive.

• The endings of the third person singular are stressed:
-ò, -é, -ì.

• Although there are a considerable number of irregular verbs,
it is worth noting that they all follow a pattern, for example:

accendere 'switch/turn on'

accesi	**accendesti**	**accese**
accendemmo	**accendeste**	**accesero**

The first and third person singular and the third person plural
are the irregular forms. However, once you know the first person then you can form the other two by replacing -i with -e or
-ero respectively. The second person singular and the first and
second person plural are formed from the stem of the verb.
This guideline can be applied to most irregular verbs. For common irregular verbs that do not conform to this pattern, consult
the Verb Tables [➤19g, 19h].

Unlike the regular conjugations, irregular verbs are not stressed on
the third person singular.

(vii) Imperfect subjunctive [➤16]

To obtain the stem remove the ending of the infinitive. The only
difference in the endings of the imperfect subjunctive is that
each conjugation retains the characteristic vowel of the
infinitve. The endings are:

-**are** verbs

-assi	-assi	-asse	-assimo	-aste	-assero

-**ere** verbs

-essi	-essi	-esse	-essimo	-este	-essero

-**ire** verbs

-issi	-issi	-isse	-issimo	-iste	-issero

Note the following group of verbs. Some have stem changes, others use -**ere** endings when you would expect those of the -**are** group.

bere	**bevessi**	drink
dare	**dessi**	give
dire	**dicessi**	say, tell
fare	**facessi**	do, make
stare	**stessi**	be, stay, remain

Note also verbs ending in -**durre** and -**arre**

produrre	**producessi**	produce
trarre	**traessi**	pull, draw

(viii) Formation of compound tenses

The following compound tenses are formed with the auxiliary verb **avere** 'have' or **essere** 'be' + the past participle [➤10f(i)]:

Indicative
- perfect [➤13a]
- pluperfect [➤13d]
- past anterior [➤13e]
- future perfect [➤14b]
- conditional perfect [➤14e]

Subjunctive
- perfect and pluperfect [➤16]

[For information on which verbs take **avere** or **essere** ➤11c(i)-(ii).]

18d Formation of non-finite parts

➤ Formation of the imperative ➤15b.
Formation of the gerund ➤10d(i).

(i) Past participle [➤10f(i)]

To form the past participle remove the infinitive ending and replace it with -**ato** (-**are** verbs), -**uto** (-**ere** verbs) or -**ito** (-**ire** verbs).

parlato	**venduto**	**dormito**

 Many past participles are irregular. The following are a few of the most common:

assistere	**assistito**	attend, be present at
chiudere	**chiuso**	close
correggere	**corretto**	correct
discutere	**discusso**	discuss
distruggere	**distrutto**	destroy
dividere	**diviso**	divide
muovere	**mosso**	move
offrire	**offerto**	offer
prendere	**preso**	take
ridere	**riso**	laugh
risolvere	**risolto**	solve
rispondere	**risposto**	reply
scendere	**sceso**	go down, get out of
sciogliere	**sciolto**	dissolve
spendere	**speso**	spend
succedere	**successo**	happen
tradurre	**tradotto**	translate
uccidere	**ucciso**	kill

[For other irregular past participles ➤19h.]

Any compound forms of the above examples will form their past participles in the same way.

18e Compound verbs

(i) Prefixes: **s-, ri-, mal-**

A prefix can be added to any base verb as long as it makes sense.

s- often serves to create the opposite meaning:

coprire	cover	**scoprire**	uncover, discover
gelare	freeze	**sgelare**	thaw

ri- can be used like the English 're-', i.e. to indicate repetition:

cominciare	begin	**ricominciare**	begin again
leggere	read	**rileggere**	reread
fare	do	**rifare**	redo

mal- gives the meaning of *bad*, *badly* or *evil*.

trattare	treat	**maltrattare**	treat badly
intendere	understand	**malintendere**	misunderstand

(ii) -porre, -tenere, -venire

A large number of verbs are derived from these three base verbs.
Porre 'put' has derivatives which often correspond to English verbs ending in '-pose'.

comporre	compose	**decomporre**	decompose
disporre	dispose, arrange	**imporre**	impose
opporre	oppose	**posporre**	postpone
presupporre	presuppose	**proporre**	propose
supporre	suppose		

Tenere 'hold' has derivatives which correspond to English verbs ending in '-tain':

contenere	contain	**detenere**	detain, stop
mantenere	maintain	**ritenere**	retain
sostenere	sustain	**trattenere**	entertain; hold up; detain

Venire 'come' has a number of derivatives:

avvenire	happen	**convenire**	agree, suit
divenire	become	**intervenire**	intervene
provenire	come from, originate from	**sopravvenire**	arrive, happen (suddenly, unexpectedly)
svenire	faint		

(iii) -durre

Sometimes the base verb does not exist. For example, there is no verb **durre** yet there are several verbs based on this ending, corresponding to the English verbs ending in '-duce' or '-duct'.

condurre	conduct, lead, drive	**dedurre**	deduce
indurre	induce, induct	**introdurre**	introduce, insert
produrre	produce	**ridurre**	reduce
riprodurre	reproduce	**sedurre**	seduce

Verb Tables

19a Regular verbs

The three conjugations (or groups) of Italian verbs which follow a regular pattern have infinitives ending in **-are, -ere** and **-ire**. The model verbs we shall use for each group are:

parlare	speak
vendere	sell
dormire	sleep

Unless otherwise stated, the *stem*, i.e. the part of the verb you add the endings to, is what you are left with when you remove the **-are, -ere** or **-ire** of the infinitive.

19b Conjugation of regular -are verbs

Present	**Perfect**
parlo	ho parlato
parli	hai parlato
parla	ha parlato
parliamo	abbiamo parlato
parlate	avete parlato
parlano	hanno parlato

Imperfect	**Pluperfect**
parlavo	avevo parlato
parlavi	avevi parlato
parlava	aveva parlato
parlavamo	avevamo parlato
parlavate	avevate parlato
parlavano	avevano parlato

Future	**Future perfect**
parlerò	avrò parlato
parlerai	avrai parlato
parlerà	avrà parlato
parleremo	avremo parlato
parlerete	avrete parlato
parleranno	avranno parlato

Conditional
parlerei
parleresti
parlerebbe
parleremmo
parlereste
parlerebbero

Conditional perfect
avrei parlato
avresti parlato
avrebbe parlato
avremmo parlato
avreste parlato
avrebbero parlato

Past definite
parlai
parlasti
parlò
parlammo
parlaste
parlarono

Past anterior
ebbi parlato
avesti parlato
ebbe parlato
avemmo parlato
aveste parlato
ebbero parlato

Present subjunctive
parli
parli
parli
parliamo
parliate
parlino

Perfect subjunctive
abbia parlato
abbia parlato
abbia parlato
abbiamo parlato
abbiate parlato
abbiano parlato

Imperfect subjunctive
parlassi
parlassi
parlasse
parlassimo
parlaste
parlassero

Pluperfect subjunctive
avessi parlato
avessi parlato
avesse parlato
avessimo parlato
aveste parlato
avessero parlato

Imperative
–
parla
parli
parliamo
parlate
parlino

Present participle
parlante

Past participle
parlato

Present gerund
parlando

Past gerund
avendo parlato

19c *Verbs ending in -are with minor changes*

(i) *Verbs with infinitives in -care and -gare*

Whenever the **c** or **g** of the stem of verbs of this type is followed by **i** or **e**, an **h** must be put in to retain the hard sound. Examples of this type are **cercare** 'look for' and **pagare** 'pay for'.

Present

cerco
cerchi
cerca
cerchiamo
cercate
cercano

Future

cercherò etc.

Conditional

cercherei etc.

The **h** will be retained throughout the future and conditional

Present subjunctive

cerchi
cerchi
cerchi
cerchiamo
cerchiate
cerchino

Imperative

–
cerca
cerchi
cerchiamo
cercate
cerchino

Pagare, and others ending in **-gare**, follow *exactly* the same pattern as **cercare**.

(ii) *Verbs with infinitives in -iare*

Verbs ending in **-iare** with an unstressed **i**, for example **studiare** 'study' have only *one* **i** in the forms referred to below, not the double **i** you would expect.

studi (second person singular present tense)
studi   studi   studi (first three persons of the present subjunctive)
studi (polite form, singular, of the imperative)

Verbs ending in **-iare** that have a stressed **i**, for example **sciare** 'ski', have a double **i** in all the above forms, i.e. **sci**i.

(iii)   *Verbs in -ciare, -giare and -sciare*

Examples of verbs in this category are **cominciare** 'begin', **viaggiare** 'travel' and **lasciare** 'leave'.
These verbs will also have just one **i** in all the forms mentioned in 19c(ii) above. However, these same verbs drop the **i** of the stem throughout the future and conditional.

Future

comincerò	comincerai etc.
viaggerò	viaggerai etc.
lascerò	lascerai etc.

Conditional

comincerei	cominceresti etc.
viaggerei	viaggeresti etc.
lascerei	lasceresti etc.

19d   *Conjugation of regular -ere verbs*

Present	**Perfect**
vendo	ho venduto
vendi	hai venduto
vende	ha venduto
vendiamo	abbiamo venduto
vendete	avete venduto
vendono	hanno venduto

Imperfect	**Pluperfect**
vendevo	avevo venduto
vendevi	avevi venduto
vendeva	aveva venduto
vendevamo	avevamo venduto
vendevate	avevate venduto
vendevano	avevano venduto

Future

venderò
venderai
venderà
venderemo
venderete
venderanno

Future perfect

avrò venduto
avrai venduto
avrà venduto
avremo venduto
avrete venduto
avranno venduto

Conditional

venderei
venderesti
venderebbe
venderemmo
vendereste
venderebbero

Conditional perfect

avrei venduto
avresti venduto
avrebbe venduto
avremmo venduto
avreste venduto
avrebbero venduto

Past definite

vendei (vendetti)
vendesti
vendé (vendette)
vendemmo
vendeste
venderono (vendettero)

Past anterior

ebbi venduto
avesti venduto
ebbe venduto
avemmo venduto
aveste venduto
ebbero venduto

Present subjunctive

venda
venda
venda
vendiamo
vendiate
vendano

Perfect subjunctive

abbia venduto
abbia venduto
abbia venduto
abbiamo venduto
abbiate venduto
abbiano venduto

Imperfect subjunctive

vendessi
vendessi
vendesse
vendessimo
vendeste
vendessero

Pluperfect subjunctive

avessi venduto
avessi venduto
avesse venduto
avessimo venduto
aveste venduto
avessero venduto

Imperative

–
vendi
venda
vendiamo
vendete
vendano

Present participle	**Past participle**
vendente	venduto

Present gerund	**Past gerund**
vendendo	avendo venduto

19e Conjugation of regular -ire verbs

Present	**Perfect**
dormo	ho dormito
dormi	hai dormito
dorme	ha dormito
dormiamo	abbiamo dormito
dormite	avete dormito
dormono	hanno dormito

Imperfect	**Pluperfect**
dormivo	avevo dormito
dormivi	avevi dormito
dormiva	aveva dormito
dormivamo	avevamo dormito
dormivate	avevate dormito
dormivano	avevano dormito

Future	**Future perfect**
dormirò	avrò dormito
dormirai	avrai dormito
dormirà	avrà dormito
dormiremo	avremo dormito
dormirete	avrete dormito
dormiranno	avranno dormito

Conditional
dormirei
dormiresti
dormirebbe
dormiremmo
dormireste
dormirebbero

Conditional perfect
avrei dormito
avresti dormito
avrebbe dormito
avremmo dormito
avreste dormito
avrebbero dormito

Past definite
dormii
dormisti
dormì
dormimmo
dormiste
dormirono

Past anterior
ebbi dormito
avesti dormito
ebbe dormito
avemmo dormito
aveste dormito
ebbero dormito

Present subjunctive
dorma
dorma
dorma
dormiamo
dormiate
dormano

Perfect subjunctive
abbia dormito
abbia dormito
abbia dormito
abbiamo dormito
abbiate dormito
abbiano dormito

Imperfect subjunctive
dormissi
dormissi
dormisse
dormissimo
dormiste
dormissero

Pluperfect subjunctive
avessi dormito
avessi dormito
avesse dormito
avessimo dormito
aveste dormito
avessero dormito

Imperative
–
dormi
dorma
dormiamo
dormite
dormano

Present participle
dormiente

Past participle
dormito

Present gerund
dormendo

Past gerund
avendo dormito

19f Verbs that have -isc between the stem and the ending

There are a considerable number of verbs that belong to the third conjugation, i.e. which end in **-ire,** that insert **-isc** between the stem and the ending. This happens in the present indicative, the present subjunctive and the imperative and these will be written out completely, using **capire** 'understand' as the model. The other parts of the verb will not be listed as they are formed as in 19e above.

Present	Present subjunctive	Imperative
capisco	capisca	–
capisci	capisca	capisci
capisce	capisca	capisca
capiamo	capiamo	capiamo
capite	capiate	capite
capiscono	capiscano	capiscano

• Other verbs of this type are:

abolire	abolish
agire	act, behave
approfondire	deepen, examine closely
arricchire	enrich
arrossire	blush
chiarire	clarify
colorire	colour/color
colpire	hit, strike
condire	season (a dish)
contribuire	contribute
costruire	build
custodire	look after, guard
definire	define, make clear
demolire	demolish
digerire	digest
diminuire	decrease, reduce
distribuire	distribute
esaurire	exhaust, use up
esibire	exhibit, display
esordire	begin (one's career)
fallire	fail, go bankrupt
favorire	favour/favor, encourage
ferire	hurt, injure
finire	finish
fiorire	flower, blossom, flourish

garantire	guarantee
gradire	welcome, accept, like
guaire	whine, yelp
guarire	heal, cure
impadronirsi	take hold of, seize
impallidire	turn pale
impazzire	go mad
impedire	prevent, hinder
infastidire	annoy, bother
ingerire	swallow
inserire	insert, put, introduce
istituire	found, set up
istruire	teach, instruct
marcire	go bad, rot, decay
munire	provide, equip
obbedire (ubbidire)	obey
patire	suffer, endure
preferire	prefer
proibire	prohibit
pulire	clean
punire	punish
rapire	kidnap
reagire	react
restituire	return, give back
riunire	assemble, get/put together
sbalordire	astonish, amaze
seppellire	bury
smarrire	lose, mislay
smentire	deny, prove wrong
sostituire	substitute, replace
sparire	disappear
spedire	send
stabilire	establish, fix
starnutire	sneeze
stupire	amaze, astonish
suggerire	suggest
svanire	disappear
tradire	betray
trasferire	transfer
trasgredire	transgress, violate, disobey
unire	unite, join, bring together
usufruire	benefit, profit

Note: Some -**ire** verbs can take either pattern with or without -**isc**. The most common of these are:

applaudire	applaud
assorbire	absorb
inghiottire	swallow
mentire	lie
nutrire	nourish
tossire	cough

Scomparire 'disappear', and **comparire** and **apparire** 'appear' can also follow the **capire** pattern, although the forms more commonly used are listed under the Irregular verbs section [➤19h].

19g   *The irregular verbs* avere *and* essere

(i)   *Avere 'have'*

Present	**Perfect**
ho	ho avuto
hai	hai avuto
ha	ha avuto
abbiamo	abbiamo avuto
avete	avete avuto
hanno	hanno avuto

Imperfect	**Pluperfect**
avevo	avevo avuto
avevi	avevi avuto
aveva	aveva avuto
avevamo	avevamo avuto
avevate	avevate avuto
avevano	avevano avuto

Future	**Future perfect**
avrò	avrò avuto
avrai	avrai avuto
avrà	avrà avuto
avremo	avremo avuto
avrete	avrete avuto
avranno	avranno avuto

Conditional
avrei
avresti
avrebbe
avremmo
avreste
avrebbero

Conditional perfect
avrei avuto
avresti avuto
avrebbe avuto
avremmo avuto
avreste avuto
avrebbero avuto

Past definite
ebbi
avesti
ebbe
avemmo
aveste
ebbero

Past anterior
ebbi avuto
avesti avuto
ebbe avuto
avemmo avuto
aveste avuto
ebbero avuto

Present subjunctive
abbia
abbia
abbia
abbiamo
abbiate
abbiano

Perfect subjunctive
abbia avuto
abbia avuto
abbia avuto
abbiamo avuto
abbiate avuto
abbiano avuto

Imperfect subjunctive
avessi
avessi
avesse
avessimo
aveste
avessero

Pluperfect subjunctive
avessi avuto
avessi avuto
avesse avuto
avessimo avuto
aveste avuto
avessero avuto

Imperative
–
abbi
abbia
abbiamo
abbiate
abbiano

Present participle
avente

Past participle
avuto

Present gerund
avendo

Past gerund
avendo avuto

(ii) *Essere* 'be'

Present	**Perfect**
sono	sono stato/a
sei	sei stato/a
è	è stato/a
siamo	siamo stati/e
siete	siete stati/e
sono	sono stati/e

Imperfect	**Pluperfect**
ero	ero stato/a
eri	eri stato/a
era	era stato/a
eravamo	eravamo stati/e
eravate	eravate stati/e
erano	erano stati/e

Future	**Future perfect**
sarò	sarò stato/a
sarai	sarai stato/a
sarà	sarà stato/a
saremo	saremo stati/e
sarete	sarete stati/e
saranno	saranno stati/e

Conditional	**Conditional perfect**
sarei	sarei stato/a
saresti	saresti stato/a
sarebbe	sarebbe stato/a
saremmo	saremmo stati/e
sareste	sareste stati/e
sarebbero	sarebbero stati/e

Past definite	**Past anterior**
fui	fui stato/a
fosti	fosti stato/a
fu	fu stato/a
fummo	fummo stati/e
foste	foste stati/e
furono	furono stati/e

Present subjunctive	Perfect subjunctive
sia	sia stato/a
sia	sia stato/a
sia	sia stato/a
siamo	siamo stati/e
siate	siate stati/e
siano	siano stati/e

Imperfect subjunctive	Pluperfect subjunctive
fossi	fossi stato/a
fossi	fossi stato/a
fosse	fosse stato/a
fossimo	fossimo stati/e
foste	foste stati/e
fossero	fossero stati/e

Imperative

–
sii
sia
siamo
siate
siano

Present participle	Past participle
essente	stato/a/i/e

Present gerund	Past gerund
essendo	essendo stato

19h   *Other irregular verbs*

The following are the most common irregular verbs in Italian.
Only irregularly formed tenses are mentioned. In the future and
conditional, only the stem can be irregular - the same endings
are always used. Any irregularity in the future will therefore
apply to the conditional, so it is not listed separately. For the
formation of the imperative and any commonly used irregular
forms ➤15b.

accendere *switch/turn on*

Past definite
accesi accendesti accese accendemmo acendeste accesero

Past participle
acceso

Also all verbs ending in **-endere**, such as:

apprendere	learn	**comprendere**	understand, include
difendere	defend	**intendere**	intend
offendere	offend	**rendere**	give back, make
scendere	descend, get out of	**sorprendere**	surprise
sospendere	suspend, put off	**spendere**	spend

---

accorgersi *notice, realize, become aware of*
mi accorsi ti accorgesti si accorse ci accorgemmo vi accorgeste si accorsero

Past participle
accorto

Also

porgere	hand, hold out	**sporgersi**	lean out

---

andare *go*

Present indicative
vado vai va andiamo andate vanno

Present subjunctive
vada vada vada andiamo andiate vadano

Future
andrò

---

apparire *appear*

Present indicative
appaio appari appare appariamo apparite appaiono

Present subjunctive
appaia appaia appaia appariamo appariate appaiano

Past definite
apparvi apparisti apparve apparimmo appariste apparirono

Past participle
apparso

Also

comparire	appear	**scomparire**	disappear

aprire *open*

Past participle
aperto

Also

coprire	cover	**offrire**	offer
scoprire	discover	**soffrire**	suffer

assumere *employ, assume*

Past definite
assunsi assumesti assunse assumemmo assumeste assunsero

Past participle
assunto

Also **riassumere**   re-employ, reassume, summarize

bere *drink*

Present indicative
bevo bevi beve beviamo bevete bevono

Present subjunctive
beva beva beva beviamo beviate bevano

Future
berrò

Past definite
bevvi bevesti bevve bevemmo beveste bevvero

Imperfect indicative
bevevo

Imperfect subjunctive
bevessi

Present participle
bevente

Past participle
bevuto

Gerund
bevendo

cadere *fall*

> **Future**
> cadrò
>
> **Past definite**
> caddi cadesti cadde cademmo cadeste caddero
>
> Also **accadere** happen

---

chiedere *ask*

> **Past definite**
> chiesi chiedesti chiese chiedemmo chiedeste chiesero
>
> **Past participle**
> chiesto
>
> Also **richiedere** request

---

cogliere *pick, gather*

> **Present indicative**
> colgo cogli coglie cogliamo cogliete colgono
>
> **Present subjunctive**
> colga colga colga cogliamo cogliate colgano
>
> **Past definite**
> colsi cogliesti colse cogliemmo coglieste colsero
>
> **Past participle**
> colto
>
> Also all verbs based on **cogliere**

accogliere	welcome	**raccogliere**	gather, pick
sciogliere	dissolve	**togliere**	remove

---

condurre *take, lead, conduct*

> **Present indicative**
> conduco conduci conduce conduciamo conducete conducono
>
> **Present subjunctive**
> conduca conduca conduca conduciamo conduciate conducano
>
> **Imperfect indicative**
> conducevo

Imperfect subjunctive
conducessi

Past definite
condussi conducesti condusse conducemmo conduceste condussero

Present participle
conducente

Past participle
condotto

Gerund
conducendo

Also all verbs ending in **-durre**

---

conoscere *know, meet*

Past definite
conobbi conoscesti conobbe conoscemmo conosceste conobbero

Past participle
conosciuto

Also **riconoscere** recognize

---

correre *run*

Past definite
corsi corresti corse corremmo correste corsero

Past participle
corso

Also any derivatives, such as

accorrere	run, rush	**percorrere**	go through, travel
ricorrere	resort, turn to	**soccorrere**	aid, assist
trascorrere	spend (time)		

---

dare *give*

Present indicative
do dai dà diamo date dano

Present subjunctive
dia dia dia diamo diate diano

Future
darò

Past definite
diedi desti diede demmo deste diedero

Imperfect subjunctive
dessi dessi desse dessimo deste dessero

---

decidere *decide*

Past definite
decisi decidesti decise decidemmo decideste decisero

Past participle
deciso

Also

dividere	divide	**ridere**	laugh
sorridere	smile	**uccidere**	kill

---

dire *say, tell*

Present indicative
dico dici dice diciamo dite dicomo

Present subjunctive
dica dica dica diciamo diciate dicano

Imperfect indicative
dicevo

Imperfect subjunctive
dicessi

Past definite
dissi dicesti disse dicemmo diceste dissero

Present participle
dicente

Past participle
detto

Gerund
dicendo

Also

contraddire	contradict	**disdire**	cancel

dovere *have to, must, owe*

Present indicative
devo (debbo) devi deve dobbiamo dovete devono (debbono)

Present subjunctive
deva/debba deva/debba deva/debba dobbiamo dobbiate devano/debbano

Future
dovrò

fare *do, make*

Present indicative
faccio fai fa facciamo fate fanno

Present subjunctive
faccia faccia faccia facciamo facciate facciano

Future
farò

Imperfect indicative
facevo

Imperfect subjunctive
facessi

Past definite
feci facesti fece facemmo faceste fecero

Present participle
facente

Past participle
fatto

Gerund
facendo

Also
soddisfare satisfy

giungere *arrive at, reach*

Past definite
giunsi giungesti giunse giungemmo giungeste giunsero

Past participle
giunto

Also

aggiungere add		**raggiungere**	reach, attain

leggere *read*

Past definite
lessi leggesti lesse leggemmo leggeste lessero

Past participle
letto

Also
proteggere protect

mettere *put*

Past definite
misi mettesti mise mettemmo metteste misero

Past participle
messo

Also any derivatives, such as:

ammettere	admit	**commettere**	commit
permettere	permit	**promettere**	promise
smettere	stop, cease		

morire *die*

Present indicative
muoio muori muore moriamo morite muoiono

Present subjunctive
muoia muoia muoia moriamo moriate muoiano

Future
morirò (or morrò)

Present participle
morente

Past participle
morto

Gerund
morendo

nascere *be born*

Past definite
nacqui nascesti nacque nascemmo nasceste nacquero

Past participle
nato

nascondere *hide*

Past definite
nascosi nascondesti nascose nascondemmo nascondeste nascosero

Past participle
nascosto

Also
rispondere reply

parere *seem*

Present indicative
paio pari pare paiamo parete paiono

Present subjunctive
paia paia paia paiamo paiate paiano

Future
parrò

Past definite
parvi paresti parve paremmo pareste parvero

Present participle
parvente

Past participle
parso

Gerund
parendo

perdere *lose*

Past definite
persi perdesti perse perdemmo perdeste persero

Past participle
perso (perduto)

persuadere *persuade*

Past definite
persuasi persuadesti persuase persuademmo persuadeste persuasero

Past participle
persuaso

Also

evadere	escape	**invadere**	invade

piacere *please*

Present indicative
piaccio piaci piace piacciamo piacete piacciono

Present subjunctive
piaccia piaccia piaccia piacciamo piacciate piacciano

Past definite
piacqui piacesti piacque piacemmo piaceste piacquero

Past participle
piaciuto

Also

dispiacere	mind, be sorry	**giacere**	be situated, lie
tacere	be silent		

piangere *cry*

Past definite
piansi piangesti pianse piangemmo piangeste piansero

Past participle
pianto

Also
rimpiangere regret

porre *put*

Present indicative
pongo poni pone poniamo ponete pongono

Present subjunctive
ponga ponga ponga poniamo poniate pongano

Future
porrò

Imperfect indicative
ponevo

Imperfect subjunctive
ponessi

Past definite
posi ponesti pose ponemmo poneste posero

Present participle
ponente

Past partciple
posto

Gerund
ponendo

Also all compounds [➤18e(ii)]

---

potere *be able, can*

Present indicative
posso puoi può possiamo potete possono

Present subjunctive
possa possa possa possiamo possiate possano

Future
potrò

---

rimanere *remain, stay*

Present indicative
rimango rimani rimane rimaniamo rimanete rimangono

Present subjunctive
rimanga rimanga rimanga rimaniamo rimaniate rimangano

Future
rimarrò

Past definite
rimasi rimanesti rimase rimanemmo rimaneste rimasero

Past participle
rimasto

rompere *break*

Past definite
ruppi rompesti ruppe rompemmo rompeste ruppero

Past participle
rotto

---

salire *go up, get on board*

Present indicative
salgo sali sale saliamo salite salgono

Present subjunctive
salga salga salga saliamo saliate salgano

---

sapere *know, know how to*

Present indicative
so sai sa sappiamo sapete sanno

Present subjunctive
sappia sappia sappia sappiamo sappiate sappiano

Future
saprò

Past definite
seppi sapesti seppe sapemmo sapeste seppero

Present participle
sapiente

---

scegliere *choose*

Present indicative
scelgo scegli sceglie scegliamo scegliete scelgono

Present subjunctive
scelga scelga scelga scegliamo scegliate scelgano

Past definite
scelsi scegliesti scelse scegliemmo sceglieste scelsero

Past participle
scelto

scrivere *write*

Past definite
scrissi scrivesti scrisse scrivemmo scriveste scrissero

Past participle
scritto

Also

descrivere	describe	**iscrivere**	enrol
friggere	fry	**sconfiggere**	defeat

scuotere *shake*

Past definite
scossi scuotesti scosse scuotemmo scuoteste scossero

Past participle
scosso

Also

commuovere   move, affect (emotion)

muovere	move	**promuovere**	promote

sedere *sit*

Present indicative
siedo siedi siede sediamo sedete siedono

Present subjunctive
sieda sieda sieda sediamo sediate siedano

Also
possedere   possess

spingere *push*

Past definite
spinsi spingesti spinse spingemmo spingeste spinsero

Past participle
spinto

Also

distinguere	distinguish	**dipingere**	paint
fingere	pretend	**tingere**	dye

stare *be, stay*

> *Present indicative*
> sto stai sta stiamo state stanno
>
> *Present subjunctive*
> stia stia stia stiamo stiate stiano
>
> *Future*
> starò
>
> *Past definite*
> stetti stesti stette stemmo steste stettero
>
> *Imperfect subjunctive*
> stessi stessi stesse stessimo steste stessero

---

stringere *clasp, grip, hold tight*

> *Past definite*
> strinsi stringesti strinse stringemmo stringeste strinsero
>
> *Past participle*
> stretto
>
> Also
> **costringere** force, compel

---

tenere *hold*

> *Present indicative*
> tengo tieni tiene teniamo tenete tengono
>
> *Present subjunctive*
> tenga tenga tenga teniamo teniate tengano
>
> *Future*
> terrò
>
> *Past definite*
> tenni tenesti tenne tenemmo teneste tennero
>
> Also any compounds [➤18e(ii)]

trarre *draw, pull*

Present indicative
traggo trai trae traiamo traete traggono

Present subjunctive
tragga tragga tragga traiamo traiate traggano

Imperfect indicative
traevo

Imperfect subjunctive
traessi

Past definite
trassi traesti trasse traemmo traeste trassero

Present participle
traente

Past participle
tratto

Gerund
traendo

Also any compounds

uscire *go out*

Present indicative
esco esci esce usciamo uscite escono

Present subjunctive
esca esca esca usciamo usciate escano

Also
riuscire   manage, succeed

valere *be worth*

Present indicative
valgo vali vale valiamo valete valgono

Present subjunctive
valga valga valga valiamo valiate valgano

Future
varrò

Past definite
valsi valesti valse valemmo valeste valsero

Past participle
valso

Also
prevalere   prevail

---

vedere *see*

Future
vedrò

Past definite
vidi vedesti vide vedemmo vedeste videro

Past participle
visto

Also
prevedere   foresee, arrange

---

venire *come*

Present indicative
vengo vieni viene veniamo venite vengono

Present subjunctive
venga venga venga veniamo veniate vengano

Future
verrò

Past definite
venni venisti venne venimmo veniste vennero

Past participle
venuto

Also
avvenire	happen	**pervenire**	reach, arrive
svenire	faint		

vincere *win*

> *Past definite*
> vinsi vincesti vinse vincemmo vinceste vinsero

> *Past participle*
> vinto

> Also
> **convincere** convince

vivere *live*

> *Future*
> vivrò

> *Past definite*
> vissi vivesti visse vivemmo viveste vissero

> *Past participle*
> vissuto

> Also
> **sopravvivere** survive, outlive

volere *want, wish*

> *Present indicative*
> voglio vuoi vuole vogliamo volete vogliono

> *Present subjunctive*
> voglia voglia voglia vogliamo vogliate vogliano

> *Future*
> vorrò

> *Past definite*
> volli volesti volle volemmo voleste vollero

D

PEOPLE, THINGS AND IDEAS: NOUNS & NOUN PHRASES

20 Labelling the world: nouns

20a What does a noun do?

Nouns answer the questions **Chi è?** 'Who is it?' and **Cos'è?** 'What is it?' They are the labels we attach to everything in the world around us or in our own minds: people, animals, things, events, processes, ideas.

Oggi è il mio *compleanno*. Per festeggiarlo vado al *ristorante* italiano con i miei *genitori* e alcuni miei *amici*.	Today is my *birthday*. To celebrate it I am going to the Italian *restaurant* with my *parents* and some of my *friends*.

20b Adding detail: the noun phrase

More often than not, nouns have other words or groups of words (phrases or clauses) attached to them, making what is known as a noun phrase. The additional items may take the form of:

- determiners [➤21];
- adjectives and adjectival phrases [➤22];
- relative clauses [➤5b, 23m];
- prepositional phrases [➤25b(i)-(ii)].

To avoid repetition, nouns (and therefore noun phrases) are often replaced by pronouns [➤23].

20c Proper, common and collective nouns

(i) Proper nouns

A *proper noun* is the name of a particular person, animal, place or thing. For example:

Michelangelo
Federico Fellini
il Papa
il Colosseo
gli Appennini

il Monte Bianco
il Chianti
il Portogallo
la Toscana
il Giro d'Italia

(ii) Common nouns

A *common noun* refers to a member of a group or species, such as:

una sedia	a chair	**un fiume**	a river
un uomo	a man	**una mosca**	a fly
un fiore	a flower		

(iii) Collective nouns

Nouns that refer to groups of individuals (people or animals) are called *collective nouns*.

la clientela	clientele	**la famiglia**	family
la folla	crowd	**la gente**	people
la polizia	police	**il pubblico**	public
il bestiame	cattle	**lo stormo**	swarm, flock

Although these nouns have a plural meaning they take a singular verb.

C'*era* troppa gente alla festa.	There *were* too many people at the party.

(iv) Use of capital letters

There are a number of instances in Italian where capital letters are not used with proper nouns (days of the week, months of the year, names of languages, titles) [▶2a(ii)].

Note: It is worth remembering also that while some names are always proper nouns, such as **Roma, Maria, Fiat,** others may be used as common nouns in different contexts. Much depends on the emphasis that the writer wishes to place on a particular word, for example:

Quel *palazzo* è molto bello.	That *palace* is very beautiful.

but

Quello lì è il *Palazzo* Pitti.	That is the Pitti *Palace*.

20d   *Gender of nouns in Italian*

The word *gender* means 'kind' or 'type'. There are only two genders in Italian - *masculine* and *feminine*. As there is no neuter gender, this means that all Italian nouns are categorized into masculine or feminine, whether they are living creatures or not. The gender of a noun may often be established by meaning or by ending but, as there are many illogicalities and exceptions, the most advisable thing to do is to learn the noun *with the definite article* [➤21c], for example **il libro** 'book', **la rivista** 'magazine', not just **libro, rivista**. The majority of nouns in the following examples are shown with the definite article. On some occasions, it is more appropriate to learn the noun with the indefinite article [➤21e].

20e   *Gender by meaning*

(i)   *General*

(A) In the case of human beings, common domestic animals and a few others, male beings are normally masculine and female ones feminine:

Masculine

l'uomo	man
il marito	husband
il ragazzo	boy
il nonno	grandfather
il fratello	brother
il gatto	cat
il cane	dog

Feminine

la donna	woman
la moglie	wife
la ragazza	girl
la nonna	grandmother
la sorella	sister
la gatta	she-cat
la cagna	bitch

However, there are some nouns whose gender does not necessarily indicate the sex of the person or animal being referred to, and the following examples illustrate this point:

la guida	guide	**la vittima**	victim
la persona	person	**l'orso**	bear
il topo	mouse	**la giraffa**	giraffe

Despite the masculine or feminine article, each of the above nouns can refer to a male or female person or animal.

(B) The names of trees tend to be masculine:

l'abete	fir tree	**il frassino**	ash
il larice	larch	**il pino**	pine tree
il pioppo	poplar	**il salice**	willow

There are quite a number, however, that are feminine, such as:

la betulla	birch	**la magnolia**	magnolia
la palma	palm tree	**la quercia**	oak tree

(C) Many fruit trees are masculine and their fruit feminine:

il pero	pear tree	**la pera**	pear
il pesco	peach tree	**la pesca**	peach
il melo	apple tree	**la mela**	apple
il ciliegio	cherry tree	**la ciliegia**	cherry

Some exceptions to this general rule include:

il limone	lemon/lemon tree
il fico	fig/fig tree
il pompelmo	grapefruit/grapefruit tree
il lampone	raspberry/raspberry bush

Note also that exotic fruits are mainly masculine:

l'ananas	pineapple	**il kiwi**	kiwi
il mango	mango		

(D) Names of cities, regions, islands, countries and continents are mostly feminine:

la Lombardia	Lombardy	**la Calabria**	Calabria
la Sardegna	Sardinia	**la Sicilia**	Sicily
la Spagna	Spain	**la Norvegia**	Norway
l'Africa	Africa	**l'Europa**	Europe
l'America	America	**la Roma**	Rome

Note: The definite article is not normally used before the names of cities [➤21c(viii)D].

Some exceptions to the above are the following Italian regions:

il Piemonte
il Veneto
il Molise
l'Abruzzo (gli Abruzzi)
il Trentino-Alto Adige
il Lazio
il Friuli

Note also the following countries that are masculine:

il Belgio	Belgium	**il Brasile**	Brazil
il Canada	Canada	**l'Egitto**	Egypt
il Giappone	Japan	**il Messico**	Mexico
il Portogallo	Portugal	**gli Stati Uniti**	United States

(E) Names of rivers, lakes, seas, oceans and mountains are mostly masculine:

il Po	the Po
il Tevere	the Tiber
il (lago di) Garda	Lake Garda
il Mediterraneo	the Mediterranean
l'Atlantico	the Atlantic
il Monte Bianco	Mont-Blanc
gli Appennini	the Apennines

Some exceptions:

le Alpi	the Alps	**le Dolomiti**	the Dolomites
la Loira	the Loire	**la Senna**	the Seine

(F) Languages are always masculine:

il tedesco	German
il portoghese	Portuguese
l'inglese	English

(G) The days of the week and months of the year [➤30a, 30b] are masculine with the exception of **domenica** 'Sunday'.

(H) The names of metals and chemical elements tend to be masculine:

l'oro	gold	**l'argento**	silver
il bronzo	bronze	**l'alluminio**	aluminium

il piombo	lead	il mercurio	mercury
il rame	copper	lo zinco	zinc
l'ossigeno	oxygen		

(I) The names of the cardinal points are masculine:

il nord (il settentrione)	the north
il sud (il meridione/il mezzogiorno)	the south
l'est (l'oriente/il levante)	the east
l'ovest (l'occidente/il ponente)	the west

Any compounds of the above would also be masculine, for example, **il nord-ovest** 'the north-west', **il sud-est** 'the south east', etc.

Note that it is possible to use capital letters if reference is being made to a geographical area, for example, **il Mezzogiorno** 'the South (of Italy)', **il Medio-Oriente** 'the Middle East'.

(J) Subjects of study, areas of knowledge and arts are mostly feminine:

la matematica	mathematics	la fisica	physics
la geografia	geography	la storia	history
la grammatica	grammar	la filosofia	philosophy
l'architettura	architecture	la pittura	painting

(K) Metric weights, measures and fractions are mostly masculine:

un etto	100 gram(me)s	un chilo	a kilo
un metro	a metre/meter	un quarto	a quarter
un litro	a litre/liter	un quinto	a fifth

(L) Foreign words introduced into the language, particularly if they end in a consonant, are mostly masculine:

il bar
il jazz
lo sport
il tram
il walkman

(M) Many abstract nouns are feminine:

l'allegria	cheerfulness	la bellezza	beauty
la delusione	disappointment	la giustizia	justice
l'intelligenza	intelligence	la miseria	poverty
la pace	peace	la tristezza	sadness
la vergogna	shame		

However, in this category there are also a number of masculine words:

l'amore	love	il buonumore	good mood
il coraggio	courage	il diritto	law, right
il disaccordo	disagreement	il dolore	pain

20f Gender by ending

(i) -o, -a *masculine, feminine*

In many of the above examples you will have noticed that the nouns ending in **-o** are masculine and those ending in **-a** are feminine. This is indeed the case with most Italian nouns ending in **-o** and **-a**.

il negozio	shop	la cartolina	postcard
il lago	lake	la finestra	window

 With some nouns, the **-o/-a** ending not only changes the gender but also the meaning.

il porto	port
la porta	door
il pero	pear tree
la pera	pear [▶20e(i)C]
il tappo	plug, stopper
la tappa	stop, stage (of journey)

(ii) Exceptions

There are some exceptions to the general rule.

(A) Nouns ending in **-o** which are feminine include:

l'auto	car	la foto	photo
la mano	hand	la moto	motorbike
la radio	radio		

Note that four of the above are abbreviations of nouns that are feminine by origin: **l'automobile, la fotografia, la motocicletta** and **la radiotrasmettitrice**.

(B) Nouns ending in **-a** which are masculine include many ending in **-ma**. (A great number of these words are of Greek origin.)

il fantasma	ghost	il clima	climate
il dramma	drama	il panorama	panorama

il pigiama	pyjama	il problema	problem
il programma	program(me)	il sistema	system
lo schema	plan	il sintoma	symptom
il telegramma	telegram(me)	il tema	theme, topic

(C) There are nouns ending in **-a, -ista** and **-cida** which can be either masculine or feminine:

l'atleta	athlete	il/la collega	colleague
il/la dentista	dentist	lo/la specialista	specialist
il/la tennista	tennis player	il/la turista	tourist
l'omicida	murderer	il/la suicida	suicide

(iii) *-e ending*

Nouns ending in **-e** can be either masculine or feminine.

la fine	end	la salute	health
la voce	voice	il mestiere	trade, profession
il pettine	comb	il sole	sun

(iv) *Other endings*

Other endings can also indicate gender.

(A) Feminine

• Most nouns ending in **-ione, -udine, -ite** (includes many medical terms that end in '-itis' in English), **-igine** and **-ice** (often used to refer to female professions):

la decisione	decision	la lezione	lesson
la nazione	nation	la televisione	television
l'abitudine	habit	la solitudine	solitude
l'appendicite	appendicitis	la meningite	meningitis
la tonsillite	tonsilitis	l'origine	origin
l'attrice	actress	la pittrice	painter

• Nouns that end in **-tà** or **-tù**:

la bontà	goodness	la città	city
la felicità	happiness	l'università	university
la volontà	will	la gioventù	youth
la virtù	virtue		

• Most nouns ending in **-i** (many of which correspond to the English ending '-sis'):

| l'analisi | analysis | la crisi | crisis |
| la diagnosi | diagnosis | l'enfasi | emphasis |

| la sintesi | synthesis | **la tesi** | thesis |

A commonly used word that is masculine is **il brindisi** 'toast' (drink to).

- Nouns ending in **-ie**:

la specie	sort, kind
la superficie	surface
la serie	series

(B) Masculine

- Nouns ending in **-ore**:

il colore	colour/color	**il fattore**	factor
il fiore	flower	**il motore**	motor
l'odore	smell	**il settore**	sector
il valore	value		

- Most nouns ending in **-ame, -ale, -ile** and **-ere**:

il catrame	tar	**il bestiame**	cattle
il rame	copper	**il rottame**	scrap
il canale	canal	**il giornale**	newspaper
lo schienale	back (of chair)	**il temporale**	storm
il tribunale	(law-)court	**il barile**	barrel
il canile	kennel	**il fienile**	barn
il benessere	well-being, welfare	**il carcere**	prison
il malessere	malaise, discomfort	**il potere**	power

The gender of **il carcere** 'prison' changes to feminine in the plural: *le* **carceri**.

20g Formation of feminines

You have already seen in 20e(i) and 20f(ii)C how to form the feminine equivalent of some masculine nouns. In some instances, the noun remains the same and the gender is indicated by the article:

| **il/la nipote** | nephew/niece |
| **il/la tennista** | male/female tennis player |

In some cases, the feminine form is obtained by changing **-o** to **-a**:

| **il ragazzo/la ragazza** | boy/girl |
| **il figlio/la figlia** | son/daughter |

In others, a completely different word is required:

l'uomo	man
la donna	woman
il marito	husband
la moglie	wife

(i) *Other general guidelines*

• A great many masculine nouns ending in **-e** have a feminine form in **-a**:

il cameriere	waiter
la cameriera	waitress
l'infermiere	male nurse
l'infermiera	female nurse
il padrone	male owner/boss
la padrona	female owner/boss
il parrucchiere	male hairdresser
la parrucchiera	female hairdresser

• Some masculine nouns ending in **-o, -a** and **-e** have a feminine form in **-essa**:

l'avvocato	male lawyer
l'avvocatessa	woman lawyer
il deputato	male member of Parliament
la deputatessa	female member of Parliament
il duca	duke
la duchessa	duchess
il poeta	male poet
la poetessa	female poet
il conte	count
la contessa	countess
il professore	male teacher
la professoressa	female teacher

• There are a number of nouns ending in **-tore,** many of which refer to professions, that have a feminine equivalent form in **-trice**:

l'attore	actor	**l'attrice**	actress
il conoscitore	connoisseur	**la conoscitrice**	connoisseuse
il redattore	male editor	**la redattrice**	female editor
lo scrittore	male writer	**la scrittrice**	female writer
lo scultore	sculptor	**la scultrice**	sculptress

il vincitore	male winner	**la vincitrice**	female winner

Note that where there is no feminine equivalent then either the masculine noun is used for both genders or the distinction can be made by placing **una donna** in front of the masculine noun, for example **una donna poliziotto** 'a police woman', **una donna controllore** 'a female ticket inspector'.

A similar rule applies to animals where a single noun form exists, of which the gender cannot be changed:

il pavone	peacock	**la giraffa**	giraffe

To express the idea of a female peacock one has to say **il pavone femmina** or **la femmina del pavone**.
A male giraffe would be **la giraffa maschio** or **il maschio della giraffa**.

• There are a few masculine nouns whose feminine equivalent does not conform to a regular pattern.

l'eroe	hero	**l'eroina**	heroine
il gallo	cock	**la gallina**	hen
il re	king	**la regina**	queen

20h   *One or more? Plural of nouns*

(i)   -i, -e

The rules for making most nouns plural in Italian are as follows:

• Masculine nouns ending in **-o** or **-a** change to **-i**:

il ragazzo	**i ragazzi**	boy(s)
il problema	**i problemi**	problem(s)

• Feminine nouns ending in **-a** change to **-e**:

la finestra	**le finestre**	window(s)

• Masculine and feminine nouns ending in **-e** change to **-i**:

la luce	**le luci**	light(s)
il costume	**i costumi**	custom(s), habit(s)

(ii)   *Exceptions*

• There is a small number of feminine nouns ending in **-o** that do not change in the plural, for example:

la moto	le moto	motorcycle(s)
la radio	le radio	radio(s)

[See also ➤20h(iv).]

One commonly used feminine noun ending in **-o** has a plural form in **-i:**

la mano	le mani	hand(s)

• The following feminine nouns ending in **-a** change to **-i** in the plural:

l'ala	le ali	wing(s)
l'arma	le armi	weapon(s)

• Some masculine nouns ending in **-o** in the singular form their plural in **-a**. In the plural these nouns change their gender to feminine:

un centinaio	about a hundred	**centinaia**	hundreds
un migliaio	about a thousand	**migliaia**	thousands
il miglio	le miglia	mile(s)	
il paio	le paia	pair(s)	
l'uovo	le uova	egg(s)	

Another important numeral that is masculine in the singular and feminine in the plural is **mille** 'one thousand', **duemila** 'two thousand'. There is also a spelling change as **mila** has one **l**.

• Some masculine nouns form their plurals according to the rules explained under 20h(i) but their plural form has a stem change:

il bue	i buoi	ox/oxen
il dio	gli dei	god(s)
l'uomo	gli uomini	man/men

(iii) *Other plurals*

• Nouns ending in **-ca** and **-ga** in the singular form their plural in **-che** and **-ghe** if they are feminine and **-chi** and **-ghi** if they are masculine. This preserves the hard sound of the **c** and **g**.

l'amica	le amiche	friend(s)
la collega	le colleghe	colleague(s)
il monarca	i monarchi	monarch(s)
il collega	i colleghi	colleague(s)

But

il Belga	i Belgi	Belgian(s)

• Nouns ending in **-cia** and **-gia** retain the **i** in the plural if it is stressed and omit it if it is unstressed:

la farmacia	le farmacie	chemist's/chemists'/drugstore(s) (stressed **i**)
la bugia	le bugie	lie(s) (stressed **i**)
la faccia	le facce	face(s) (unstressed **i**)
la spiaggia	le spiagge	beach(es) (unstressed **i**)

However, the unstressed **i** is sometimes retained in the plural to avoid ambiguity between words that would otherwise have the same spelling, for example:

la camicia	le camic*i*e	shirt(s)

(to avoid confusion with **il camice** 'surplice')

l'audacia	le audac*i*e	courage/daring deeds

(to avoid confusion with the adjective **audace** 'daring')

It is normal to retain the **i** whenever the **-cia** or **-gia** is preceded by a vowel, as in **la valigia/le valigie** 'suitcase/s' and omit it when these endings are preceded by a consonant, as in **la goccia/le gocce** 'drop/s'.

• Nouns ending in **-io** have a double **i** in the plural when the **i** of **-io** is stressed and just one **i** if unstressed:

lo zio	gli zii	uncle(s)
il negozio	i negozi	shop(s)

There are occasions where the plurals of words ending in **-io** are identical to those of other nouns or adjectives. In the written form, an accent or a double **i** is used to avoid confusion:

il conservatorio	i conservatòri	conservatory
conservatore	conservatori	conservative
il principe	i prìncipi	prince
il principio	i princìpi	principle

In the spoken language, the distinction between these words is made by sound - the open **o** of **conservatorio** and the closed **o** of **conservatore**, the stress on the first **i** of **principe** and the second **i** of **principio**.

il tempio	i tempii (or more commonly i templi)	temple

(double **i** in the plural to avoid confusion with:)

il tempo	i tempi	time
l'omicidio	gli omicidii	murder

(double **i** in the plural to avoid confusion with the adjective)

omicida	omicidi	murderous

Without the doubling of the **i** the pronunciation of the plural forms would be identical.

• Nouns ending in **-co** and **-go** form their plurals in **-chi** or **-ci** and **-ghi** or **-gi**. Because there are a number of exceptions, it is not easy to provide clearcut rules. When you come across unfamiliar words with these endings it would be advisable to check their plural form in a dictionary. However, the following general guidelines should be of some help:

(A) Many nouns that have the stress on the penultimate syllable form their plurals in **-chi** and **-ghi**. These nouns preserve the hard **c/g** sound.

il fuoco	i fuochi	fire(s)
il parco	i parchi	park(s)
l'albergo	gli alberghi	hotel(s)
il lago	i laghi	lake(s)
il luogo	i luoghi	place(s)

But

l'amico	gli amici	friend(s)
il greco	i greci	Greek(s)
il porco	i porci	pig(s)

The above nouns undergo a sound change in the plural. The **i** after the **c** softens the sound. The same applies when the **g** is followed by **i**, as in the examples below. The **-ci** and **-gi** are pronounced in the same way as the **C** and **G** of the Italian alphabet [➤2a(i)].

(B) If the stress falls before the penultimate syllable, the general tendency for these nouns is to form their plurals in **-ci** or **-gi**:

il medico	i medici	doctor(s)
il portico	i portici	porch(es)
l'asparago	gli asparagi	asparagus
il teologo	i teologi	theologian(s)

But

l'obbligo	gli obblighi	obligation(s)
il profugo	i profughi	refugee(s)

Note that there are some nouns that have two possible plural forms:

il farmaco	i farmaci/i farmachi	drug(s) (medicine)

| lo stomaco | gli stomaci/stomachi | stomach(s) |
| il chirurgo | i chirurgi/chirurghi | surgeon(s) |

• Nouns in **-logo** tend to change to **-logi** when they refer to *people* and **-loghi** when they refer to *things*.

l'archeologo	gli archeologi	archaeologist(s)
lo psicologo	gli psicologi	psychologist(s)
il catalogo	i cataloghi	catalogue(s)
il dialogo	i dialoghi	dialogue(s)/dialog(s)

(iv) Nouns that do not change in the plural

• Abbreviated noun forms:

l'auto	le auto	car(s)
la bici	le bici	bicycle(s)
il cinema	i cinema	cinema(s)/movie theater(s)
la foto	le foto	photo(s)

[See also ➤20h(ii).]

The complete forms of these nouns change from singular to plural in the normal way [➤20h(i)]:

| l'automobile | le automobili |
| la fotografia | le fotgrafie |

• Nouns ending in a consonant:

l'autobus	gli autobus	bus(es)
il bar	i bar	bar(s)
lo sport	gli sport	sport(s)

• Monosyllabic nouns:

il re	i re	king(s)
la gru	le gru	crane(s)
lo sci	gli sci	ski(s)

• Nouns ending in an accented vowel:

la città	le città	town(s)
il tè	i tè	tea(s)
la virtù	le virtù	virtue(s)
il falò	i falò	bonfire(s)
il lunedì	i lunedì	Monday(s)

 The article is not normally used with days of the week in the singular. **Lunedì** without the article conveys both 'Monday' and 'on Monday'. **Il lunedì** is used to express 'on Mondays' [➤30a].

• Nouns ending in **-i**:

l'analisi	**le analisi**	analysis/analyses
la crisi	**le crisi**	crisis/crises
l'ipotesi	**le ipotesi**	hypothesis/hypotheses

• Nouns ending in **-ie**:

la serie	**le serie**	series

But

la moglie	**le mogli**	wife/wives
la superficie	**le superfici**	surface(s)

• Others:

il paria	**i paria**	outcast(s)
il sosia	**i sosia**	double(s)
il vaglia	**i vaglia**	money order(s)

(v) Nouns used only in the plural

Some nouns are generally used only in the plural. They include:

• Nouns denoting pairs of things:

le forbici	scissors
le manette	handcuffs
gli occhiali	spectacles
i pantaloni/i calzoni	trousers/pants *(US)*

• Nouns which refer to things or events that have a plural sense:

le posate	cutlery
le stoviglie	dishes
i viveri	provisions
i dintorni	surroundings
le ferie	holidays/vacation
le macerie	ruins

Note also:

le nozze	wedding

(vi) Nouns used only in the singular

Some nouns are generally used only in the singular. They include:

- Many nouns referring to food products, because they are non-countable:

l'aceto	vinegar	**il pane**	bread
il sale	salt	**lo zucchero**	sugar

- The names of the months:

gennaio, febbraio, etc	January, February, etc.

- Metals and chemical elements:

l'oro	gold	**l'ossigeno**	oxygen

- Abstract nouns:

il coraggio	courage	**l'orgoglio**	pride

(vii) Nouns with two plural forms

- There is a small number of nouns that have two plural forms, one masculine and one feminine. The difference in gender also carries a difference in meaning.

il braccio	**i bracci**	arms (of cross, etc.), wings (of building)
	le braccia	arms (of body)
il ciglio	**i cigli**	edges (of ditch, road)
	le ciglia	eyelashes
il corno	**i corni**	horns (instrument)
	le corna	horns (of animal)
il dito	**i diti**	fingers (considered individually)
	le dita	fingers (considered collectively)
il filo	**i fili**	threads, wires
	le fila	threads (of plot)
il fondamento	**i fondamenti**	basic principles
	le fondamenta	foundations (of building)
il frutto	**i frutti**	fruits (different individual fruits or fruits of work)
	le frutta (la frutta)	fruit (in a collective sense)
il grido	**i gridi**	cries (of animal)
	le grida	cries (of human)
il labbro	**i labbri**	lips (of a wound)
	le labbra	lips (of mouth)
il lenzuolo	**i lenzuoli**	sheets (two or more, i.e. considered separately)

	le lenzuola	pair of sheets (to make the bed)
il membro	i membri	members (of group, etc.)
	le membra	limbs (of body)
il muro	i muri	walls (of house)
	le mura	walls (of city)
l'osso	gli ossi	bones (considered individually or bones for a dog, etc.)
	le ossa	bones (of a human skeleton)

Note that you use the feminine plural **le ciglia, le dita,** etc. in a collective sense but the masculine plural **uno dei cigli, uno dei diti,** etc. when used in a partitive sense, i.e. '*one of* the eyelashes', '*one of* the fingers', etc. Similarly **uno dei lenzuoli,** '*one of* the sheets'.

• The following nouns have two singular and two plural forms, with no difference in meaning.

l'orecchio	l'orecchia	ear
gli orecchi	le orecchie	ears
l'arancio	l'arancia	orange
gli aranci	le arance	oranges

(viii) *Plural of compound nouns [➤3a(i)]*

Compound nouns in Italian are formed by combining words together. The formation of the plural depends on the components that make up the compound word. As there are various inconsistencies it is only possible to give the following general guidelines.

• Compound nouns comprising adjective + noun or adjective + adjective form their plural by changing the ending of the *second* part:

l'altoparlante	gli altoparlant*i*	loudspeaker(s)
il francobollo	i francoboll*i*	stamp(s) (adjective + noun)
il pianoforte	i pianofort*i*	piano(s)
il sordomuto	i sordomut*i*	deaf and dumb person, deaf mute

• Compound nouns made up of noun + adjective form their plural by changing the ending of *both* parts:

| il caposaldo | i cap*i*sald*i* | stronghold(s) |
| la cassaforte | le cass*e*fort*i* | safe(s) |

• Compounds comprising two nouns of the *same* gender normally make the *second* noun plural:

| l'arcobaleno | gli arcobalen*i* | rainbow(s) (both nouns are masculine) |
| la madreperla | le madreperl*e* | mother-of-pearl (both nouns are feminine) |

However, if the compound comprises two nouns of *different* genders then you normally make the *first* noun plural:

il capostazione	i cap*i*stazione	stationmaster(s)
il pescespada	i pesc*i*spada	swordfish
But		
la banconota	le banconot*e*	banknote(s)
la ferrovia	le ferrovi*e*	railway(s)

The reason for the second noun changing to plural and not the first is that **banco** and **ferro** are used adjectivally and therefore you have the adjective + noun combination previously explained.

• Compounds comprising verb + *plural* noun do not change in the plural:

| il cavatappi | i cavatappi | corkscrew(s) |
| la lavastoviglie | le lavastoviglie | dishwasher(s) |

• Compounds comprising verb + singular *feminine* noun remain unchanged in the plural:

il cacciavite	i cacciavite	screwdriver(s)
il salvagente	i salvagente	lifebelt(s)
But		
l'asciugamano	gli asciugamani	towel(s)

• Compounds comprising verb + singular *masculine* noun make the *noun* plural:

| il passaporto | i passaport*i* | passport(s) |
| il portafoglio | i portafogl*i* | wallet(s) |

• Compounds comprising two verbs remain *unchanged* in the plural:

| l'andirivieni | gli andirivieni | coming(s) and going(s) |
| il fuggifuggi | i fuggifuggi | rush, scramble |

• Nouns comprising either preposition + noun or adverb + noun form their plurals in a variety of ways. It would be advisable, therefore, to check the plural form in a dictionary.

il senzatetto	i senzatetto	homeless person(s)
il dopopranzo	i dopopranzi	afternoon(s)
il soprannome	i soprannomi	nickname(s)
il sottopassaggio	i sottopassaggi	subway(s)/underpass(es)

20i Adjectives used as nouns

Adjectives are frequently used as nouns in Italian.

(i) Implied noun

Sometimes the noun is strongly implied:

Molti *giovani* hanno lasciato il paese in cerca di lavoro. Per loro, l'*importante* è di guadagnarsi la vita. Adesso la maggior parte degli abitanti del paese è composta da *anziani*.	Many *young people* have left the village in search of work. For them, *the important thing* is to earn a living. Now the majority of the inhabitants of the village is made up of *elderly people*.

(ii) Abstract nouns

Adjectives can also stand alone to represent abstract nouns. In this case they are masculine:

A dire *il vero*, i giovani hanno perfettamente ragione di andare altrove in cerca di lavoro.	To tell the *truth*, the young people are perfectly right to go elsewhere in search of work.

(iii) Colours/Colors

When a colour/color is used as a noun it is masculine.

Il rosso e *il verde* sono i miei colori preferiti.	*Red* and *green* are my favourite colours/favorite colors.

Note: An adjective can be used to agree with a noun that has been omitted but is understood.

Quale camicia ti piace? – *La bianca*.	Which shirt do you like? – *The white one.*

20j   Nouns formed from other parts of speech

Prepositions are occasionally used as nouns in Italian:

Bisogna considerare *il pro* e *il contro*.	We must consider *the pros* and *cons* (of the argument).

[For infinitives used as nouns ►10a(iii).]

20k   Suffixes and prefixes

(i)   Suffixes

Suffixes are endings that are added to nouns to modify their meaning. It is not possible to modify the meaning of *all* nouns in this way and it is advisable to use only those formations that you have seen or heard. Italian uses a range of suffixes, such as:

- **-ino/a, etto/a, -ello/a**, generally used as *diminutives*:

mio fratello	my brother
il mio fratell*ino*	my *little* brother
un libro	a book
un libr*etto*	a *small* book, a book*let*
una casa	a house
una cas*etta*	a *small* house, a cottage
un paese	a country, a village
un paes*ello*	a *small* village, hamlet

Note that the gender of the suffix is normally that of the original noun.

- **-one/-ona** is an *augmentative* denoting size:

una barca	a small boat	**un barc***one*	a *big* boat
una donna	a woman	**un donn***one*	a *huge* woman

 Care has to be taken when adding the suffix **-one**, as even feminine words tend to become masculine.

- **-astro/a, -accio/a** tend to create a *negative* meaning:

un poeta	a poet	**un poet*astro***	a *worthless* poet
una sorella	a sister	**una sorell*astra***	a *half-/step*-sister
una parola	a word	**una parol*accia***	a *swear* word

- **-ista** is frequently used to denote a profession or a sport:

il bar	bar	**il bar*ista***	bar*man*
il tennis	tennis	**il tenn*ista***	tennis *player*

 A number of words ending in the above suffixes can have a completely different meaning.

il padre	father	**il padrino**	godfather
la carta	paper	**il cartone**	cardboard
il cavallo	horse	**il cavalletto**	trestle, easel

(ii) Prefixes

Italian also uses a large number of prefixes. These are placed before nouns, and like suffixes, they serve to modify their meaning.

- **s-, in-** and **dis-** are often used to give the opposite meaning:

la fortuna	fortune, luck	**la *s*fortuna**	*mis*fortune
il vantaggio	advantage	**lo *s*vantaggio**	*dis*advantage
la disciplina	discipline	**l'*in*disciplina**	*in*discipline
la felicità	happiness	**l'*in*felicità**	*un*happiness
l'ubbidienza	obedience	**la *dis*ubbidienza**	*dis*obedience
il piacere	pleasure	**il *dis*piacere**	*dis*pleasure

- **sovra-, sopra-** denote excess:

l'affollamento	crowding
il *sovra*ffollamento	*over*crowding
la popolazione	population
la *sovra*ppopolazione	overpopulation
il nome	name
il *sovra*nnome	*nick*name
il peso	weight
il *sovra*ppeso	*excess* weight, *over*weight

Note the doubling of the initial consonant after **sovra-** and **sopra-**.

- **sotto-** conveys 'under':

lo sviluppo	development
il *sotto*sviluppo	*under*development
la valutazione	estimation
la *sotto*valutazione	*under*estimation

[For suffixes and prefixes with adjectives ➤22g; for suffixes
with adverbs ➤26c.]

21 Specifying nouns: determiners

21a   What are determiners?

You will not find the word *determiner* in older grammars, but it is a very useful term, which takes in some of the most common words in any language. Determiners are used with nouns to place them in a context, to say whether they are assumed to be known or not, to whom they belong, how many there are, and so on. So, for example, a noun such as **casa** 'house' can be introduced by different determiners according to the context:

La casa è troppo piccola.	*The* house is too small. (not just any house, but a particular one)
Cerchiamo *una* casa più grande.	We are looking for *a* bigger house. (not specified – could be any bigger house)
Questa casa ha una vista sul mare.	*This* house has a sea view. (emphatic reference to a particular house)
La nostra casa si trova in periferia.	*Our* house is on the outskirts. (belongs to us)
I miei amici hanno *due* case.	My friends have *two* houses. (number specified)
Quali amici?	*Which* friends? (asking for specification)

These examples serve to remind us of an important difference between Italian and English in the use of determiners. Most determiners in Italian have to *agree with* the noun, that is they may vary according to whether the noun is masculine or feminine (gender), singular or plural (number).

21b   The interrogative determiner: Which? What?

*   *singular* (masculine and feminine) **quale?**
*   *plural* (masculine and feminine) **quali?**

Quale film vuoi vedere?	*Which* film/movie do you want to see?
Quali film ti piacciono?	*Which* films/movies do you like?

Quale can be separated from its noun by a form of the verb **essere**:

Qual è l'ultimo film che hai visto?	*What* is the last film/movie you saw?

Note that it is normal to drop the -**e** of the singular **quale** before the verb **essere**. An apostrophe is *not* used to indicate this omission.

• **Che** 'What?' is another commonly used interrogative determiner and, in most cases, fulfils the same function as **quale.** It is invariable.

Che film vuoi vedere?	*What* film/movie do you want to see?

21c   *Already known: the definite article 'the'*

The definite article is used most frequently in English to introduce nouns which refer to specific items, either because they have already been mentioned, or because it is obvious from the context that one is referring to a particular item. In Italian, the definite article is used on many occasions with nouns where in English no article would be required. This is described later in this chapter [▶21c(viii)].

(i)   *Forms*

singular	plural
masculine	
il	**i**
lo, l'	**gli**
feminine	
la, l'	**le**

(ii)   il/i

Il and **i** are used before masculine nouns beginning with a consonant:

il giardino   **i giardini**   garden(s)

These articles are also used before foreign words beginning with **j-** and **w-**, for example **il jazz, il judo**, **il walkman, il windsurf**.

(iii)   lo/gli

Lo and **gli** are used before masculine nouns beginning with **s-** followed by another consonant or with **z-**:

lo studente	**gli studenti**	student(s)
lo sbaglio	**gli sbagli**	mistake(s)
lo spazio	**gli spazi**	space(s)
lo zio	**gli zii**	uncle(s)
lo zaino	**gli zaini**	rucksack(s)

These articles are also used before the few nouns that begin with **gn-**, **ps-**, **pn-**, **x-**, or with **y/i-** + a vowel:

lo gnocco	**gli gnocchi**	dumplings
lo psicologo	**gli psicologi**	psychologist(s)
lo pneumatico	**gli pneumatici**	tyre(s)/tire(s)
lo xenofobo	**gli xenofobi**	xenofobe(s)
lo yogurt	**gli yogurt**	yoghurt(s)
lo Ionio		Ionian sea

(iv)   l', gli

L' and **gli** are used before masculine nouns beginning with a vowel:

l'adulto	**gli adulti**	adult(s)
l'indirizzo	**gli indirizzi**	address(es)

The -**i** of **gli** is hardly ever elided (**gl'**) nowadays and it is better to keep the complete form.

gli Italiani   *not* *gl'*Italiani   Italians

(v)   la, le

La and **le** are used before feminine nouns beginning with a consonant:

la ragazza	le ragazze	girl(s)

(vi)   *l', le*

L' and **le** are used before feminine nouns beginning with a vowel:

l'amica	**le amiche**	friend(s)
l'uscita	**le uscite**	exit(s)

 If the definite article is separated from its noun by, for example, an adjective, then the choice of article depends on the adjective, according to the rules 21c(i) to 21c(vi):

il **giorno**   day

> but

*l'*altro giorno   the other day
lo spettacolo   show

> but

il primo spettacolo   the first show
*l'*amica   friend

> but

la mia amica   my friend

(vii)   *a, da, di, in, su* + definite article

When the prepositions **a, da, di, in** and **su** [➤25c(i)-(vi)] are used in front of the definite articles [➤21c], they combine to produce the compound forms below.

	il	lo	la	l'	i	gli	le
a	al	allo	alla	all'	ai	agli	alle
da	dal	dallo	dalla	dall'	dai	dagli	dalle
di	del	dello	della	dell'	dei	degli	delle
in	nel	nello	nella	nell'	nei	negli	nelle
su	sul	sullo	sulla	sull'	sui	sugli	sulle

Stamattina, per andare in città, sono uscita di casa *alle* nove. Sono salita *sull'*autobus *alla* fermata di fronte a casa mia.	This morning, to go to town, I left the house *at* nine o'clock. I got *on the* bus *at the* stop opposite my house.

Arrivata in città, sono andata subito *dal* fioraio perché volevo comprare *dei* fiori per la Festa *della* Mamma. Poi sono andata *nel* supermercato accanto per comprare *del* pane e *dello* zucchero. Dopo, sono corsa *all'*agenzia di viaggi per chiedere informazioni *sui* voli charter per Londra.	Having arrived in town, I went straight *to the* florist's because I wanted to buy *some* flowers for Mother's Day . Then I went *into* the supermarket next door to buy *some* bread and *some* sugar. After that, I rushed *to the* travel agent's to ask for information *on the* charter flights to London.

(viii)   *Use of the definite article*

The definite article is used:

(A) As in English, to make it clear that a particular item is being referred to:

Questo non è *il* libro che ti ho prestato.	This isn't *the* book that I lent you.
Hai imbucato *le* lettere?	Have you posted *the* letters?

(B) When generalizing or using abstract nouns:

Lo sport non mi piace per niente.	I don't like *sport* at all.
Non mangiamo mai *la carne*.	We never eat *meat*.
La disoccupazione è un grosso problema.	*Unemployment* is a big problem.
Il denaro è la fonte di tutti i mali.	*Money* is the root of all evil.

 You will see from the above examples, and the ones that follow, that in English the article is often omitted altogether when generalizing or using abstract terms. Remember that this is not possible in Italian.

(C) With titles when referring to the person in question, but not when addressing them directly:

Mi dispiace ma *il dottor* Zambetti non è ancora arrivato.	I'm sorry but *Doctor* Zambetti hasn't arrived yet.
Buon giorno, dottor Zambetti.	Good morning, Doctor Zambetti.

Note also that titles such as **dottore, professore** 'teacher', **ingegnere** 'engineer' and **ragioniere** 'accountant' drop the final -e in front of a person's name.

(D) When referring to names of continents, countries and other named geographical features – regions, lakes, large islands, rivers, mountain ranges:

L'Italia è un bellissimo paese.	*Italy* is a very beautiful country.
Per me, *la Toscana* è la regione che conosco meglio.	For me, *Tuscany* is the region that I know best.

Names of towns and cities are not accompanied by the definite article unless they are an integral part of the name as in **L'Aquila** and **La Spezia**.

If, however, the name of the town or city is qualified or emphasised in some way then the article is used:

La Roma della mia gioventù.	*The Rome* of my youth.

 When you wish to say 'to go to' (**andare in**) a country, the article is omitted if the country is singular or is not qualified by an adjective.

Quest'anno vogliamo andare *in Danimarca*.	This year we want to go *to Denmark*.
but	
L'anno scorso siamo andati *negli Stati Uniti*.	Last year we went *to the United States*. (plural)
L'Emilia Romagna si trova *nell'Italia centrale*.	Emilia Romagna is *in Central Italy*. (qualified by an adjective)

Note also:

*nell'*Africa del Nord   *in* North Africa

(E) With possessive adjectives and pronouns:

Lo pago *il mio* caffè e tu paghi *il tuo*.	I'll pay for *my* coffee and you pay for *yours*.

[For the use of article with possessive adjectives when referring to members of the family ►21h(v).]

(F) With expressions of time and age:

È *l'una.*   It is *one o'clock.*
Sono *le undici.*   It is *eleven o'clock.*

     but

È **mezzogiorno.**   It is midday.
È **mezzanotte.**   It is midnight.

Per me, *il 1975* è stato un anno significativo.	For me, *1975* was a significant year.
La settimana scorsa ho visto il mio ex professore di matematica.	*Last week* I saw my former maths/math teacher.
Questo ristorante è sempre chiuso *la domenica.* but	This restaurant is always closed *on Sundays.* (*every* Sunday)
Sono partiti *venerdì.*	They left *on Friday.* (article omitted when referring to a *particular* day)
Quella signora dimostra tra *i cinquanta* e *i sessant'anni.* but	That lady looks between *fifty* and *sixty years old.*
Mia sorella ha *trent'anni.*	My sister is *thirty.* (article omitted after **avere** when expressing *age*)

(G) When referring to languages:

Quale lingua preferisci, *il francese* o *l'italiano*?	Which language do you prefer, *French* or *Italian*?

No article is required after **parlare** 'speak' unless it is separated from the language by another part of speech:

Parli *tedesco*? but	Do you speak *German*?
Parli molto bene *l'inglese.*	You speak *English* very well.

(H) When referring to parts of the body, particularly when they are the object of a verb, or with reflexive verbs when the possessor is often the indirect object of the verb [➤8e(iv), 21h(vi)]:

Metti giù *i piedi*!	Put *your feet* down!
Dammi *la mano.*	Give me *your hand.*
Gli fa male *la schiena.*	*His back* hurts.
Mi sono lavato *i capelli.*	I washed *my hair.*
Mi sono rotto *il braccio.*	I have broken *my arm.*

(I) When expressing speeds and prices per quantity (in English the indefinite article 'a' or 'an' is used here) and also percentages:

La sua auto fa 180 chilometri *all'ora/l'ora.*	His car does 180 kilometres/kilometers *an hour.*
Quanto vengono *al chilo*?	How much do they cost *a kilo*?
L'ottanta per cento degli studenti nella mia classe d'italiano sono ragazze.	*Eighty per cent* of the students in my Italian class are girls.

(J) Before nouns preceded by expressions such as **entrambi/ tutti e due** 'both':

Abbiamo già visto *tutti e due i film.*	We have already seen *both films/movies.*

(ix) Omission of the definite article

You have already seen a number of examples in the preceding section [➤21c(viii)] where the definite article is omitted in Italian. The article is also omitted:

(A) In a number of adverbial expressions:

L'ho guardato *per curiosità.*	I watched it *out of curiosity.*
Ha salito le scale *di corsa.*	She ran up the stairs. (She went up the stairs *running*).
Hanno reagito *con calma.*	They reacted *calmly.*

Note also the omission of the article in constructions such as verb + adverbial expression of place. This is particularly the case when the adverbial expression is introduced by **in**:

Vado *in banca.*	I am going *to the bank.*

Andiamo *in chiesa*.	We are going *to church.*
Abitano *in campagna*.	They live *in the country.*
Sono entrati *in casa*.	They went *into the house.*
Domani mattina non vado *a*	Tomorrow morning, I'm not going
***scuola*, rimango *a casa*.**	*to school*, I'm staying *at home.*

(B) In a number of verbal expressions such as:

avere caldo	be hot	**avere freddo**	be cold
avere fame	be hungry	**avere sete**	be thirsty
avere ragione	be right	**avere torto**	be wrong
avere voglia (di)	want to, feel like	**perdere tempo**	lose/waste time

(C) When listing things:

Devi comprare *latte, pane,*	You must buy *milk, bread, butter,*
burro, zucchero...	*sugar...*

(D) Before a noun in apposition to another noun [►3e]:

***Roma, capitale* d'Italia, è ricca di**	*Rome, capital* of Italy, is full of
storia.	history.

21d   The demonstrative determiners 'this', 'that'

Demonstratives are like a strong definite article. They refer to something very specific, usually indicating whether it is near to or far from the speaker in time and place. The demonstratives in Italian are:

- **questo**   *this* (near the speaker)
- **quello**   *that* (away from both the speaker and the person addressed)

(i)   Questo

Masculine
questo ragazzo	this boy
questi ragazzi	these boys

Feminine
questa ragazza	this girl
queste ragazze	these girls

(ii)   Quello

You will see from the following examples that **quello** has forms like the definite article [➤21c(i)-(vi)] when it *precedes* the noun:

Masculine

quel ragazzo	*that* boy
quei ragazzi	*those* boys
quello studente	*that* student
quegli studenti	*those* students
*quell'*indirizzo	*that* address
quegli indirizzi	*those* addresses

Feminine

quella ragazza	*that* girl
quelle ragazze	*those* girls
*quell'*isola	*that* island
quelle isole	*those* islands

Le piace *questa* camicetta? – Sì, ma prima vorrei provare *quella* camicetta rossa che ho visto in vetrina.	Do you like *this* blouse? – Yes, but first I would like to try on *that* red blouse I saw in the window.

(iii)   Stesso/a/i/e 'same'

È la *stessa* camicetta che pensavo di comprare io.	It's the *same* blouse as I thought of buying.

Medesimo/a/i/e fulfils the same function as **stesso** but it is used less frequently, especially in spoken Italian.

[For **questo** and **quello** as demonstrative pronouns ➤23j(i).]

21e   Unknown individuals: the indefinite article un, uno, una, un' 'a (an)'

(i)   Un, uno

Un and **uno** are the two masculine forms of the indefinite article. **Un** is used before words beginning with a consonant or vowel. **Uno** is used with words beginning with **s-** + another consonant, **gn-, pn-, ps-, x-, z-,** and with **y/i-** + a vowel. It follows exactly the same rules as the definite article **lo** [➤21c(iii)].

un regalo	a present
un amico	a friend
uno studente	a student
uno zio	an uncle

(ii) Una, un'

Una and un' are the feminine forms of the indefinite article. **Un'** is used in place of **una** in front of words beginning with a vowel:

una stanza	a room	**un'amica**	a friend

 If the indefinite article is separated from its noun by, for example, an adjective, then the choice of indefinite article depends on the adjective, according to the rules 21e(i-ii):

uno zio   an uncle

but

un **caro zio**   a dear uncle
*un'***amica**   a friend

but

una **buon'amica**   a good friend

(iii) Use

When the indefinite article is used we know what type of person or thing the noun refers to but not which individual.

Per il mio compleanno, i miei genitori mi hanno regalato *un* orologio e *una* bicicletta.

For my birthday, my parents gave me *a* watch and *a* bicycle.

(iv) Some other uses

The indefinite article is also used:

(A) For emphasis:

Ho *una* sete!   I have *such a* thirst!

(B) To convey approximation:

Quant'è di qui all'autostrada? – **Un dieci chilometri.**	How far is it from here to the motorway/highway? – *About ten kilometres/kilometers.*

(v) Omission of the indefinite article

The use of the indefinite article in Italian is often much the same as in English, but there are a number of other occasions where it is not used.

(A) After **essere** 'be' and **diventare** 'become' with a noun complement denoting a profession, nationality, religion or civil status, unless the noun is qualified by an adjective or other phrase.

Mio fratello, Gino, *è professore*. Tutti dicono che *è un professore eccezionale*. Quando era più giovane, voleva *diventare dentista*. *È* ancora *scapolo* ma credo che la sua libertà stia per finire. Si è innamorato di una ragazza che ha conosciuto al mare durante le vacanze estive. Si chiama Barbara ed *è americana*. Lei è *una bravissima giornalista*.	My brother, Gino, *is a teacher*. Everyone says that *he is an exceptional teacher*. When he was younger, he wanted *to become a dentist*. *He is* still *a bachelor* but I think that his freedom is about to end. He has fallen in love with a girl he met at the seaside during the summer holidays/vacation. Her name is Barbara and *she is American*. She *is a very good journalist*.

(B) In the following type of construction, composed of verb + **da** + noun, to convey 'in the manner of':

Ho fatto da interprete. *Agisce da persona onesta.* *Ti sei comportato da vigliacco.*	*I acted as interpreter.* *He behaves like an honest person.* *You behaved like a coward.*

(C) After certain time expressions introduced by **da**:

Da giovane, ero un appassionato del calcio. L'ho conosciuta *da studentessa*.	*As a young man,* I was a football/soccer fan. I knew her *as a student.*

(D) After **Che...!** 'What a...!' in exclamations:

Che bella giornata!	What a pity!
Che peccato!	What a beautiful day!

(E) Before **mezzo/a**:

un'ora e *mezza*	an hour and *a half*
tre chili e *mezzo*	three kilos and *a half*

21f   Unknown quantities: the partitive article

In Italian **un, uno,** etc. have no plural forms. To convey 'some' or 'any' you can use the partitive article (**di** + the definite article [►21c(vii)]). There are occasions where no article is used in English where one would be required in Italian:

Quando fai la spesa non dimenticare di comprare *del* **prosciutto e** *della* **frutta.**	When you do the shopping don't forget to buy *ham* and *fruit*.
Abbiamo *dello zucchero?*	Do we have *any sugar?*
Penso di sì. Comprami anche *delle cartoline* **e** *dei francobolli.*	I think so. Buy me *some postcards* and *(some) stamps* as well.
Mi puoi dare *dei soldi* **perché non ne ho abbastanza?**	Can you give me *some money* because I haven't got enough?

(i)   Omission of the partitive article

The partitive article is *always* omitted:

(A) In negative sentences before plural nouns:

Non **ho** *soldi.*	I have*n't any money.*
Non **hanno** *figli.*	They have *no children.*

(B) After the preposition **di**:

Ha bisogno *di riposo.*	He needs *(some) rest.*

Se perdo l'ultima corriera, posso sempre stare a casa *di amici*.	If I miss the last bus, I can always stay with *friends*.

(C) The partitive article can be omitted when there is no great emphasis on the idea of 'some' or 'any' and the phrase is merely expressing an indefinite quantity of an article or product:

Non ti preoccupare, abbiamo *tempo*.	Don't worry, we have (*some*) time.
Per pranzo abbiamo mangiato *spaghetti*.	For lunch we had (*some*) spaghetti.
Hai *spiccioli*?	Do you have (*some/any*) change?

(ii) *Other ways of expressing 'some' and 'any'*

(A) The plural forms **alcuni** (masculine) and **alcune** (feminine):

Ho comprato *alcuni* libri e *alcune* riviste.	I have bought *some* books and *a few* magazines.

(B) Qualche:

Hai *qualche* rivista inglese?	Have you *some* (*any*) English magazines?

 Although **qualche** conveys a *plural* sense, it can *only be used with singular, countable nouns*.

(C) Un po' di:

Metti *un po' di* zucchero sulle fragole.	Put *a little* (*some*) sugar on the strawberries.
Per chi vuole, c'è ancora *un po' di* caffè.	For whoever wants it, there is still *a little* coffee.
Hai *un po' di* carta da lettere?	Have you *any* writing paper?
Ho già risparmiato *un po' di* soldi per le vacanze di Pasqua.	I have already saved *a bit of* money for the Easter holidays/vacation.

(D) 'Any' in its widest sense is **qualsiasi** or **qualunque**:

I miei amici farebbero *qualsiasi* (*qualunque*) cosa per aiutarmi.	My friends would do *any*thing to help me.

21g   *Other indefinite determiners in Italian*

In addition to the use of the indefinite and partitive articles above [➤21e, 21f], the following forms should be noted:

(i)   Alcuno, nessuno

'No, not any' are expressed by **alcuno** or **nessuno**. These words have the same rules of agreement as the indefinite article **un, uno,** etc. [➤21e(i)-(ii)]. They can only be used with the *singular* of *countable* nouns. Like all negative words, if they follow the verb, the verb is preceded by **non**.

Non ho *nessuna/alcuna* difficoltà a capire il tuo italiano. Quando parli non fai *nessun/alcun* errore di grammatica.	I have *no* difficulty in understanding your Italian. When you speak you don't make *any* grammatical errors.

• As can be seen from the above examples, **alcuno** and **nessuno** are used for *emphasis*. If there is no great emphasis on the negative quantity of the article or product then the quantifier is omitted.

Non ho difficoltà a capire il tuo italiano. Quando parli non fai errori di grammatica.	I have*n't any* difficulty in understanding your Italian. When you speak you do*n't* make *any* grammatical errors.

(ii)   Altro/a/i/e

'Other' is expressed by the appropriate form of **altro**.

Se vuoi *altre* idee, devi comprarti un *altro* libro.	If you want *other* ideas, you must buy yourself an*other* book.

(iii) Ogni

Ogni 'each, every', exists only in this invariable singular form.

Vorrei andare in Italia *ogni* **anno.**	I would like to go to Italy *every* year.
L'anno scorso il nostro professore ha organizzato uno scambio e *ogni* **membro della classe ci ha partecipato.**	Last year our teacher organized an exchange and *every* member of the class took part in it.

• Like 'every' **ogni** can be used before numerals:

Il nostro professore va in Italia *ogni sei* **mesi.**	Our teacher goes to Italy *every six* months.

(iv) Tutto/a/i/e

'All' is expressed by the appropriate form of **tutto**.

Tutti **i suoi parenti abitano nel sud d'Italia e gli piace trascorrere** *tutta* **l'estate con loro.**	*All* his relatives live in the south of Italy and he likes to spend *all* summer with them.

Note: The notion of 'every' can be expressed in two ways:

ogni anno every year   **tutti gli anni** every year

 Care should be taken not to confuse the meaning of 'all' and 'every'.

Il mio professore va in Italia *tutti* **gli anni. Una volta ci è rimasto** *tutto* **l'anno.**	My teacher goes to Italy *every* year. Once he remained there *the whole (all)* year.

(v) Ciascuno

'Each, every' can also be conveyed by **ciascuno**, which has forms like those of the indefinite article **un, uno**, etc. [21e(i)-(ii)].

| *Ciascun* membro della classe ha deciso di partecipare allo scambio. | *Each* member of the class has decided to take part in the exchange. |

(vi) 'Both'

'Both' is translated by **entrambi/e, tutti e due/tutte e due** or **ambedue**.

| *Tutti e due* gli scambi ai quali ho partecipato finora sono stati stupendi. *Entrambe/ambedue* le visite sono state utili da diversi punti di vista. | *Both* exchanges I have taken part in up to now have been marvellous. *Both* visits were useful from various points of view. |

(vii) Molto/a/i/e

The appropriate form of **molto** is used to express 'much, many, a lot'.

| Durante il nostro soggiorno in Italia non avremo *molto* tempo libero. Siccome ci fermiamo per solo una settimana, il professore preferisce organizzare *molte* gite. | During our stay in Italy we shall not have *much* free time. As we are there for only a week, our teacher prefers to organize *lots of* trips. |

(viii) Troppo/a/i/e

Troppo means 'too much, too many'.

| Ci sono *troppe* cose da fare. | There are *too many* things to do. |

(ix) Tanto/a/i/e

Tanto means 'so much, so many'.

| Ci sono *tanti* posti da vedere. | There are *so many* places to see. |

(x)   Parecchi/parecchie, vari/varie, diversi/e

'Several' can be expressed by **parecchi/parecchie, vari/varie** or **diversi/e,** which are, of course, always plural.

Ho già letto *parecchi/vari/diversi* libri sulla regione che visiteremo.	I have already read *several* books on the region we shall be visiting.

Note: **Molto** 'very', **troppo** 'too', **tanto** 'so' and **parecchio** 'rather (a lot)/quite (a lot)' are also *invariable* adverbs [➤26b(ii)].

I libri che ho letto sono *molto* interessanti.	The books I've read are *very* interesting.

(xi)   Poco/poca/pochi/poche

The appropriate form of **poco** is used to express, 'not much, little, a little, few'. It is the opposite of **molto.**

Il professore è stato malato e perciò gli rimane *poco tempo* per organizzare tutto. Purtroppo, *pochi* colleghi sono in grado di aiutarlo.	The teacher has been ill and so he has *little (not much)* time left to organize everything. Unfortunately, *few (not many)* colleagues are in a position to help him.

(Italian often prefers to use **poco** where in English we would say 'not much'.)

Be careful to distinguish between **poco,** which has a negative connotation and means 'not much' and **un poco di** [➤23l(i)], which means 'a little/some' and has a more positive emphasis.

C'è *poco* tempo prima della nostra partenza. Ho ancora *un po' di* tempo per ripassare quello che abbiamo fatto in classe.	There's *little (not much)* time before our departure. I still have *a little* time to go over what we have done in class.

(xii) *Certo/a/i/e*

Certo means 'certain'.

Prima che partiamo farò uno sforzo per imparare *certi verbi* e *certe* espressioni.	Before we leave I shall make an effort to learn *certain* verbs and (*certain*) expressions.

(xiii) *Tale/i*

Tale means 'such'.

Per me, sarà la prima volta che avrò partecipato a un *tale* scambio.	For me, it will be the first time that I will have taken part in *such* an exchange.

(xiv) *Quanto/a/i/e*

Quanto means 'how much, how many'.

Mi sono già dimenticato. Per *quanto* tempo andate in Italia?	I have already forgotten. For *how long* (*how much* time) are you going to Italy?

(xv) *Altrettanto/a/i/e* 'as much, as many'

Durante il nostro soggiorno, visiteremo molte chiese e *altrettanti* musei.	During our stay, we shall visit many churches and *as many* museums.

(xvi) *Più* and *meno*

'More' is **più** and 'less' is **meno**. They are both invariable, that is, they never change, and generally present few problems in their use. 'More and more'/'less and less' are **sempre più/sempre meno**.

Ogni anno ci sono *più* studenti che si interessano allo scambio con l'Italia.	Every year there are *more* students who are interested in the exchange with Italy.

Il nostro professore organizza scambi con altri paesi ma c'è *meno* interesse. È un peccato perché ci sono *sempre più* studenti dagli altri paesi che vogliono venire da noi.	Our teacher organizes exchanges with other countries but there is *less* interest. It's a pity because there are *more and more* students from other countries who want to come to us.

[For further uses of **più/meno** with comparatives ➤22f(i)(iii).]

[For indefinite determiners in this section that can also be used as pronouns ➤23k(i).]

21h   *Belonging together: possessive determiners*

Possessives are used to show that the noun *belongs* to somebody or something. They take their form from the *possessor* and their gender and number from the *thing possessed*. The words 'belong' and 'possessor' are used loosely here: possessives are also used for all kinds of other relationships between people and things.

(i)   *Italian possessive determiners*

Singular		Plural		
Masculine	*Feminine*	*Masculine*	*Feminine*	
il mio	la mia	i miei	le mie	my
il tuo	la tua	i tuoi	le tue	your (informal)
il suo	la sua	i suoi	le sue	his, her, its
il Suo	la Sua	i Suoi	le Sue	your (formal)
il nostro	la nostra	i nostri	le nostre	our
il vostro	la vostra	i vostri	le vostre	your (informal)
il loro	la loro	i loro	le loro	their
il Loro	la Loro	i Loro	le Loro	your (formal)

[These same forms are also used for the possessive pronouns ➤23l.]

Il mio desiderio è di parlare perfettamente l'italiano.	*My* wish is to speak Italian perfectly.

> Frequento un corso serale da quasi un anno. *La nostra* professoressa è bravissima e *le sue* lezioni sono sempre interessanti. Purtroppo, non tutti gli studenti hanno il tempo per fare *i loro* compiti.

> I have been attending an evening class for almost a year. *Our* teacher is very good and *her* lessons are always interesting. Unfortunately, not all the students have the time to do *their* homework.

(ii) Your

Be careful to distinguish between the different words for 'your'. Which form you choose will depend on whom you are addressing. [For more detail see also the corresponding forms of the subject pronouns ➤23b.]

> Dove sei andato con *i tuoi* amici?
> Questa è *la Sua* macchina, signorina?

> Where did you (*tu*) go with *your* friends?
> Is this *your* (*Lei*) car, Miss?

- The formal **il Suo, la Sua**, etc. is used when speaking to *one* person and **il Loro, la Loro**, etc. when addressing *more than one* person. (The same rule applies to the informal **il tuo, la tua** etc. and **il vostro, la vostra**.)

> *La Loro* camera è al quinto piano.   *Your* room is on the fifth floor.

- The formal **Suo** and **Loro** have been written in capitals in the list of possessives but it is fairly common nowadays to write them in small letters.

- **loro** is the one form that remains invariable. The gender and number of the 'thing' or 'person' possessed is indicated by the accompanying article.

(iii) Avoiding ambiguity

As **il suo** can mean 'his, her, your, its' and **il loro** 'your, their', it is not difficult to imagine that this could give rise to confusion and ambiguity, particularly in writing.

Maria legge *il suo* giornale.

This sentence could have *three* possible meanings:

– Maria is reading *her* newspaper.
– Maria is reading *his* newspaper.
– Maria is reading *your* newspaper.

Fortunately, we rarely deal with sentences in isolation, but rather in a wider context, in which case the *possessor* of the newspaper would usually be obvious. Should, however, there be a need to avoid ambiguity then this can be achieved by using:

- **di** + the disjunctive pronoun [➤23h]:

Maria legge il giornale *di lui*.	Maria is reading *his* newspaper.
Maria legge il giornale *di lei*.	Maria is reading *her* newspaper.
Maria legge il giornale *di Lei*.	Maria is reading *your* newspaper. (polite form with a capital **L**)

- the adjective **proprio** 'own':

Maria legge il *proprio* giornale.	Maria is reading *her (own)* newspaper.

- the capital **S** when **suo** means 'your':

Maria legge *il Suo* giornale.	Maria is reading *your* newspaper.

 Remember that the possessive determiners must agree in gender and number with the *thing or person possessed* and NOT with the *possessor*. Thus, in the above example the masculine singular form **il suo** must be used to agree with the masculine noun **il giornale**. English speakers sometimes get confused and use the feminine **la sua** because they are influenced by the fact that the possessor is a female ('her').

(iv) Possessive determiners and the definite article

You have already seen in the above examples that the possessive determiners are accompanied by the definite article **il, la, i, le** and this is generally the case. There are many occasions when the definite article is replaced by another part of speech.

un mio parente	*a* relative of mine
questa mia amica	*this* friend of mine
quel nostro zio	*that* uncle of ours
alcuni miei amici	*some* of my friends

tre **tuoi conoscenti**	*three* of your acquaintances
dei **loro colleghi**	*some* of their colleagues

(v) Omission of the definite article

There are a number of occasions when the definite article preceding the possessive is omitted:

* With members of the family and family relationships in the *singular*

nostra zia	our aunt
tuo fratello	your brother

The article *must be used* however:

* With *plural* forms of the above:

le **nostre zie**	our aunt*s*
i **tuoi fratelli**	your brother*s*

* When the possessive determiner is **loro**

mio **fratello**	*my* brother

but

il loro **fratello**	*their* brother

* When the noun is qualified by *another adjective* in addition to the possessive

mio **nipote**	*my* nephew

but

il **mio** *caro* **nipote**	*my dear* nephew

* When the noun has a *suffix* [➤20k]

nostra **sorella**	*our* sister

but

la **nostra sorell***ina*	*our little* sister

The use of the article is *optional* :

* With terms of endearment such as **babbo, papà** 'dad', **mamma** 'mum/mom', **nonno** 'grandad' and **nonna** 'gran'.

mio babbo or **il mio babbo**	my dad

The definite article is also omitted:

• With certain set expressions

Vado a casa loro.	I am going to their house.
Non è colpa mia.	It's not my fault.
Non sono affari tuoi.	It's none of your business.
Lasciamolo fare a modo suo.	Let's leave him do as he wants/pleases.

• In exclamations

mamma mia!	my goodness!
amici miei!	my friends!
Dio mio!	my God!

In both sets of examples you will have noticed that the possessive is placed *after* the noun.

• With particular expressions

a mio avviso/parere	in my opinion
a tua disposizione	at your disposal

[For omission of the definite article when **il mio,** etc. is used as a possessive pronoun ➤23b(iii).]

(vi) *Omission of the possessive determiner*

The possessive is not normally used with actions performed to parts of the body or clothing, where the indirect object pronoun [➤8e(iv), 23l(i)] identifies the possessor.

Mi **sono lavato** *la faccia*.	I washed *my face*.
Il signore *si* **è tolto** *il cappello*.	The gentleman took off *his hat*.

Neither is it required when the identity of the possessor is obvious from the context.

La ragazza ha chiuso *gli occhi*.	The girl shut *her eyes*.
Hai fatto *i compiti*?	Have you done *your homework*?

22 Describing nouns: adjectives

22a What do adjectives do?

Adjectives describe nouns. They can be used either as part of a phrase containing a noun [➤22b] or in the predicate of the sentence [➤22c].

(i) Agreement of adjectives

Adjectives in Italian agree in gender and number with the noun(s) they describe.

(A) The many adjectives ending in **-o** have *four* forms: masculine singular and plural, feminine singular and plural.

il ragazzo italian**o**	the *Italian* boy
i ragazzi italian**i**	the *Italian* boys
la ragazza italian**a**	the *Italian* girl
le ragazze italian**e**	the *Italian* girls

Note: Adjectives of nationality are written with a small letter [➤2a(ii)].

(B) Adjectives ending in **-e** have the same ending for masculine and feminine singular. The plural is also the same for both genders and ends in **-i**.

il libro interessant**e**	the *interesting* book
i libri interessant**i**	the *interesting* books
la rivista interessant**e**	the *interesting* magazine
le riviste interessant**i**	the *interesting* magazines

(C) Adjectives ending in **-a** have the same ending for masculine and feminine singular. However, the masculine plural ends in **-i** and the feminine plural in **-e**.

il professore entusiast**a**	the *enthusiastic* teacher
i professori entusiast**i**	the *enthusiastic* teachers
la professoressa entusiast**a**	the *enthusiastic* teacher
le professoresse entusiast**e**	the *enthusiastic* teachers

(D) Adjectives ending in **-one** have a feminine form in **-ona**. The plural endings are **-oni** and **-one** respectively.

lo studente chiacchier**one**	the *talkative* student

gli studenti chiacchier*oni*	the *talkative* students
la studentessa chiacchier*ona*	the *talkative* student
le studentesse chiacchier*one*	the *talkative* students

(ii) Adjectives that combine to form a single unit

When two adjectives combine to form a single unit the first remains unchanged but the second agrees in the normal way.

il programma *socio-economico*	the *socio-economic* program(me)
i programmi *socio-economici*	the *socio-economic* program(me)s

Care has to be taken when using these forms as the spelling of the first adjective is often modified in some way so, for example, the 'Italian-French agreement' is **l'accordo italo-francese.**

[For adjectives used as nouns ➤20i.]

(iii) Agreement: exceptions

There is a small number of adjectives that are invariable, i.e. they have only *one* form irrespective of the gender or number of the noun they describe. They include the following:

(A) Some adjectives of colour – these are adjectives of foreign origin or they exist as nouns in their own right.

la giacca *blu*	the *blue* jacket
le giacche *blu*	the *blue* jackets
il fiore *rosa*	the *pink* flower
i fiori *rosa*	the *pink* flowers
la maglia *viola*	the *purple* sweater
le maglie *viola*	the *purple* sweaters
la scarpa *marrone*	the *brown* shoe
le scarpe *marrone*	the *brown* shoes

(B) Adjectives ending in **-i**

un numero par*i*	an *even* number
i numeri dispar*i*	the *odd* numbers
la lotta impar*i*	the *unequal* struggle

22b Accompanying the noun: attributive adjectives

Attributive adjectives form part of the same phrase as a noun, though sometimes the noun is *understood*, that is, left out because it is obvious [➤22b(vi)].

(i)   *Normal position of adjectives*

The adjective normally follows the noun in Italian.

Un tè *freddo* per me e un bicchiere di vino *bianco* per Marco.	A *cold* tea for me and a glass of *white* wine for Marco.

- This goes especially for adjectives denoting nationality, religion, shape, colour/color as well as past participles used adjectivally.

un amico *francese*	a *French* friend
un prete *cattolico*	a *Catholic* priest
una stanza *rettangolare*	a *rectangular* room
una camicia *bianca*	a *white* shirt
una casa *demolita*	a *demolished* house

However, a number of common adjectives normally precede the noun. Those marked with an asterisk below have irregular forms when they precede a noun [►22d(i)-(iii)].

bello*	una bella giornata	a beautiful day
buono*	un buon riposo	a good rest
breve	una breve pausa	a short break
brutto	una brutta notizia	bad news
cattivo	un cattivo gusto	a bad taste
giovane	un giovane autista	a young driver
grande*	una grande casa	a large house
grosso	un grosso problema	a big problem
largo	un largo viale	a wide avenue
lungo	una lunga passeggiata	a long walk
piccolo	un piccolo giardino	a small garden
vecchio	una vecchia casa	an old house

(ii)   Even adjectives that normally precede a noun sometimes follow it. The change of position is important when one wishes to shift the emphasis and create other shades of meaning.

È un *piccolo* appartamento.	It's a *small* flat/apartment.
È un appartamento *piccolo*.	It's a *small* flat/apartment.

The positioning of the adjective after the noun emphasizes its *size*. Similarly, adjectives that are normally placed after the noun may precede it for emphasis.

Dobbiamo prendere una decisione *difficile*.	We have to take a *difficult* decision.
La *difficile* decisione che abbiamo preso è stata giustificata.	The *difficult* decision we took has been justified.

(iii) Adjectives that normally precede the noun *must* follow the noun when they are qualified by an adverb.

una *bella* ragazza	a *beautiful* girl
but	
una ragazza *molto bella*	a *very beautiful* girl
una *grande* casa	a *big* house
but	
una casa *abbastanza grande*	*quite a big* house

Note: If two or more adjectives are used with the same noun, they all keep their normal positions, but any that come together are joined by **e** 'and'.

una bella ragazza simpatica	a nice, beautiful girl
but	
una ragazza simpatica *e* intelligente	a nice, intelligent girl
una grande *e* bella casa	a big, beautiful house

(iv) A number of adjectives have a different meaning according to whether they precede or follow the noun:

alto	l'alta marea	high tide
	un uomo alto	a tall man
basso	la bassa marea	low tide
	un numero basso	a small/insignificant number
buono	un buon attore	a good/capable actor
	un vino buono	a good wine
caro	un caro amico	a dear friend
	un libro caro	an expensive book
cattivo	un cattivo odore	a bad/nasty smell
	una ragazza cattiva	a bad/wicked girl

certo	una certa somiglianza	a certain/some similarity
	una notizia certa	reliable news
diverso/vario	diverse/varie volte	various/several times
	riviste diverse/varie	different (not the same) magazines
dolce	la dolce vita	the good/sweet life
	l'acqua dolce	fresh (not salty) water
grande	un grand'uomo	a great man
	un uomo grande	a big/tall man
grosso	un grosso errore	a big/serious mistake
	un signore grosso	a big/well-built gentleman
nuovo	una nuova maglia	another sweater
	una maglia nuova	a new sweater
numeroso	numerose famiglie	numerous/many families
	famiglie numerose	large families
povero	una povera famiglia	a poor/unfortunate family
	una famiglia povera	a poor (not well-off) family
santo	tutta la santa settimana	all (blessed) week
	la Settimana Santa	Holy Week (before Easter)
semplice	una semplice idea	just/simply an idea
	un'idea semplice	a simple/uncomplicated idea
unico	l'unica occasione	the one (and only) opportunity
	un attore unico	a unique actor
vero	un vero disastro	a real disaster
	una storia vera	a true story

Generally speaking the adjectives in the above list have a *literal* meaning when they follow the noun and a more *figurative* meaning when they precede the noun. Many of these adjectives have a variety of meanings when used in other contexts, as you will find when you consult a dictionary.

(v) Qualcosa, niente + adjective

Qualcosa 'something' and **niente** 'nothing' combine with **di** before an adjective (which is always in the masculine singular form).

Hai fatto *qualcosa di bello* ieri sera?	Did you do *something nice* last night?
Non ho *niente di nuovo* da dirti.	I have *nothing new* to tell you.

(vi) 'Understood' noun

When the noun is understood, the adjective continues to agree with it as if it were there.

Vuole provare queste scarpe marrone o *quelle nere*?	Do you want to try on these brown shoes or *the black ones*?

22c At a distance: predicative adjectives

(i) What is a predicative adjective?

Predicative means *in the predicate* [➤4c]. These adjectives are usually the complement of the verb, that is they are linked to the subject by a verb such as **essere** 'be', **diventare** 'become', **sembrare** 'seem'. Although separated from the noun they relate to, they nonetheless agree in number and gender exactly as when used attributively [➤22b].

Sono venuto a vivere in questa zona sei mesi fa. I dintorni sono veramente *belli*, il clima è *mite* e la gente è *simpatica*. Ora tutto è *tranquillo*, le strade sono *deserte*. Ma fra poco arriva l'estate e ho sentito dire che la zona diventa *affollata* di turisti. Forse non mi sembrerà più così *idillico*!	I came to live in this area six months ago. The surroundings are really *beautiful*, the climate is *mild* and the people are *nice*. Now everything is *calm*, the streets are *deserted*. But summer will be here shortly and I have heard that the area becomes *crowded* with tourists. Perhaps it will no longer seem so *idyllic* to me!

(ii) Agreement with more than one noun

When the same adjective describes two or more nouns of the same gender, it is plural and agrees with the common gender:

Oggi il teatro e il cinema sono *chiusi*. La panetteria e la macelleria sono *aperte*.	Today the theatre/theater and the cinema/movie house are *closed*. The baker's and the butcher's are *open*.

If the nouns in the same sentence are of different genders, the adjective is in the masculine plural:

La farmacia e il fioraio sono *aperti*.	The chemist's/drugstore and the florist's are *open*.

When an adjective precedes two nouns of different genders and is used to describe both, then it is possible to repeat the adjective and make it agree with its respective noun:

Ho visitato *molti* musei e *molte* chiese.	I visited *many* museums and (*many*) churches.

or the adjective is used with the first noun of the group and agrees with it:

Ho visitato *molti* musei e chiese.	I visited *many* museums and churches.

Although it would be normal not to repeat the adjective in cases where you have a series of nouns, it often makes more sense, and would be more correct to do so, when it is a question of two nouns of different gender or different number.

***Mio* fratello e *mia* sorella non vengono con noi.**	*My* brother and (*my*) sister are not coming with us.
Andiamo a trovare *mio* zio e *i miei* nonni.	We are going to see *my* uncle and *my* grandparents.

(iii)   Agreement with *si*

When the impersonal pronoun **si** 'one' [➤23d] is followed by a verb + adjective, then the adjective must always be in the masculine plural form.

Dopo una giornata di lavoro *si torna* a casa *stanchi*. Quando *si è giovani* non è un problema ma quando *si è vecchi*...	After a day's work *you come back* home *tired*. When *you are young* it's not a problem but when *you are old*...

(iv)   *Avere fame,* etc.

A number of everyday expressions which in English are rendered by 'to be' + adjective are expressed in Italian using **avere** (*not* **essere**) + noun. They include:

avere caldo	be hot (referring to people)
avere fame	be hungry
avere freddo	be cold (referring to people)
avere paura	be afraid
avere ragione	be right
avere sete	be thirsty
avere sonno	be sleepy
avere torto	be right
avere vergogna	be ashamed

In these expressions, **caldo, fame, freddo,** etc. are nouns and therefore invariable: no agreement is required. However, adjectives that may accompany them, such as **molto** 'very', must agree in the normal way.

Se hai fredd*o* Daniela, mettiti la giacca.	If you are *cold* Daniela, put your jacket on.
Mamma, abbiamo molt*a* sete.	Mum/Mom, we are *very thirsty*.

[For **avere** to express age ➤30e.]

(v) Weather

The same thing happens in weather expressions using **fa, c'è**, etc.:

fa caldo	it's hot
fa freddo	it's cold
c'è la nebbia	it's foggy
c'è il sole	it's sunny
tira vento	it's windy

Non vado al mare a quest'ora perché *fa* troppo *caldo*.	I am not going to the seaside at this hour because *it's* too *hot*.

Note: **Caldo** and **freddo** can be used both as nouns and adjectives.

22d Irregular adjectives

There are a few adjectives that have irregular forms when they *precede* the noun. When they follow the noun they are formed regularly [➤22a(i)].

(i) Bello, quello

Bello 'beautiful' and the demonstrative determiner **quello** 'that' have forms like those of the definite article [➤21c(i)-(vi)].

Masculine singular	*Masculine plural*
bello	begli
bell'	begli
bel	bei

Feminine singular	*Feminine plural*
bella	belle
bell'	

un *bel* sorriso	a *beautiful* smile
dei *bei* bambini	some *beautiful* children
un *bell'* uomo	a *handsome* man
un *bello* specchio	a *beautiful* mirror
che *begli* occhi!	what *beautiful* eyes!
una *bella* ragazza	a *beautiful* girl
delle *belle* ragazze	some *beautiful* girls
una *bell'*isola	a *beautiful* island

[For the demonstrative determiner **quello** ➤21d(ii).]

(ii) *Buono*

Buono 'good' is irregular in the singular only and has forms like those of the indefinite article [➤21e(i-ii)].

un *buon* amico	a *good* friend
buon divertimento!	have a *good* time!
un *buono* studente	a *good* student
buona fortuna	*good* luck
una *buon'*attrice	a *good* actress

[**Alcuno** and **nessuno** also follow this same pattern in the singular ➤21g(i).]

(iii) *Grande*

Grande 'great/large/big' may be shortened to **grand'** before a vowel and **gran** before nouns beginning with a consonant, with the exception of **s-** + another consonant, **z-, gn-, ps-** and **x-**. However, the use of the complete form **grande** is now much more common.

una *grand'/grande* opportunità	a great opportunity
un *gran/grande* signore	a *great* gentleman
una *gran/grande* finestra	a *large* window
una *grande* scoperta	a *big* discovery

Note: The shortened form is used in expressions that convey *strong* feelings, such as:

Abbiamo un *gran* desiderio di tornare in Italia.	We have a *great* desire to go back to Italy.

(iv)   *Santo*

Santo 'saint/holy' has the following shortened forms when it precedes a noun:

• **sant'** before masculine and feminine nouns beginning with a vowel:

*sant'***Antonio**	*Saint* Anthony
*sant'***Anna**	*Saint* Anne

• **san** before masculine nouns beginning with a consonant other than **s-** + consonant:

san **Paolo**	*Saint* Paul
san **Pietro**	*Saint* Peter

However, the complete form is used:

• before masculine nouns beginning with **s-** + a consonant:

santo **Stefano**	*saint* Stephen

• before feminine nouns beginning with a consonant:

santa **Chiara**	*saint* Claire

22e   *Plural formation of other adjectives*

There are a considerable number of adjectives that form their plurals in the same way as nouns [▶20h(iii)].

(i)   *-io*

Adjectives ending in **-io** form their masculine plural in **-ii** when the **i** of **-io** is *stressed,* and in a single **-i** when *unstressed.*

stant*io*	**stant*ii***	stale
	but	
amp*io*	**amp*i***	wide

(ii) -co, -go

Masculine adjectives ending in **-co** and **-go** form their plural in **-chi** and **-ghi** when the stress falls on the *penultimate* syllable.

bianco	**bian*chi***	white
largo	**lar*ghi***	wide

An exception is:

greco	**greci**	Greek

Adjectives where the stress falls *before* the penultimate syllable generally form their plural in **-ci**:

magnifico	**magnifi*ci***	magnificent

An exception is:

carico	**carichi**	loaded, laden

Note: As there are a number of exceptions to the rules governing the plurals of adjectives ending in **-co** and **-go** it is always advisable to check the formation of the plural in a good dictionary.

(iii) -ca, -ga

Feminine adjectives ending in **-ca** and **-ga** form their plural with **-che** and **-ghe**.

magnifica	**magnifi*che***	magnificent
lunga	**lun*ghe***	long

(iv) -cia, -gia

Feminine adjectives ending in a consonant + **-cia** and **-gia** form their plural with **-ce** and **-ge**.

li*scia*	**li*sce***	smooth
selva*ggia*	**selva*gge***	wild

When these same endings are preceded by a vowel the plural ends in **-cie** and **-gie**.

rand*agia*	**rand*agie***	stray

22f *'More' and 'most': comparative and superlative*

Most (though not all) adjectives can be used to make comparisons: for this we use the *comparative* form. If we are comparing more than two people or things, then we use the *superlative*.

(i)   Comparative

The comparative in Italian is formed by putting **più** 'more' before the adjective and, where necessary, **che** or **di** 'than' after it.

Ho due fratelli, Gino e Marco. Gino è *più giovane di* Marco. Gino è *più bravo* a scuola ma solo perché è *più diligente*. A Marco piace uscire quanto possibile e, in genere, è un tipo molto *più attivo di noi.*	I have two brothers, Gino and Marco. Gino is *younger than* Marco. Gino is *better* at school but only because he is *more diligent.* Marco likes to go out as much as possible and, generally, he is a much *more active* type *than we are.*

Note: **Di** is used before nouns (**di Marco**), pronouns (**di noi**), and numerals:

La settimana scorsa ha speso *più di 50.000* mila lire.	Last week he spent *more than 50,000* lire.

Che is used before adjectives, adverbs, prepositions, participles and infinitives.

Marco è più attivo *che passivo.*	Marco is more active *than passive.*
Quando fa i suoi compiti, li fa sempre più velocemente *che correttamente.*	When he does his homework, he always does it more quickly *than correctly.*
È un po' più diligente a scuola *che a* casa.	He is a bit more diligent at school *than at* home.
È più interessato allo svago *che motivato* dai suoi studi.	He is more interested in entertainment *than motivated* by his studies.
Per lui, è più importante uscire *che studiare.*	For him, it is more important to go out *than to study.*

When the comparison is between two nouns or pronouns that are complements or objects of the *same* verb, 'than' is expressed by **che** and not **di**:

Per lui, *è più importante lo svago che la scuola.*	For him, *entertainment is more important than school.*
I miei genitori *aiutano più me che lui.*	My parents *help me more than him.*

[For the use of the subjunctive after a comparative ➤16g.]

(ii) *Superlative*

The superlative is formed by using the definite article + the comparative, which may come before or after the noun, or may stand without the noun if it is understood. Note, however, that the article is *not* repeated when the adjective follows the noun.

Marco è *lo* studente *più dotato* ma Gino è *il più diligente*.	Marco is *the most gifted* student but Gino is *the most diligent*.

• After a superlative, use **di** for 'in':

Marco è *Il più dotato della* classe.	Marco is the *most gifted in* the class.

• Sometimes the prepositions **fra** or **tra** [➤25c(ix)] are used in place of **di**:

Marco è *il più dotato fra/tra* tutti gli studenti della sua classe.	Marco is the *most gifted of* all the students in his class.

(iii) *Meno* 'less', 'least'

The comparative and superlative forms introduced by **meno** 'less', 'least' follow exactly the same patterns of formation and use as **più**.

Marco è senz'altro *meno ambizioso di* Gino, infatti penso che sia *il meno ambizioso* della sua classe.	Marco is certainly *less ambitious than* Gino, in fact I think he is *the least ambitious* in his class.

(iv) *Tanto...quanto/così...come*

When comparing people or things as equals, use either **tanto...quanto...** or **così...come...** 'as...as...' or **non tanto...quanto/non così...come...** 'not as/so...as...' in the negative.

Io sono *tanto diligente quanto* mio fratello Gino ma *non* sono *così ambizioso come* lui.	I'm *as diligent as* my brother Gino but I'm *not as/so ambitious as* him.

* **Tanto** and **così** are frequently omitted:

Io sono *diligente quanto* mio fratello Gino ma *non* sono *ambizioso come* lui.	I'm *as diligent as* my brother Gino but I'm *not as ambitious as* him.

 Tanto/quanto are invariable when they qualify adjectives as in the example above. However, when they qualify nouns they must agree in number and gender:

Nella mia classe ci sono *tanti ragazzi quante ragazze*.	In my class there are *as many boys as girls*.

(v)   *-issimo*

To say something is 'very', 'extremely', etc. + adjective you can add **-issimo** to the adjective after removing the final vowel. The **-issimo** ending agrees with the noun in the usual way. This form is known as the *absolute superlative*.

I miei compagni di scuola sono *simpaticissimi* **e facciamo** *tantissime* **cose insieme.**	My school companions are *extremely nice* and we do *a great many* things together.

* Remember that some adjectives need spelling adjustments before adding **-issimo,** for example, adjectives ending in **-co** and **-go** that form their plurals in **-chi** and **-ghi** [➤22e(ii)].

bianco	bian**ch**issimo	very white
largo	lar**gh**issimo	very wide

* Adjectives ending in **-io** drop both final vowels before adding **-issimo**.

vecchio	vechissimo	very old

(vi)   *Alternative forms to -issimo*

Adjectives may also be emphasized:

- by placing an adverb such as **molto/assai** 'very', **veramente** 'really', **incredibilmente** 'incredibly' in front of the adjective:

Sei *molto* gentile.	You are *very* kind.
Sono *assai* motivati.	They are *very* motivated.
Gino è *veramente* studioso.	Gino is *really* hard-working.
Suo fratello è *incredibilmente* pigro.	His brother is *incredibly* lazy.

- by means of a prefix such as **arci-, stra-, super-, ultra-:**

Come studente, Gino è *arci*contento.	As a student, Gino is *extremely* happy.
Frequenta una scuola *ultra*moderna.	He attends an *ultra*modern school.
Non è *super*intelligente ma fa del suo meglio.	He is not *super*intelligent but he does his best.
I nostri genitori non sono *stra*ricchi, altrimenti l'avrebbero mandato a una scuola privata.	Our parents are not *very* rich, otherwise they would have sent him to a private school.

- by repeating the adjective:

Abitiamo in una casa *piccola piccola*.	We live in a *very* small house.

- by adding another adjective that strengthens the meaning of the first.

Stamattina sono arrivato a scuola bagnato *fradicio*.	This morning I arrived at school *soaking* wet.
L'autobus era pieno *zeppo*.	The bus was *packed* full.
Ieri sera eravamo tutti stanchi *morti*.	Last night we were all *dead* tired.
Mia sorella non riesce a concentrarsi a scuola perché è innamorata *cotta*.	My sister can't concentrate at school because she is *head over heels* in love.

- by other expressions such as the following:

Abitiamo in campagna e in pieno inverno fa un freddo *da morire*.	We live in the country and in the middle of winter it's *bitterly* cold.

| Una vecchia zia abita con noi. È ancora molto vivace ma è *sorda come una campana*. | An old aunt lives with us. She is still very lively but she's *as deaf as a post*. |

(vii)   Più...più... 'The more...the more...', etc.

These express the consequences of doing something.

| *Più* studio, *più* imparo. | *The more* I study, *the more* I learn. |

Meno...meno... 'the less...the less...' is used in the same way. It is also possible to use a combination of these forms, as in the following example:

| *Più* imparo, *meno* capisco. | *The more* I learn, *the less* I understand. |

[For comparative and superlative forms of adverbs ➤26b(iv).]

(viii)   Adjectives with two forms

There are a small number of Italian adjectives that have irregular forms in addition to the regular ones:

	Comparative	Superlative	Absolute superlative
buono	**migliore**	**il migliore**	**ottimo**
good	better	the best	very good
cattivo	**peggiore**	**il peggiore**	**pessimo**
bad	worse	the worst	very bad
grande	**maggiore**	**il maggiore**	**massimo**
big	bigger	the biggest	very big
piccolo	**minore**	**il minore**	**minimo**
small	smaller	the smallest	very small
alto	**superiore**	**il superiore**	**supremo**
high	higher	the highest	very high
basso	**inferiore**	**l'inferiore**	**infimo**
low	lower	the lowest	very low

• There are some occasions where you can use either form of the comparative or superlative without affecting the meaning:

Questo vino è *buonissimo/ottimo*. Infatti, è *il migliore/il più buon* vino che abbia mai bevuto.	This wine is *very good*. In fact, it's *the best* wine I've ever drunk.

[For use of the subjunctive after a superlative ➤16f(iii).]

• In other cases, the different form gives rise to a different meaning:

Delle due case la nostra è *più grande*.	Of the two houses ours is *bigger*. (in size)
Il mio fratello *maggiore* si chiama Roberto.	My *older* (age) brother is called Roberto.
Il costo dei danni causati dal maltempo è stato *maggiore* di quanto pensassimo .	The cost of the damage caused by the bad weather was *greater* (more substantial) than we thought.

Note: **Più piccolo** 'smaller' (in size) and **minore** 'younger' (in age) and 'lesser' (in importance) are used in a similar way to **più grande** and **maggiore**.

The other comparative and superlative forms listed can also be used in different contexts to convey various meanings. It is, therefore, worth consulting a good dictionary to study in greater depth the range of options available.

Note: Adjectives may be formed from the present participle [➤10c(iii)] and past participle [➤10f(ii)] of verbs.

Adjectives may also be used as nouns [➤20i].

22g   *Prefixes and suffixes*

(i)   *Prefixes*

In English, we often make the opposite, usually the negative, of the adjective by using such prefixes as 'un-' or 'dis-', as in 'unable' or 'disorganized'. In Italian many opposites are formed by using the prefixes **in-**, **dis-** and **s-**

felice	happy	*in*felice	*un*happy
accettabile	acceptable	*in*accettabile	*un*acceptable
simile	similar, like	*dis*simile	*dis*similar, unlike
occupato	employed	*dis*occupato	*un*employed

fortunato	fortunate	***sfortunato***	*un*fortunate
carico	loaded	***scarico***	*un*loaded

As you can see from the examples the English 'un-' can be conveyed in Italian by three different prefixes: **in-, dis-, s-**.

Do not attach prefixes to adjectives without first consulting a dictionary to ensure that the word really does exist.

Another fairly common way of making the opposite is the use of **poco** + adjective.

Lei è *poco* motivata.	She's *un*motivated. (*not very* motivated)
Questi libri sono *poco* interessanti.	These books are *un*interesting.

Poco is always invariable in these constructions.

(ii)   *Suffixes*

The meaning of some adjectives can be modified by suffixes. These include:

* the diminutives **-ino, -ello, -etto, -otto**:

caro	dear	**car*ino***	*pretty, cute*
cattivo	naughty	**cattiv*ello***	*rather* naughty
povero	poor	**pover*etto***	poor *thing*
vecchio	old	**vecchi*otto***	*rather* old, oldish

* the augmentative **-one**:

pigro	lazy	**pigr*one***	*very* lazy

Note: An augmentative – the opposite of diminutive – adds strength to the meaning of the adjective and conveys the idea of size. Remember that the feminine form is **-ona**.

* **-accio** which is used in a pejorative sense:

povero	poor	**pover*accio***	poor *wretch*

Note: Before adding the suffix remove the final vowel of the adjective.

As in the case of prefixes, it is safer to use the suffixes with adjectives you have seen or heard to avoid the risk of creating non-existent words.

Representing nouns: pronouns

23a   What pronouns do

The word *pronoun* means 'in place of a noun'. Pronouns are constantly used instead of nouns as a way of avoiding repetition. The types of pronoun discussed in paragraphs 23i to 23l below have corresponding determiners [➤21].

Pronouns take:

• their *gender* (masculine/feminine) and *number* (singular/ plural) from the noun they refer to (although Italian has a number of 'neuter' pronouns, some of which are explained in paragraph 23g below);

• their *form* from the sentence they are in.

23b   Personal pronouns

These are the most neutral pronouns – they simply replace nouns without adding any further information. They may refer to the person(s) speaking (first person), the person(s) spoken to (second person), or the person(s) or thing(s) spoken about (third person).

(i)   *Subject pronouns*

Singular

First person	**io**	I
Second person	**tu**	you (informal)
	Lei	you (formal)
Third person	**lui (egli)**	he
	lei (ella)	she
	esso	it (masculine)
	essa	it (feminine)

Plural

First person	**noi**	we
Second person	**voi**	you (informal)
	Loro	you (formal)
Third person	**loro (essi)**	they (masculine)
	loro (esse)	they (feminine)

Because the subject – the doer – of the action [➤4b] is contained in the verb ending in Italian, the subject pronouns are only used for *emphasis, contrast* or *to avoid confusion*, and *when they stand alone*. **Lei/Loro** are perhaps used more frequently, mainly because of the possible ambiguity over the shared third person verb endings, but also sometimes to emphasize deference to the person(s) addressed.

Cosa facciamo stasera? – *Tu* **puoi fare quello che vuoi ma** *io* **preferisco stare a casa. Cosa fanno Gianni e Barbara? –** *Lui* **va a vedere la partita di pallacanestro mentre** *lei* **va al cinema. Perché non vai alla partita** *anche tu*? **–** *Io*, **ma scherzi, sai che detesto lo sport.**	What are we doing this evening? – *You* can do what you want but *I* prefer to stay at home (contrast between you and I). What are Gianni and Barbara doing? – *He* is going to the basketball game while *she* is going to the cinema/movies (contrast between he and she). Why don't *you* go to the game *too*? (emphasis) – *Me*, you must be joking, you know that I hate sport (subject stands alone without the verb).

Note: In the example **Perché non vai** *anche tu*? the subject pronoun **tu** is used for reasons of emphasis but it must be used anyway after adverbs such as **anche, neanche,** etc.

Non ci voglio andare *neanch'io*.	*I* don't want to go there *either*.

• Subject pronouns usually follow the verb when they are used for emphasis:

Se non vai *tu*, **vado** *io*. **Chi parla? – Sono** *io* **Barbara. – Ah, sei** *tu*.	If *you* don't go, *I* will. Who's speaking? – It's *me*, Barbara. – Ah, it's *you*.

• It is a good idea to use the subject pronoun with the singular of the present subjunctive to avoid confusion as the first three persons have an identical form [➤18c(ii),19].

 Although the formal **Lei** and **Loro** 'you' have been listed under the second person, it is very important to remember that they not only take the third person of the verb, but that in all other functions they take *third person pronouns* and *possessives* [➤23b(ii), 23l, 21h(i)].

- **Egli/ella** 'he'/'she' and **esso/essa** 'it' are rarely used nowadays in speech. They have been replaced by **lui/lei**. Similarly, in the third person plural **essi/esse** 'they' have been replaced by **loro**. You will, however, come across these forms in the written language, especially in reference to inanimate nouns.

- The polite forms **Lei** and **Loro** are sometimes written with a small I in informal writing.

- **Formal and informal address**
In Italian it is very important to distinguish between the use of the informal **tu** and the formal **Lei**. **Tu** is used when addressing family, friends, children and animals. You should use **Lei** in formal settings – at a bank, hotel, restaurant, travel agency, etc. – unless of course one of the employees is a friend of yours. A reasonable guideline is that people on a first name basis would use the informal **tu**, whereas if you were addressing someone by title, such as **signore, signora, signorina, dottore, professore, etc.** you would certainly use **Lei**.

Foreigners often find themselves in a kind of dilemma when they first meet people of similar age. The safest thing to do is to use **Lei** until you are invited to do otherwise! (**Diamoci del tu.** – Let's use the **tu** form.) There is an increasing tendency in the spoken language to replace the formal plural **Loro** with **voi**, which is also of course the informal plural.

Come stai, Elena? – Bene grazie, e *tu*?	How are you Elena? – Well, thank you, and *you*?
Come sta, signora Bianchi? – Non c'è male grazie, e *Lei*?	How are you Mrs.Bianchi? – Not bad thank you, and *you*?
Elena e Marco, statemi a sentire un attimo, dove andate (*voi*) in vacanza quest'anno?	Elena and Marco, just listen to me a moment, where are *you* going on holiday/vacation this year?
A che ora partono (Loro)/partite (voi)?	At what time are *you* leaving?

(ii) *Direct object pronouns [➤8d]*

Singular		**Plural**	
mi	me	ci	us
ti	you (informal)	vi	you (informal)
La	you (formal, masculine + feminine)	Li	you (formal, masculine)
		Le	you (formal, feminine)
lo	him, it	li	them (masculine)
la	her, it	le	them (feminine)

Perché non vai al cinema con Barbara? – Danno lo stesso film della settimana scorsa e *l'*ho già visto. A proposito, Gianni e Barbara *ci* hanno invitato a pranzo domenica. *Mi* ascolti o no? – Certo che *ti* ascolto e mentre stai in piedi spegni la televisione. – *L'* ho spenta cinque minuti fa.	Why don't you go to the cinema/movies with Barbara? – They are showing the same film/movie as last week and I have already seen *it*. By the way, Gianni and Barbara have invited *us* to lunch on Sunday. Are you listening to *me* or not? – Of course I'm listening *to you* and while you are on your feet turn off the television. – I turned *it* off five minutes ago.

Ascoltare means 'listen *to*' and takes a direct object [➤8h(vii)].

• **Lo** and **la** elide (**l'**) before a vowel or **h**. Although elision is possible with **mi, ti, ci** and **vi**, it happens less frequently. One notable exception with **ci** is of course the expression **c'è** 'there is'. Never elide the plural forms **li** and **le**.

[For agreement of past participle with direct object pronouns ➤11d(i).]

(iii) *Indirect object pronouns [➤8e]*

Singular

mi	to me
ti	to you (informal)
Le	to you (formal)
gli	to him, to it
le	to her, to it

Plural

ci	to us
vi	to you (informal)
Loro	to you (formal)
loro (gli)	to them (masculine + feminine)

• There is an increasing tendency to use **gli** for 'to them' in place of **loro** in the spoken language. **Loro**, however, is still used in more formal situations as well as in the written language.

Loro is the one indirect pronoun that always follows a verb and can never be attached to an infinitive, gerund, imperative or past participle [➤23b(iv)].

Ho detto *loro* che veniamo or *Gli* ho detto che veniamo.	I told *them* that we are coming.

• Although the indirect object means 'to' or 'for' someone, in English this is not always clear, and care should be taken to use the correct object pronoun in Italian. It is helpful sometimes to put the word 'to' before the object. If this makes sense, then the object is *indirect*.

Dove hai messo la lettera che ti ho dato stamattina?	Where have you put the letter I gave (*to*) *you* this morning?

However, some verbs take an indirect object in Italian but not in English.

Perché non *mi* hai chiesto prima di accettare l'invito?	Why didn't you ask *me* before accepting the invitation?

[For other verbs that take an indirect object [➤8e(i)].

• When there is both an indirect and a direct object pronoun, with the exception of **loro** 'to them', the indirect always precedes the direct [➤23b(v)].

Perché non *me l*'hai detto prima?	Why didn't you tell *me it* before?

Note: 'It' is often omitted in English in sentences such as the one above but Italian usually includes **lo/l'** to complete the sense. [For other examples ➤23g(i)].

(iv) *Position of object pronouns*

With the exception of **loro** all object pronouns immediately precede the verb.

Ma quando *ti* dico qualcosa non *mi* ascolti mai.	But when I tell *you* something you never listen to *me*.

• In compound tense forms the object pronoun comes before the auxiliary verb.

***Ti* ho già detto due volte.** **– Non è vero, non *mi* hai detto nemmeno una volta.**	I have already told *you* twice. – It's not true, you haven't told *me* even once.

Note also that in negative sentences the object pronouns still retain the same position immediately in front of the verb.

• Object pronouns are attached to the end of an infinitive after the final -e of the infinitive is removed. (For verbs modelled on **tradurre** 'translate' and **porre** 'put' remove the final **-re** before attaching the object pronoun.)

Spero di veder*li* domani mattina.	I hope to see *them* tomorrow morning.

• With modal verbs [➤9] + infinitive, the object pronoun(s) can either be placed before the modal verb or be attached to the following infinitive.

***Gli* posso dire che hai un altro impegno.** or **Posso dir*gli* che hai un altro impegno.**	I can tell *them* that you have something else on.

• With **stare/andare** + gerund [➤8k(i)-(ii)] the object pronouns normally come before **stare/andare** but it is also possible to attach them to the end of the gerund.

Cosa *mi* stavi dicendo? or (less common) **Cosa stavi dicendo*mi?***	What were you saying *to me*?

The object pronouns must, however, be attached to both the simple and compound forms of the gerund when it stands alone.

Accettando*lo*, avremo modo di conoscere i loro cugini che sono appena tornati dall'America.	By accepting *it*, we shall have the opportunity to meet their cousins who have just returned from America.
Avendo*lo* accettato, non posso dire di no.	Having accepted *it*, I can't say no.

• Object pronouns must be attached to past participles standing alone:

Accettato*lo*, non posso dire di no.	Having accepted *it*, I can't say no.

and also to **ecco** 'here is/are', 'there is/are':

Ecco*li*!	There *they* are!
Ecco*mi*!	Here *I* am!

[For position of pronouns with imperative ➤15b(ii)-(iii).]

(v) *Order of object pronouns*

When two object pronouns occur together the *indirect* precedes the *direct*. The list below also includes the reflexive pronoun **si**, which will be dealt with in paragraph ➤23c. You will notice that **mi, ti, ci, vi** and **si** become **me, te, ce, ve** and **se** when they precede the direct object pronoun. **Gli** ' to him', **le** 'to her' and **Le** 'to you' (formal) become **glie** before combining with the direct object pronoun to give *one word*.

me lo	me la	me li	me le
te lo	te la	te li	te le
glielo	gliela	glieli	gliele
se lo	se la	se li	se le
ce lo	ce la	ce li	ce le
ve lo	ve la	ve li	ve le

• When **me lo,** etc. precede the verb they are written separately but they too join to form one word when attached to an infinitive, gerund, past participle and **ecco** [➤23b(iv) above].

Te lo manderò ma non posso mandar*telo* subito.	I shall send *it to you* but I can't send *it to you* immediately.

Glie combined with another third person direct object pronoun could mean 'to him/her' or 'to you' (formal). As there is a growing tendency to use **gli** in place of **loro,** especially in spoken language, then the meanings could also include 'to them' and 'to you' (formal plural). The person being addressed, however, is usually obvious from the context.

Hai detto a tuo fratello che è invitato a pranzo? – Sì, *glie'*ho **detto.**	Have you told your brother that he is invited to lunch? – Yes, I've told *him.*

• **Gli** also combines with **ne** [➤23f(i)] to become **gliene:**

Gliene **ho parlato.**	I've spoken *to him about it.*

(vi) *'Redundant' object pronouns*

Noun objects, both direct and indirect, are often 'doubled' in Italian by the addition of the object pronoun, especially – but not necessarily – when the noun object precedes the verb.

Questo invito, **non** *lo* **voglio rifiutare.**	I don't want to turn down *this invitation.*
Ma *a te,* **cosa** *ti* **hanno detto esattamente?**	But what did they tell *you* exactly?

23c *Reflexive pronouns*

(i) *Use of reflexive pronouns*

Reflexive pronouns are object pronouns which refer back to the subject of the sentence, as when you do something to yourself. In the first person (**mi** 'me', **ci** 'us'), and the second person (**ti** 'you', **vi** 'you' *informal*), Italian uses the normal personal object pronouns as reflexives. But there is a special third person reflexive which is both singular and plural: **si,** which means 'himself', 'herself', 'itself', 'themselves' and also 'yourself' and 'yourselves' for **Lei** and **Loro,** which – remember! – use *third person pronouns.*

If you use the ordinary third person object pronouns **lo/la/li/le/gli,** etc.[➤23b(ii)-(iii)], then the action is being done to someone or something else, not to the subject.

Si **è comprata un bell'abito da sera.**	*She* bought *herself* a beautiful evening dress.
Gli **ha comprato una cravatta.**	*She* bought *him* a tie.

Si è svegliato presto.	*He* woke (*himself*) up early.
*L'*ha svegliata più tardi.	*He* woke *her* up later.

Note: Actions performed to parts of one's own body or clothing are usually expressed by a reflexive verb rather than a possessive [➤21h(vi)].

Mi sono storto *la* caviglia.	*I* twisted *my* ankle.
Si è lavata *i* capelli.	*She* washed *her* hair.

(ii) 'Each other'

Plural reflexive pronouns (**ci, vi, si**) can also be used *reciprocally*, that is, when people do something not to themselves but to each other.

Che peccato che tuo fratello non possa venire a pranzo domenica, non *ci vediamo* da almeno due mesi, e chi sa quando è l'ultima volta che lui e i miei cugini *si sono incontrati*!	What a pity that your brother can't come to lunch on Sunday, *we haven't seen each other* for at least two months, and who knows when he and my cousins last *met* (*each other*).

 Do not confuse reflexives with the words we use to emphasize that it was *the subject* that did something, not anyone else. To obtain this emphasis, simply use **stesso** 'self', agreeing in gender and number, after the subject pronoun [➤23b(i)].

Ha accettato l'invito *lei stessa*.	She accepted the invitation *herself*.

23d The indefinite pronoun 'one'
(i) Si

To express the idea of the English indefinite pronoun 'one', 'you', 'we', 'they', 'people' in a general sense, Italian normally uses the third person reflexive pronoun **si** with the third person singular of the verb.

Si vede che per tuo fratello domenica sarà impossibile.	*One can see* that for your brother Sunday will be impossible.

Forse *si può* organizzare qualcos'altro. – Ma con lui, non *si sa* mai cosa fare.	Perhaps *we can* organize something else. – With him, *you* never *know* what to do.

 Care should be taken not to confuse the impersonal pronoun **si** 'one' with the **si passivante** [➤17e(i)].

• When used with a reflexive verb **si** changes to **ci** to avoid repetition and confusion with the third person reflexive pronoun which is also **si**.

***Ci* si abitua alla sua indecisione.**	*One* gets used to his indecision.

• When **si** is used with a compound tense [➤11b], the auxiliary is *always* **essere**. The past participle of verbs that are normally conjugated with **essere** is *always* in the plural.

***Si è detto* che i tuoi cugini torneranno in America alla fine delle vacanze.** ***Ci* si è abituat*i* alla sua indecisione.** **Basta, *si* è tornat*i* sullo stesso discorso di prima.**	*People have said* that your cousins will be going back to America at the end of the holidays. *One* has got used to his indecision. That's enough, *we* have come back to the same subject of conversation as before.

Note: Dire 'say','tell' is normally conjugated with **avere** so **detto** is singular.

[For **si** + verb + *plural adjective* ➤22c(iii).]

• All object pronouns precede **si** with the exception of **ne** [➤23f(iii)], which follows it. **Si** becomes **se** when it precedes **ne**.

***Gli* si dice di essere un po' più socievole.** **Dimmi a che ora devo venire domenica e poi non se *ne* parla più.**	People tell *him* to be a bit more sociable. Tell me at what time I have to come on Sunday and then we won't talk *about it* any more.

(ii) **Uno**

The indefinite pronoun **uno** is sometimes used in place of **si**.

Quando *uno* si comporta così è difficile.	When *one* (*someone*) behaves like that it's difficult.

 The rules governing the use of **si** + compound tense, reflexive verb, etc. explained under ►23d(i) *do not apply* when using **uno**.

23e The pronouns **ci**, **vi**

(i) *Ci* or *vi* 'there'

In addition to their function as object pronouns **ci** and, less frequently, **vi** are used as adverbs meaning 'there'.

Sei mai stata in America, Silvia? – No, non *ci* sono mai stata.	Have you ever been to America, Silvia? – No, I've never been *there*.

Note that very often no word for **ci** is present in English:

Ma spero di andar*ci* un giorno.	But I hope to go one day.

Ci is also used:

• to replace other adverbial expressions indicating location, such as 'in there', 'by there':

I tuoi genitori sono *a casa*? – No, non *ci* sono, sono andati a trovare mia nonna. *Ci* passano ogni sera perché abita da sola.	Are your parents *at* home? – No, they're not, they've gone to see my grandmother. They drop by (*there*) every evening because she lives alone.

• to replace **a** + a noun or pronoun:

Penso ancora *alla indecisione* di mio fratello. *Ci* penso spesso. Non capisco perché voglia rinunciare *a questo invito*.- Lascialo stare, avrà i suoi motivi per rinunciar*ci*.	I'm still thinking *about* my brother's *indecisiveness*. I often think *about it*. I don't understand why he wants to decline *this invitation*. – Leave him be, he must have his own reasons for not accepting *it*.

When used in this way, **a** can only refer to a thing or things, *never* to people. To refer to people use a disjunctive pronoun [►23h]:

È strano perché pensa spesso a ***loro.***	It's strange because he often thinks about *them*.

- to replace **a** + an infintive or an entire phrase:

Allora non sei riuscita *a convincerlo*. – No, purtroppo, non *ci* sono riuscita.	So you didn't manage *to convince him*. No, unfortunately, I didn't.
Forse si è abituato *a stare a casa*. – Hai ragione, *ci* si è abituato.	Perhaps he's got used *to staying at home*. – You're right, he's got used *to it*.

- in a number of more idiomatic expressions to convey meanings such as 'about/of/to/on/from it':

Dimmi, cosa *ci* posso fare?	Tell me, what can I do *about it*?
Non *ci* capisco più niente.	I can't make any sense *of it* any more.
Per quanto riguarda quell'altra faccenda, *ci* penserò io.	As for that other matter, I shall see *to it*.
Ma ti ho detto che puoi contare sul mio aiuto. – Lo so che *ci* posso contare.	But I told you that you can count on my help. – I know that I can count *on it*.
Se vendi il tuo appartamento adesso, cosa *ci* guadagni?	If you sell your flat/apartment now, what do you gain *from it*?
Il doppio di quello che ho pagato. – Non *ci* credo.	Double what I paid for it. – I don't believe *it*.
Comunque, i soldi non *c'*entrano!	However, money doesn't come *into it*!

- in some other idiomatic expressions in combination with **la**:

Questo appartamento è troppo grande per me, c'è sempre tanto lavoro e non *ce la* faccio.	This flat/apartment is too big for me, there is always so much work to do and I can't manage.
Mia sorella *ce l'*ha sempre con me.	My sister is always angry with me.

- with **avere** in expressions like:

Hai il mio indirizzo? – No, non *ce* **l'ho.**	Have you got my address? – No, I haven't.
Ce **le hai tu le foto del mio appartamento? – Sì,** *ce* **le ho.**	Have you got the photos of my flat/apartment? – Yes, I have.

Ci in such expressions is for purposes of reinforcement, as **l'ho** and **le ho** on their own sound rather odd.
[**Ci** becomes **ce** in front of another object pronoun ➤23b(v).]

Note also:

Ci **ho sonno.**	I am tired.
Ci **hai fame?**	Are you hungry?

 This is a very colloquial use of **ci** which you will come across in the spoken language but which should not be used in writing.

(ii) *Position*

When it is used in combination with other pronouns, **ci** comes first [➤23b(v)]. However, it comes after **mi** and **ti**.

Se vai da Gianni domani sera, ti *ci* **vedrò.**	If you go to Gianni's tomorrow evening, I shall see you *there*.

[For position when used on its own ➤23b(iv).]

Note: In place of **ci** meaning 'there' it is possible to use **lì** or **là**. These must *never* be attached to a verb form.

Se vai da Gianni domani sera, ti vedrò lì.	If you go to Gianni's tomorrow evening, I shall see you *there*.

23f   *The pronoun* ne
(i)   *Ne* replaces *di*

The pronoun **ne** replaces **di** (or one of its forms) + a noun or pronoun. Given the range of uses of **di** in Italian, **ne** covers a wide range of meanings such as 'of him/her/them', 'of it/this/that', 'some', 'any'.

Come sta tua zia? – Da quando è andata a vivere a Venezia non *ne* **so niente.**	How is your aunt? – Since she went to live in Venice I know nothing *about her.*
Ma ti avrà mandato almeno una cartolina? – No, nemmeno una, ma non voglio parlar*ne.*	But she must have sent you at least a postcard? – No, not even one, but I don't want to talk *about it.*
Ma può darsi che stia male, cosa *ne* **pensi?**	But maybe she's ill/sick, what do you think (*about it*)?
Cambiando il discorso, hai comprato dei fiori per il compleanno di tua sorella? – No, non *ne* **ho comprati, vado a comprar***ne* **subito.**	Changing the subject, have you bought some flowers for your sister's birthday? – No, I haven't bought *any*, I shall go and buy *some* at once.

(ii)   *With expressions of quantity*

Ne often appears with expressions of quantity as a great number of them are followed by **di**.

Se vai dal fioraio, compra due mazzi di fiori, uno per te e uno per me. – Va bene, *ne* **compro due.**	If you go to the florist's, buy two bunches of flowers, one for you and one for me. – All right, I'll buy two (*of them*).
Quanti soldi hai? – *Ne* **ho abbastanza.**	How much money do you have? – I have enough (*of it*).
Se passi dal mercato, compra delle banane. – *Ne* **comprerò due chili.**	If you go by the market, buy some bananas. – I'll buy two kilos (*of them*).

(iii)   *Other uses*

Ne is also used:

• with an adverbial function, meaning 'from there/here':

Quando *ne* **torni, ti faccio un bel caffè.**	When you come back (*from there*), I shall make you a nice coffee.

• on occasions to replace **di** + an entire phrase or sentence, particularly after verbs like **dimenticarsi** 'forget' and **rendersi conto** 'realize', which are followed by **di**.

Sapevi che volevo vendere il mio appartemento, vero? – Sì, mi avevi detto una volta ma poi me *ne* sono dimenticata.	You knew that I wanted to sell my flat/apartment? – Yes, you had told me once but I forgot *about it*.
Ti rendi conto che avrai difficoltà a venderlo adesso? – Sì, comincio a renderme*ne* conto.	You realize that you will have difficulty in selling it now? – Yes, I'm beginning to realize.

 As the above examples illustrate **ne** is required in Italian, where in many cases in English its equivalent is absent or understood.

Note: **Ne** could be similarly used with a number of the verbs listed under 8h(ii).

[For agreement of **ne** with the past participle in compound tenses ➤11d(i).]

(iv) Position

Ne follows other object pronouns, including reflexives:

Te *ne* vai adesso?	Are you off now?
Non dimenticare, comprame*ne* due chili.	Don't forget, buy two kilos of them for me.
Sono già le undici e non ce *ne* siamo accorti!	It's already eleven o'clock and we didn't realize it!

[For position when used on its own ➤ 23b(iv).]

23g Neuter pronouns

(i) Lo

Apart from its more frequent use as 'him/it', **lo** is also used as a neuter object or complement in cases where English would omit it or perhaps use 'so' or even 'one'.

Mio fratello è incapace di prendere una decisione. – *Lo* so, me *l*'hai detto cento volte.	My brother is incapable of making a decision. – I know (*it*), you've told me *so* a hundred times.

Finiti gli studi, vuole diventare chirurgo ma non *lo* diventerà mai.	When he has finished his studies, he wants to become a surgeon but he will never become *one*.
Pensa di essere un tipo molto estroverso ma non *lo* è.	He thinks he's a very extrovert type but he isn't.

(ii)   'It'

The English impersonal subject pronoun 'it' has no real equivalent in Italian, as the subject is contained in the verb ending. There are, however, plenty of impersonal verbs, such as weather expressions like **fa freddo** 'it's cold' and expressions such as **è difficile** 'it is difficult'. These are dealt with fully in paragraph 8f.

23h   *Prepositions and personal pronouns: disjunctive pronouns*

Disjunctive means here *not related directly to the verb*. These pronouns are sometimes also called *prepositional* pronouns since their main use is after prepositions.

Singular		*Plural*	
me	me	**noi**	us
te	you (informal)	**voi**	you (informal)
Lei	you (formal)	**Loro**	you (formal)
lui	him	**loro**	them (masculine + feminine)
lei	her		
esso/a	it	**essi/e**	them

(i)   Note that except for **me** and **te**, the form is the same as the subject pronouns in 23b(i).

Non posso venire *con te*. Devo andare da mia nonna perché due volte alla settimana faccio la spesa *per lei*.	I can't come with you. I have to go to my grandmother's because twice a week I do the shopping *for her*.

There are some prepositions that require an additional preposition **di** before a disjunctive pronoun. They include the following:

contro	against	**dentro**	inside
dietro	behind	**dopo**	after
fra/tra	among, between	**senza**	without
sopra	above, upon	**sotto**	under, below
su	on, above	**verso**	towards

Conta molto *su di me*.	She depends a lot on me.
Dice sempre che non ce la farebbe *senza di me*.	She is always saying that she couldn't manage *without me*.

Note: **Di** is sometimes omitted after **fra/tra**.

Remember that disjunctive pronouns are used after verbs that take a prepositional object [▶8h].

(ii) *Other uses*

Disjunctive pronouns are also used:

• for emphasis, in which case they replace an object pronoun:

***A lei*, non piace uscire la sera.** (emphatic)	*She* doesn't like going out in the evening.
Non le piace uscire la sera. (unemphatic)	
Ma quando io avevo dei problemi, lei aiutava *me*. (emphatic)	But when I had problems, she used to help *me*.
Ma quando io avevo dei problemi, lei mi aiutava. (unemphatic)	

• whenever the verb has two or more direct or indirect objects:

Delle volte quando vado da mia nonna aiuto *lei* e *i suoi vicini*, che sono anziani anche loro.	Sometimes when I go to my grandmother's I help *her* and *her neighbours/neighbors*, who are also elderly. (two *direct* objects)
Do una mano *a lei* e *a loro*.	I help *her* and *them*. (two *indirect* objects)

• after **di, che, tanto...quanto.../così...come...** in comparisons [▶22f(i)(iii)(iv)]:

Comunque, aiuto più lei *che loro*.	However, I help her more *than them*.
Mia nonna non è così attiva *come loro*.	My grandmother isn't as active *as them*.
I miei genitori fanno molto più *di me*.	My parents do much more *than me*.

- in exclamations after some adjectives:

Fra poco andiamo in vacanza. – *Beati voi!*	– Shortly we are going on holiday/vacation. – *Lucky you!*
Io, invece, non andrò da nessuna parte. – *Povero te!*	Whereas I shall be going nowhere. – *Poor you!*

Note: Disjunctive pronouns plus **stesso/a/i/e** are used to convey the emphatic forms 'myself', 'yourself', etc.

Pensi solo a *te stesso*.	You think only of *yourself*.

(iii) **Sé**

There is also a third person reflexive [➤23c(i)] disjunctive pronoun **sé**, which means 'him/himself', 'her/herself', 'itself', 'oneself', 'themselves', 'yourself', 'yourselves' (**Lei/Loro**). It is used after prepositions when the object of the preposition is the same person as the subject.

Mia nonna non può fare tutto da *sé*.	My grandmother can't do everything by *herself*.
Forse questo problema che ha tuo fratello si risolverà da *sé*.	Perhaps this problem that your brother has will resolve *itself*.

This pronoun is often used together with **stesso**. When this happens **sé** is written without the acute accent.

A volte, mi fa arrabbiare perché pensa solo a *se stesso*.	At times, he makes me angry because he only thinks of *himself*.

 Be careful not to confuse the emphatic use of **me stesso,** etc. with the use of reflexive pronouns [➤23c(i)]:

Mi sono tagliato.	I've cut myself. (the 'myself' is conveyed by the reflexive pronoun **mi**)

23i *'Which one?': interrogative pronouns*

These are question words listed in paragraphs 6d(i) to 6d(iii).

(i) *Chi 'Who?' 'Whom?'*

• **Chi?** is used for 'who?' 'whom?' as subject, object and after a preposition. The preposition must *always* precede **chi**, and may not come at the end of the clause as often happens in English. **Chi** is invariable.

Chi ha telefonato? – Una ragazza.	*Who* rang? – A girl.
Con chi voleva parlare? – Non lo so, è caduta la linea.	*Whom* did she want to speak *to*? – I don't know, I was cut off.
Chi hai incontrato alla festa?	*Whom* did you meet at the party?
A chi hai prestato il tuo ombrello?	*Whom* did you lend your umbrella *to*?

(Whilst *whom* is now largely restricted to formal language in English its inclusion here is intended to be helpful in distinguishing between the subject and the object form.)

In spoken Italian it is fairly common to put the preposition and pronoun after the verb.

Voleva parlare con chi?	Who did she want to speak to?

• **Di chi ... ?** 'Whose?'

Di chi è questa giacca?	*Whose* jacket is this?
Di chi sono queste scarpe?	*Whose* shoes are these?

 Do not confuse this with the word **cui** meaning 'whose', which is a relative pronoun and is not used to ask questions [➤23m(v)].

(ii) *Cosa/che/che cosa? 'What?'*

Cosa, che or **che cosa** are used for 'what?' as subject, object or after a preposition (which must precede it).

Cos'hai fatto?	*What* have you done?
Che è successo?	What has happened?
A *che cosa* stai pensando?	*What* are you thinking *about*?
Con *che cosa* posso pagare se sono al verde?	*What* do I pay *with* if I am broke?

Note that it is possible to elide **Cosa** (**Cos'**) but never **Che**.

 Remember that you can only use **che**, not **cosa or che cosa**, as an interrogative adjective [➤21b]. So, for example, 'What type/sort of... ?' would be **Che tipo/genere di...?**

(iii)   *Quale/quali?* 'Which one(s)?'

Quale 'which one' and the plural **quali** 'which ones' can refer to both people and things.

Ho comprato due riviste. *Quale* vuoi leggere?	I've bought two magazines. *Which one* do you want to read?
Abbiamo riviste dappertutto, non possiamo tenerle tutte. Allora, *quali* buttiamo via?	We have magazines everywhere, we can't keep them all. So *which ones* shall we throw out?

Note that **quale** is shortened to **qual** before the verb **essere**. The **-e** is not replaced by an apostrophe.

Qual è la tua rivista preferita?	*Which* is your favourite/favorite magazine?
Quale dei tuoi amici ti ha prestato questa videocassetta?	*Which* of your friends lent you this video?

Qual also means 'what' in sentences such as 'what is the ... ?'

Qual è il tuo motivo per tenere tutte queste riviste?	*What* is your reason for keeping all these magazines?

(iv)
All the interrogative pronouns referred to above [23j(i)-(iii)] are used in exactly the same way in indirect speech:

Non so *chi* ha telefonato.	I don't know *who* rang.

266

Dimmi *cosa* vuoi.	Tell me *what* you want.
Mi ha chiesto *quale* volevo leggere.	He asked me *which one* I wanted to read.

23j *Pointing and showing: demonstrative pronouns*

Demonstrative pronouns are used to point out or emphasize things – the equivalent in English being 'this one', 'that one', 'these/those (ones)'. They are usually used to convey whether something is near to or far from the speaker, though sometimes this distance is mental rather than physical.

(i) *Forms*

The demonstrative pronouns in Italian are **questo** 'this' and **quello** 'that'. Like adjectives ending in **-o** [➤22a(i)] they agree in number and gender with the noun they stand for.

Quale colore preferisce, *questo* o *quello*?	Which colour/color do you prefer, *this one* or *that one*?
Di chi sono tutte queste riviste? – *Queste* sono le mie e *quelle* sono le tue.	Whose are all these magazines? – *These* are mine and *those* are yours.

To emphasize further the notions of proximity and distance, **qui/qua** 'here' and **lì/là** 'there' are added after the demonstrative pronoun. These, therefore, could be added to both of the above examples.

Quale colore preferisci, questo *qui* o quello *lì*?	Which colour/color do you prefer, this one *(here)* or that one *(there)*?

• **Qui/qua** and **lì/là** can follow nouns as well as the pronouns **questo** and **quello**:

Preferisco questo *colore qui*.	I prefer this *colour/color (here)*.

• **Questo** and **quello** also function as neuter pronouns:

Di chi è *questo*?	Whose is *this*?
Di chi è *quello*?	Whose is *that*?

- **Quello** and **questo** are used to convey 'the former' and the 'latter' respectively. The appropriate form of **il primo** and **il secondo** can also be used.

Le mie due sorelle, Daniela e Rosaria si sono iscritte all'università: *questa/la seconda* **ha scelto di fare la storia dell'arte e** *quella/la prima* **la medicina.**	My two sisters, Daniela and Rosaria, have enrolled at the university: *the latter* has chosen to do history of art and *the former* medicine.

- **Quello** (*not* **questo**) + the preposition **di** is used in the following type of construction:

Il corso che ha scelto Daniela sarà più lungo di *quello di* **Rosaria.**	The course that Daniela has chosen will be longer than Rosaria*'s*.

The Italian **quello di** 'that of' is the way of expressing the English ''. The masculine form of the pronoun **quello** replaces the masculine noun **il corso**.

[For 'those who ...', 'all those who ...' ➤Relative pronouns 23m(viii).]

(ii) **Ciò** *'that'*

Ciò 'that' is an invariable neuter pronoun used to refer to something previously mentioned. However, **questo** is preferred here in spoken Italian.

Ciò/questo **mi sembra impossibile.**	*That* seems impossible to me.

23k *'How much?' 'How many?': pronouns of quantity*

Some *quantifiers* refer to the whole or none of something, others to some part or some members of it.

(i) *Quantifier pronouns*

The following list includes most of the *quantifier pronouns* used in Italian. Many resemble closely the quantifier determiners [➤21f, 21g].

alcuni/e	some, a few
altrettanto/a/i/e	as much, as many
altro/a	other, something else, anything else
altri/e	others
ambedue, entrambi/e, tutti/e e due	both
certi/e	some
chiunque	anyone
ciascuno/a	each one
diversi/e, vari/varie	several, a number of
molto/a	much, a lot
molti/e	many, a lot
nessuno/a	no one
niente/nulla	nothing
ognuno/a	everyone, everybody
parecchio/a	quite a bit, a lot
parecchi/parecchie	several, quite a few
un poco (di)	a little (of), a bit (of)
poco/a	little, not much
pochi/e	few, not many
qualcosa/qualche cosa	something
qualcuno	someone
quanto/a?	how much?
quanti/e?	how many?
tale/i	someone, person
tanto/a	so much
tanti/e	so many
troppo/a	too much
troppi/e	too many
tutto/a	all, everything
tutti/e	all, everybody
uno/a	one, someone, somebody

Qualcuno è venuto a riparare la televisione? – No, non è venuto *nessuno*.	Has *anyone* come to repair the television? – No, *no-one* came.
Ma quando guardavo dalla finestra, ho visto *uno* suonare alla casa di fronte.	But when I was looking out of the window, I saw *someone* ringing at the house opposite.
E poi? – E poi *niente*, *nessuno* è venuto ad aprire e quel *tale* è andato via.	And then? – And then *nothing*, *no one* came to open the door and the *person* went away.

C'era *qualcosa* che volevi guardare?	Was there *something* you wanted to watch?
È ora di buttare via quel televisore, ci è già costato *parecchio* per le riparazioni, *troppo* infatti. In fin dei conti, quanti programmi interessanti ci sono da vedere? *Pochi*. *Certi* sono interessanti, *altri* meno.	It's time to throw that set away, it's already cost us *quite a lot* for repairs, *too much* in fact. When it comes down to it, how many interesting programmes/programs are there to see? *Not many*. *Some* are interesting, *others* less so.
Ieri sera, quando la televisione funzionava ancora, abbiamo guardato due film, *uno* era bello e l'*altro* no ma, come me, tu hai guardato *tutti e due* fino alla fine.	Last night, when the television was still working, we watched two films/movies, *one* was good and the *other* not but, just like me, you watched *both* right to the end.
Ma solo perché non avevo *altro* da fare.	But only because I didn't have *anything else* to do.
Ti prego, guardi sempre *tutto*.	Come on, you always watch *everything*.
Ognuno ha i suoi difetti.	*Everyone* has his faults.

(ii)   *Negative pronouns*

Negative pronouns such as **niente, nulla** and **nessuno** need **non** before the verb when they follow it [➤27a(ii)] but not when they precede it. **Non** is not needed when the verb is preceded by **senza** 'without' [➤27a(v)].

Italian	English
Lunedì sono andato a letto *senza guardare niente*.	On Monday I went to bed *without watching anything*.

(iii)   'Anyone'

Care should be taken with the equivalent of 'anyone'. 'Not… anyone' is, of course, the same as 'no one' **nessuno**. 'Someone' and 'anyone' in the sense 'Is anyone/someone there?', although different in English, are both **qualcuno** in Italian. However, 'anyone' in the very wide sense of 'anyone at all' is **chiunque: chiunque avrebbe fatto la stessa cosa** 'anyone would have done the same thing'.

This same distinction applies to 'not...anything/nothing' **niente,** and to 'is there anything/something...?' which is **qualcosa** in both cases in Italian.

C'è *qualcosa* **da bere**?	Is there *anything/something* to drink?

Note that 'anyone... who' is **chi...** [➤Relative pronouns 23m(viii)].

 Be careful not to confuse the pronoun quantifiers with their adjectival equivalents. Compare the following examples:

Ho *molti* **amici.**	I have *many* friends.
Molti **di loro sono italiani.**	*Many* of them are Italian.

In the first example **molti** is an adjective and is not followed by the preposition **di**. In the second example **molti** is a pronoun and is normally followed by **di** in front of a noun or its equivalent. This same rule applies to most of the pronoun quantifiers listed above under 23k(i).

23l   Belonging together: possessive pronouns

Possessive pronouns are unique in that they represent two different nouns at once: the *possessor* and the *thing possessed*. Like possessive determiners they take their *form* from the *possessor*, and their *gender* and *number* from the *thing possessed*. Take care not to confuse the two: one person can own several things – which means that the possessive pronoun will be the *masculine or feminine plural* form – and several people can be joint owners of one thing – which means that the possessive pronoun will be *masculine or feminine singular*.

The possessive pronouns in Italian have identical forms to the possessive adjectives [➤21h(i)].

 Remember that the third person singular pronoun **il suo,** etc. can mean 'his', 'hers', 'its' as well as 'yours' (formal). The third person plural **i loro,** etc. can mean 'theirs' and 'yours' (formal). In formal writing **suo** and **loro** are often found with an initial capital letter.

(i)   Use

Possessive pronouns are normally used with the definite article:

Questa è la mia macchina; qual è *la tua?*	This is my car; which is *yours*?
La mia* è più bella de*lla tua.	*Mine* is nicer than *yours*.

The article is sometimes omitted when the pronoun comes after the verb **essere**:

Mamma mia, quanti regali! – Allora, questo è *tuo*, questo è *suo*, quello lì è *vostro* e questo qua è *mio*.	Goodness me, what a lot of presents! – Now then, this is *yours*, this is *hers*, that is *yours* and this one is *mine*.

The article is generally retained for emphasis and to underline the idea of ownership.

 This last example shows the distinction between **tuo** – singular and for one person – and **vostro** – plural and for more than one person. Remember that, although **suo** means 'hers' in this context, the masculine form is used because it refers to **regalo**.

 'Mine', etc. is not to be expressed by the possessive pronoun in expressions such as the following:

Uno dei *miei* amici/un *mio* amico	A friend of *mine*.
Una delle *nostre* zie/una *nostra* zia	An aunt of *ours*.

In these examples, **miei, mio, nostre, nostra** are possessive *adjectives*.

23m   *Relative pronouns*

(i)   *Use*

A relative pronoun relates or links a noun to a clause which closely follows it and which defines or comments on it. The noun is known as the *antecedent*, and the clause introduced by the relative pronoun is called a *relative clause* [▶5b].

Il film *che* abbiamo visto era clamoroso.	The film/movie *that* we saw was sensational.

In the above sentence, the relative clause is **che abbiamo visto**, and its function is to give more information about **il film**. The relative pronoun is **che**, in this case the object of **abbiamo visto**.

 Beware especially of the fact that in English, relative pronouns can take a variety of forms, and are often omitted altogether: **Il film che abbiamo visto** can be expressed in English as 'The film/movie that we saw' or 'The film/movie which we saw' or 'The film/movie we saw'. This variety of alternatives does not exist in Italian and the relative pronoun *must never be omitted.*

(ii)   *Che*

Che as a relative pronoun means 'who', 'whom', 'which' and 'that'. It is used, therefore, as both a subject and an object. It is invariable.

Sono andato al cinema con due persone *che* **conosco molto bene, Marco,** *che* **lavora in banca con me, e Sonia** *che* **è appena rientrata dopo un viaggio in Africa.**	I went to the cinema/film theater with two people (*whom*) I know very well, Marco, *who* works at the bank with me, and Sonia *who* has just returned after a trip to Africa.

(iii)   *Il che*

When the relative pronoun refers to an idea or a sentence, i.e. not to a preceding noun, then the neuter pronoun **il che** must be used.

Il divo del film muore alla fine, *il che* **ci ha sconvolto.**	The star of the film/movie dies at the end, *which* upset us.

It wasn't *the end* that upset them, but *the fact that the star dies.*

(iv)   Preposition + *cui*

When the relative pronoun follows a preposition you must *never* use **che**. Use the invariable pronoun **cui**.

Dove danno il film *di cui* **ci hai parlato?**	Where are they showing the film/movie *that* you spoke to us *about*?

> **Conosco molto bene le due persone *con cui* sono andato.**
>
> I know the two people (*that*) I went *with* very well.

 In both of the above examples you see that in English the preposition comes later on in the relative clause. In Italian, the preposition *must precede* the relative pronoun. Remember also that English often omits the relative pronoun whereas this is *not possible* in Italian.

Note the following useful expressions:

il motivo/la ragione *per cui*...	the reason *why*...
il momento/il giorno *in cui*...	the moment/the day *when*...
***per cui*...**	so (that), and so...

> **Avevamo sentito dire che la fine era un po' triste e questo era il motivo *per cui* mia sorella non voleva venire con noi.**
>
> We had heard that the end was a little sad and that was *the reason why* my sister didn't want to come with us.
>
> **La fine era un po' triste, *per cui* mia sorella ha deciso di non venire.**
>
> The end was a little sad, *and so* my sister decided not to come.

(v)   Definite article + **cui**

'Whose', 'of whom', 'of which' is conveyed by placing **cui** between the definite article and the noun.

> **Il film, *il cui* regista mi è completamente sconosciuto, ha avuto un successo strepitoso.**
>
> The film/movie, *whose* director is completely unknown to me, has been an outstanding success.
>
> **Mi pare un regista per *le cui* idee simpatizzo.**
>
> He seems (to be) a director *whose* ideas I go along with.

Il cui, etc. is strictly a determiner but it is more appropriate to deal with it here.

(vi)   *Il quale*

It is possible to replace **che** or **cui** with the relative pronoun **il quale**, which has the following forms:

il quale (masculine singular)	**i quali** (masculine plural)
la quale (feminine singular)	**le quali** (feminine plural)

Il quale, etc. is seldom used in place of **che** as a subject or object. It is used:

• particularly after prepositions, and very often therefore as a substitute for **a cui, di cui,** etc. The same examples as those in paragraphs (iv) and (v) above illustrate this point:

Dove danno il film *del quale* ci hai parlato?
Conosco molto bene le due persone *con le quali* sono andato.
Il film, il regista *del quale* mi è completamente sconosciuto, ha avuto un successo strepitoso.
Mi pare un regista per le idee *del quale* simpatizzo.

• to avoid ambiguity:

L'amica di Marco, *la quale* non conosco molto bene, non è potuta venire con noi.	Marco's friend, *whom* I don't know very well, couldn't come with us.

La quale here obviously refers to **l'amica**. However, this is only useful when there is one masculine and one feminine noun.

(vii) Quello che, quel che, ciò che

Quello che, quel che and **ciò che** convey the English 'what (that which)'. All three relative pronouns refer here to things and not to persons. It does not matter which form you use.

Non voglio che mi racconti *quello che* è successo alla fine.	I don't want you to tell me *what* happened at the end.
Ciò che succede alla fine è molto triste.	*What* happens at the end is very sad.

Note: **Quello che** 'the one who' also refers to people.

Chi è Marco? – È *quello che* lavora in banca.	Who is Marco? – He is *the one who* works in the bank.

To convey 'everything', 'all that' place **tutto** before **quello che**, etc.:

| Se mi racconti *tutto quello che* è successo dall'inizio alla fine, non avrò bisogno di andare a vedere il film. | If you tell me *everything that* happened from beginning to end, I won't need to go and see the film/movie. |

(viii)   Chi

Chi can convey a whole range of meanings such as 'he/she who', 'the one(s) who', 'people who', 'those who', 'whoever', 'anyone who'. Although it can be used in a plural sense, the verb *must always be in the singular*.

Chi va a vedere questo film non sarà deluso.	*Anyone who* goes to see this film/movie will not be disappointed.
Se non vuoi sapere quello che succede alla fine, è meglio non chiedere a *chi* l'ha già visto.	If you don't want to know what happens at the end, it is better not to ask *people who* have already seen it.
Chi impara tutte queste regole grammaticali sarà premiato.	*Those who* learn all these grammar rules will be rewarded.

Chi is found in a number of proverbs:

| *Chi* dorme non piglia pesci. | The early bird catches the worm. |
| *Chi* va piano va sano e va lontano. | Slow and steady wins the race. |

• 'Those who' can also be expressed by **coloro che** and **quelli che,** which take a plural verb:

| *Coloro che vanno* a vedere questo film non *saranno* delusi. | *Those who* go to see this film/movie *will* not *be* disappointed. |

Note: **Chi** tends to be preferred to the more formal **coloro**.

• To express 'all those who' place **tutti** in front of **coloro che** or **quelli che**:

| *Tutti quelli che* avranno studiato dettagliatamente questo capitolo saranno stanchi morti. | *All those who* have studied this chapter in detail will be dead tired. |

24 Giving vent to your feelings: exclamations and interjections

24a Exclamations

Exclamations express emotions such as delight, anger, surprise or fear. The standard exclamations are introduced by words normally used as interrogatives, and may be created with whatever vocabulary is appropriate.

- Before a noun phrase **Che** is the standard device:

Che bella sorpresa!	What a lovely surprise!
Che peccato!	What a pity!
Che spavento!	What a fright!
Che delusione!	What a disappointment!
Che barba!	What a bore!
Che fregatura!	What a rip-off!
Che schifo!	How disgusting!

- **Che** + adjective is also very common:

Che bello!	How nice/lovely!
Che freddo!	Isn't it cold!
Che triste!	How sad!
Che scemo!	How stupid!

- The following type of construction is even more emphatic:

Che bravo che sei!	How good you are!
Che pignolo che sei!	How fussy you are!
Che brutte abitudini che hai!	What bad habits you have!
Che pigrone che sei!	What a lazy bones you are!

- 'How' + adjective or adverb can also be rendered by **Come** + verb + adjective or adverb:

Come siete gentili!	How kind you are!
Come sei buffo!	How funny you are!

| Come suona bene il pianoforte! | How well she plays the piano! |
| Come mangiano male! | How badly they eat! |

* 'What a lot of...!' is **Quanto...!**

Quanta gente!	What a lot of people!
Quanto lavoro!	What a lot of work!
Quanto hanno bevuto!	What a lot they have drunk!

* '(Just) look how...!' is **Guarda (un po') come...!** + verb:

| Guarda come piove! | Look how it's raining! |
| Guarda un po' come mi parla! | Just look how he speaks to me! |

24b Interjections

Interjections range from words or short phrases which are really cut-down exclamations through to the range of noises associated with emotions.

* Some are reactions to the senses – sadness, pain, taste, smell, sound, sight – and are barely words.

Ah, povero ragazzo!	*Oh*, poor boy!
Ahi, mi fai male!	*Ouch*, you're hurting me!
Eh, non c'è più speranza!	*Oh*, there's no hope left!
Puah, che puzza!	*Ugh*, what a smell!

* Some express boredom, resignation, doubt.

Uffa, che scocciatura!	*Ouf*, what a bore!
Bah, cosa ci posso fare io!	*Ah well*, what can I do about it!
Boh, penso di sì!	*Ah*, I think so!

Note that some interjections such as **ah** and **eh** can communicate different feelings in different contexts. It is worth remembering also that it is not always easy, or even possible, to express in English certain interjections used in Italian. Their meaning usually becomes more obvious in a real life situation as many interjections are accompanied by gestures.

* Some express surprise or disbelief.

| **Davvero!** | Really! |
| **Ma come?** | What!/Do you mean to say? |

Ma dai!	Come off it!
Eh!	Phew! Did it really!
Mamma mia!	Goodness gracious!
Ma insomma!	For Heaven's sake!
Ma no!	Really!/You don't say!
Ma via!	Go on!

• Some express pleading or exhortation to action.

Per l'amor di Dio!	For goodness sake!/For Heaven's sake!
Coraggio!	Don't be afraid!/Cheer up!
Dai!/Su!/Andiamo!	Come on!

• Some contain a warning or instruction.

Aiuto!	Help!
Attenzione!	Attention please!/Mind!/Look out!
Avanti!	Come in!/Move forward!/Go on!
Fermo!	Stop!/Stay where you are!/Hold it!
Fuori!	Get out!
Giù le mani!	Hands off!
Occhio!	Mind!/Watch out!
Silenzio!	Quiet!/Hush!
Smettila!	Stop it!
To'!/Tieni!	Here you are!
Voce!	Speak up!

• Some express reactions such as indignation or disappointment.

Neanche per sogno!	Not on your life!
E allora?	So what?
Accidenti!/Maledizione!	Damn!

• Others pleasure or joy.

Bravo!	Well done!/Bravo!
Fantastico!	Marvellous!/Wonderful!/Splendid!
Magnifico!	Wonderful!/Brilliant!
Stupendo!	Super!/Great!

Note: Like all languages, Italian too has its fair range of swear words. A good current dictionary will no doubt provide a fair selection of those you may require, but you should be careful about how you use them!

E

LINKING AND MODIFYING MEANINGS: PREPOSITIONS AND ADVERBIAL EXPRESSIONS

25 Prepositions and their uses

25a What does a preposition do?

A preposition is a connecting word, which is placed in front of a noun or pronoun to relate it to the rest of the sentence.

25b Prepositional phrases linked to verbs

A prepositional phrase can be linked to a verb in two ways.

(i) Free-standing adverbial expressions

The prepositional phrases may be a free-standing adverbial expression [➤27], which modifies or extends the meaning of the verb by answering questions such as **Quando?** 'When?', **Dove?** 'Where?', or **Come?** 'How?' [➤6d(vi)-(viii)].

Quando sono partiti i tuoi parenti? – *Verso le sette*.	When did your relatives leave? – *Around seven o'clock.*
Dove pensano di fermarsi stasera? – *Vicino alla frontiera*.	Where are they thinking of stopping tonight? – *Near the border.*
Come viaggiano? -*In macchina*.	How are they travelling? – *By car.*

(ii)
Certain common prepositions link particular verbs to the following noun phrases [➤8h] or to the infinitive of another verb [➤8j]. (See the paragraphs mentioned for details.)

(iii) Prepositional phrases

Prepositions like *di*, *con* and *a* are frequently used in Italian to create prepositional phrases with the value of an adjective [➤3b, 25c(iv)], a relative clause [➤25c(vi)] or an adverb [➤27b(ii)].

Chi era quella signora *di mezza età con i capelli ricci*? – Era mia zia.	Who was that *middle-aged* lady with *curly hair*? – She was my aunt.

Perché zoppicava? – Da quando si è rotta la gamba, cammina _a stento_.	Why was she limping? – Since she broke her leg, she has _difficulty_ walking.

(iv)   Verbs after prepositions

The only part of the verb which can follow a preposition is the infinitive [►10a(iv)].

Volevano partire di buon mattino _per evitare_ l'ora di punta.	They wanted to leave early _(in order) to avoid_ the rush hour.
Hanno fatto colazione _prima di partire_.	They had breakfast _before setting off_.

(v)   Verbs + prepositions; adjectives, adverbs, nouns + prepositions

A, **di** and sometimes **per** are frequently used as fixed links following particular verbs [►8j].

Abbiamo cercato _di_ convincerli _a_ rimanere ancora qualche giorno. A un certo punto stavano _per_ cambiare idea ma alla fine ...	We tried _to_ convince them _to_ stay another few days. At one point they were _about to_ change their minds but in the end ...

•   Many nouns and some adjectives are linked to a following infinitive by **di**.

Si capisce la loro decisione _di_ partire presto con la speranza _di_ evitare gli ingorghi stradali. Saranno contenti _di_ tornare a casa.	You can understand their decision _to_ leave early in the hope _of_ avoiding the traffic jams. They will be happy _to_ get back home.

[For adverbs linked to a following infinitive by **da** ►25c(iii).]

25c   Common prepositions and their use

Because prepositions are used in a variety of ways, with considerable variation of meaning both within and between languages, it is generally easier to learn them in context, that is in association with particular expressions, fixed phrases or defined uses. The meaning in English is often the least reliable clue to the choice of the appropriate preposition in Italian. Prepositions in Italian can be one word or compound prepositions of two or more words joined to the following noun or pronoun with *a* or *di*.

(i)   The simple prepositions *a, da, di, in, su, per, con*

The prepositions **a, da, di, in, su, per,** and **con** are among the most frequently used in Italian and will therefore be dealt with in some detail. **A, da, di, in** and **su** combine with the definite article to form one word [▶21c(vii)].

(ii)   *A*

- Destination, location, direction, position (to, at, in, on):

andare a casa	to go home
andare a scuola	to go to school
stare a letto	to stay in bed
stare a casa	to stay at home
a Milano	to/at/in Milan (**a** before names of towns/cities)
voltare a destra, a sinistra	to turn right/left
la prima strada a destra/sinistra	the first street on the right/left
alla televisione	on television
alla radio	on the radio
al sole	in the sun
all'ombra	in the shade
all'aperto	outdoors, in the open

- Time, age, distance, speed, measure, price (at, in, until, by):

all'una	at one o'clock
alle otto	at eight o'clock
a mezzanotte	at midnight
lavorare dalle sei alle dieci	to work from six until ten
all'alba	at dawn
a luglio	in July
a Natale/Pasqua	at Christmas/Easter

una volta al giorno/alla	once a day/a week/
settimana/al mese/all'anno	a month/a year
a presto!	see you soon!
a stasera!	see you this evening!
a trent'anni	at the age of thirty
abitare a tre chilometri dalla stazione	to live three kilometres/kilometers from the station
viaggiare a duecento chilometri l'ora	to travel at two hundred kilometres/kilometers an hour
vendere al chilo	to sell by the kilo
questi dischi si vendono a diecimila (lire)	these records are being sold at ten thousand (lire)

- Method, means, manner, use (by, on, in, with):

fatto a mano	made by hand
scrivere a matita	to write in/with a pencil
a piedi, a cavallo	on foot/on horseback
ad alta/a bassa voce	in a loud/quiet voice
ai ferri/alla griglia	grilled
una cotoletta alla milanese	a cutlet Milanese style
un panino al prosciutto	a ham roll
a braccia aperte	with open arms
imparare a memoria	to learn by heart
chiudere a chiave	to lock
una barca a vela	a sailing boat
una cucina a gas	a gas cooker
un motore a reazione	a jet engine

- Added detail or features:

una giacca a doppio petto	a double-breasted jacket
una maglia a strisce	a striped sweater
una televisione a colori	a colour/color television

- After ordinals [▶28b(i)], **solo, unico** and with some adjectives:

Erano i primi ad arrivare e gli ultimi a partire.	They were the first to arrive and the last to leave.
Il solo a dire qualcosa.	The only one to say something.
Siamo pronti a mangiare.	We are ready to eat.
Ma non siamo disposti a lavare i piatti.	But we are not willing to wash up.
È nocivo alla salute.	It is harmful to your health.

Note that **ad** often replaces **a** before a word beginning with a vowel – see the first example above – and especially if the word begins with the letter **a**.

- After the verb **giocare** to talk about games:

giocare a calcio	to play football/soccer
giocare a carte	to play cards

- In some invocations:

al fuoco!	fire!	**al ladro!**	stop thief!

- Other uses:

a prima vista	at first sight
a perdita d'occhio	as far as the eye can see
un senatore a vita	a senator for life
a poco a poco	little by little
a due a due	two by two

[For **a** with other adverbial expressions ➤27b(ii).]

- With verbs taking an indirect object in Italian but not in English:

assomigliare a	look like

[For other examples ➤8h(i).]

(iii)   Da

- Origin, movement from/to/by/through a place:

venire da Bari	to come from Bari
arrivare da Venezia	to arrive from Venice
uscire dal negozio	to go/come out of the shop/store
andare dal dentista	to go to the dentist's
passare da Bologna	to go through/via Bologna
uscire dalla finestra	to go out through the window

Note: It is worth comparing the use of **da** and **di** in the following constructions:

Da dove vieni? – Vengo *da* Bari.	Where do you come *from*? – I come *from* Bari.
But	
Di dove sei? – Sono *di* Bari.	Where are you *from*? – I'm *from* Bari.

- At someone's place, in someone's town or country:

abitare dai genitori	to live with your parents
cenare dai nonni	to have dinner at your grandparents'
da loro si mangia bene	at their house you eat well
da noi non c'è questo problema	we haven't got this problem (in our country)

- Purpose:

un abito da sera	an evening dress
un cavallo da corsa	a racehorse
una sala da giochi	a games room
una camera da letto	a bedroom
una macchina da cucire	a sewing machine
un costume da bagno	a bathing costume/suit
un bicchiere da vino	a wine glass

Note: 'A glass of wine' is **un bicchiere di vino**.

- Necessity, obligation:

la roba da lavare	things to wash/be washed
camicie da stirare	shirts to iron/be ironed
lettere da scrivere	letters to write/be written

- After adverbs such as **molto, troppo, tanto, poco** and the indefinite pronouns **qualcosa** and **niente**:

molto/troppo/tanto/poco da fare	a lot/too much/so much/little (not much) to do
qualcosa da bere	something to drink
niente da mangiare	nothing to eat

- Description:

l'uomo dal naso storto	the man with the crooked nose
la ragazza dagli occhi verdi	the girl with the green eyes
la casa dalle persiane nere	the house with the black shutters

- Manner, worthy of:

comportarsi da gentiluomo	to behave like a gentleman
mascherarsi da infermiera	to dress up as a nurse
un comportamento da gentiluomo	gentlemanly behaviour/behavior
una vita da cani	a dog's life

• After passives [➤17c]:

Molte case sono state distrutte dall'uragano.	Many houses have been destroyed by the hurricane.
Questo libro è stato scritto da un mio amico.	This book was written by a friend of mine.

• Price, value:

un biglietto da ventimila lire	a twenty thousand lire ticket
una gonna da novantamila lire	a ninety thousand lire skirt

• Cause:

morire dalla fame	to die of hunger
tremare dal freddo	to tremble with cold

• Time, age:

Imparo l'italiano da tre mesi.	I have been learning Italian for three months.
Pioveva da tre giorni.	It had been raining for three days.
Da giovane non praticavo nessuno sport.	When I was young I didn't play any sport.
Da studente la mia materia preferita era la matematica.	As a student my favourite/favorite subject was mathematics.

[For use of tenses after **da** ➤12a(iv), 13b(viii).]

• Note also the following expressions:

cieco da un occhio	blind in one eye
sordo da un orecchio	deaf in one ear

Never elide **da** before a vowel, for example, **fare** *da* **interprete** 'to act as interpreter'.

(iv) Di

• Possession, definition, specification:

l'appartamento di mio fratello	my brother's flat/apartmentt
il treno delle nove	the nine o'clock train
il professore d'italiano	the Italian teacher
il direttore dell'ufficio	the office manager
una vista del mare	a view of the sea

un uomo di mezza età	a middle-aged man
un bambino di sei mesi	a six month old baby
l'isola di Capri	the island of Capri

- After many expressions of quantity:

migliaia di turisti	thousands of tourists
un paio di volte	a couple of times
una fetta di pane	a slice of bread
un mazzo di fiori	a bunch of flowers
un grappolo d'uva	a bunch of grapes
un litro di vino	a litre/liter of wine

- In partitives, i.e. to express 'some, any, of, of the' [▶21f]:

del pane	some bread
uno di loro	one of them
una delle riviste	one of the magazines

- Material, contents:

un sacchetto di plastica	a plastic bag
una camicia di cotone	a cotton shirt
una borsa di pelle	a leather bag
una medaglia d'argento	a silver medal
una scatola di fiammiferi	a box of matches
una lattina di birra	a can of beer

- With a number of expressions of time:

di giorno	by day, in the daytime
di pomeriggio	in the afternoon
di sera	in the evening
di notte	at night, during the night
d'estate	in summer
d'inverno	in winter
alle otto di mattina	at eight o'clock in the morning/at 8 a.m.

- In adverbial expressions of manner:

vestire di nero	to dress in black
essere di buon/cattivo umore	to be in a good/bad mood
ridere di cuore	to laugh heartily
uscire di corsa	to run out

- After certain adjectives:

lieto di conoscer La	*pleased to* meet you
un paese *ricco di* materie prime	a country *rich in* raw materials
un libro *povero di* idee	a book *lacking in* ideas
non sono *responsabile del* loro comportamento	I am not *responsible for* their behaviour/behavior
un camion *carico di* legno	a lorry *loaded with* wood

- Origin, motion from a place:

sono di Parma	I am from Parma
la gente del Sud	the people from the South
uscire di casa	to leave the house
uscire di strada	to go off the road

- After **qualcosa, niente** when followed by an adjective:

niente di speciale	nothing special
qualcosa di interessante	something interesting

- Other uses:

spero di sì	I hope so
penso di no	I think not
ho detto di sì/no	I said yes/no
conoscere qualcuno di persona/di vista/di nome	to know someone personally/by sight/by name
dare del tu/del Lei a qualcuno	to address someone with the **tu/Lei** form

[For use of **di** after comparatives ➤22f(i); after superlatives ➤22f(ii); after verbs ➤8h(ii).]

(v)   In

- *To* or *in* a place

andare in città	to go to town
andare in banca	to go to the bank
lavorare in ufficio	to work in an office
abitare in periferia	to live on the outskirts
abitare in montagna	to live in the mountains

Note: **In** is similarly used with countries, continents, regions and large islands.

andare in Italia/in Europa/in Calabria/in Sicilia	to go to Italy/Europe/Calabria/Sicily

• Transport

andare in macchina/in treno/in aereo/in pullman/in bicicletta	to go by car/train/plane/coach (bus)/bike

• With many expressions of time:

in gennaio	in January
nel 1994	in 1994
in primavera/in autunno	in spring/in autumn, fall
nel Cinquecento	in the sixteenth century
arrivare in anticipo/in ritardo	to arrive early/late
il pullman è arrivato in orario	the coach/bus arrived on time
ho finito il lavoro in un'ora	I finished the work in one hour (duration, i.e. 'one hour' is *how long it took to complete the work*)

• Manner:

parlare in fretta	to speak quickly
camminare in punta di piedi	to walk on tiptoe
vivere in pace	to live in peace
parlare in dialetto	to speak in dialect
guardare in silenzio	to watch in silence

• Other uses:

se fossi in te	if I were you
la parola non viene in mente	the word doesn't come/spring to mind
stare in piedi	to stand
essere bravo in lingue	to be good at languages
essere debole in scienze	to be weak at/in sciences
siamo in pochi	there are only a few of us
eravamo in cinque	there were five of us

(vi) Su

• Place, position:

il ponte sul fiume	the bridge over the river
una città sul mare	a city by the sea

PREPOSITIONS AND ADVERBIAL EXPRESSIONS

Il giornale è sul tavolo.	The newspaper is on the table.
L'appartamento dà sul parco.	The flat/apartment overlooks the park.

- Approximation:

essere sulla settantina — to be around seventy

Il viaggio costerà sulle centomila lire.	The journey will cost about one hundred thousand lire.
Peso sui settanta chili.	I weigh approximately seventy kilos.

- About, on, concerning:

una lezione sul Rinascimento	a lesson on the Renaissance
una conferenza sulla musica classica	a lecture about classical music
informarsi sulla situazione politica	to find out about the political situation

- Out of:

otto su dieci — eight out of ten

- Other uses:

l'abbiamo letto sul giornale	we read it in the newspaper
i pantaloni fatti su misura	made-to-measure trousers/pants
prendere qualcuno sul serio	to take someone seriously

(vii) Per

- Movement to/through/around a place

partire per la Spagna	to set off for Spain
passare per la Francia	to go through France
camminare per la città	to walk round the town

- With a number of expressions of time:

Ho studiato per tre ore.	I studied for three hours.
Devo fare questo per domani.	I have to do this for/by tomorrow.
Si fermeranno per due settimane.	They will stay for two weeks.

- Because of, out of:

Per il freddo, ho deciso di stare a casa.	Because of the cold, I decided to stay at home.
L'abbiamo fatto per curiosità.	We did it out of curiosity.

• Intended for, in relation to :

Questo regalo è per te.	This present is for you.
È alto per la sua età.	He's tall for his age.

• By means of:

Le ho comunicato la notizia per telefono.	I told her the news by phone.
Ti manderò le informazioni per posta.	I shall send you the information by post/mail.

• Purpose:

Ho deciso di fare il corso per migliorare il mio italiano.	I decided to do the course (in order) to improve my Italian.
D'inverno devo sempre usare la crema per le mani.	In winter I always have to use hand cream.

• Mathematical calculations:

cinque per cinque	five times five
dividere per due	divide by two

• Other uses:

stare per	be about to [▶8c]
fare qualcosa per scherzo	do something as a joke
uno per volta	one at a time
prendere qualcuno per il braccio	take someone by the arm
andare su/giù per le scale	go up/down the stairs
per favore/per piacere/per cortesia	please
per caso	by chance
per fortuna	fortunately

(viii) *Con*

• With

PREPOSITIONS AND ADVERBIAL EXPRESSIONS

Non usciamo più con loro.	We are not going out with them again.

- Towards:

Si sono comportati male con noi.	They behaved badly towards us.

- Description:

la ragazza con i capelli corti **la signora con gli occhiali**	the girl with the short hair the lady with the glasses

- With, in view of:

Come facciamo a studiare con questo caldo?	How can we study with this heat?

- With, despite:

Con tutti i suoi problemi finanziari, è sempre di buon umore.	Despite all his financial problems, he is always in a good mood.

- Transport:

viaggiare con la macchina/con il treno   to travel by car/by train

- Manner:

fare le cose con calma   to do things calmly
accettare l'invito con piacere   to accept the invitation with pleasure
agire con prudenza   to act wisely

- Other uses:

con mia grande sorpresa   to my great surprise
con nostro grande sollievo   to our great relief

(ix)   *Other simple prepositions*

Those marked with an asterisk take the preposition **di** before a disjunctive pronoun [▶23h(i)]. This same rule also applies to **su** dealt with under 25c(vi) above.

attraverso	across	**circa**	about, regarding
contro*	against	**dentro***	inside
dietro*	behind	**dopo***	after
durante	during	**eccetto**	except
fra/tra*	among, between	**lungo**	along
malgrado	in spite of	**mediante**	by means of
nonostante	in spite of	**presso***	near, with
salvo	except, barring	**secondo**	according to
senza*	without	**sopra***	above, upon
sotto*	under, beneath	**tramite**	through, by means of
tranne	except	**verso***	towards, around

Siamo partiti *verso* le dieci di sera. Abbiamo viaggiato *durante* la notte. *Salvo* imprevisti, speriamo di arrivare alla nostra destinazione domani pomeriggio. *Malgrado* la distanza che dobbiamo percorrere, abbiamo in mente di fare il viaggio *senza* sosta. Siamo in quattro e, *tranne* Marco, sappiamo tutti guidare.

We set off *around* ten in the evening. We travelled *during* the night. *Barring* mishaps, we hope to arrive at our destination tomorrow afternoon. *Despite* the distance we have to travel, we intend to do the journey *without* stopping. There are four of us and, *except for* Marco, we can all drive.

(x)   Compound prepositions with *a*

accanto a	next to, beside
davanti a	in front of
di fronte a	opposite, facing
dirimpetto a	opposite
fino/sino a	up to, until
in cima a	at the top of
in fondo a	at the end of, at the bottom of
in mezzo a	in the middle of
in testa a	at the head of
incontro a	towards
insieme a	along with, together
intorno a	around
quanto a	as for

riguardo a	regarding
rispetto a	regarding, compared to
vicino a	near

La nostra casa è *accanto a* un bar che rimane aperto *fino a* tardi. *Di fronte al* bar c'è un locale notturno che chiude *intorno alle* due di notte. Molti giovani, quando escono dal bar o dal locale notturno, si fermano *in mezzo alla* strada a parlare. Delle volte si mettono a cantare proprio *davanti alla* mia finestra – ho una camera al pianterreno. *In fondo alla* strada c'è un grandissimo parco. Perché non vanno lì a parlare e poi non danno fastidio a nessuno? *Rispetto all'*anno scorso la situazione va sempre peggiorando.	Our house is *next to* a bar that stays open *until* late. *Opposite* the bar there is a night club which closes *around* two a.m. Many young people, when they leave the bar or night club, stop *in the middle* of the street to talk. Sometimes they start singing right *in front of* my window – I have a room on the ground floor. *At the end of* the street there is a huge park. Why don't they go there and talk and then they don't bother anyone? *Compared to* last year the situation is getting worse and worse.

(xi)   Compound prepositions with *di*

a causa di	because of, on account of
a favore di	in favour of
ad eccezione di	with the exception of
a seconda di	according to
fuori di	outside, out
invece di	instead of
nel mezzo di	in the middle of
per mezzo di	by means of
per via di	by means of, because of
prima di	before

Per via degli esami che darò fra poco, devo studiare giorno e notte *ad eccezione di* sabato, l'unico giorno in cui non faccio nulla.	*Because of* the exams that I shall be taking shortly, I have to study day and night *with the exception of* Saturday, the only day when I do nothing.

Invece di studiare, esco con i
miei amici e non vado mai a
letto *prima di* mezzanotte.
Sabato scorso sono stato *fuori
di* casa tutto il giorno.

Instead of studying, I go out with
my friends and I never go to bed
before midnight. Last Saturday I
was *out of* the house all day.

Note: Occasionaly **fuori** is used without **di**:

Mio fratello è *fuori* città.

My brother is *out of* town.

(xii) Compound prepositions with *da*

fin (sin) da   ever since, (as) from
lontano da   far from
lungi da   far from

Non abitiamo *lontano dal*
centro. *Fin da giovane* mi è
sempre piaciuta questa città. I
miei genitori pensano di
traslocarsi in campagna ma io
sono *lungi dal* fare una cosa del
genere.

We don't live *far from* the
centre/center. *Ever since* I was
young I have always liked this
town. My parents are thinking of
moving into the country but I
wouldn't *dream of* doing such a
thing.

26 Types of adverbial expression

26a What is an adverbial expression?

(i) Adverbial expressions (often shortened to *adverbials*) mainly answer the questions listed in paragraphs 6d(vi) to 6d(x). We say that they modify meanings because they complete, alter or even contradict them. They may modify the meanings of verbs, adjectives or of the whole sentence. Adverbial expressions can take the form of a single word, a phrase or a complete clause with its own verb.

Te lo spiegherò.	I shall explain it to you.
Te lo spiegherò *dopo.*	(afterwards: *adverb*)
Te lo spiegherò *dopo la conferenza.*	(after the lecture: *adverbial phrase*)
Te lo spiegherò *quando la conferenza sarà finita.*	(when the conference is over: *adverbial clause*)

Each of these three adverbials performs the same sort of function, of modifying the meaning of **Te lo spiegherò** by adding information, in this case about when the action will happen. The word **dopo** is itself an adverb, but the adverbial phrase and the adverbial clause are simply groups of words performing the same role.

[For more detail on adverbial clauses ►5a(ii).]

(ii) *Adverb + adjective/adverb*

Adverbs can modify verbs, as in the above illustration, but also adjectives and other adverbs.

È *molto* **facile da capire.**	It's *very* easy to understand. (**molto** modifies the adjective **facile**)
Capiscono *molto* **facilmente.**	They understand *very* easily. (**molto** modifies the adverb **facilmente**)

26b *Formation of adverbs*

(i) *Adverbs formed from adjectives [▶22]*

Most of these adverbs answer the question **Come?** 'How?'

The majority of adverbs in Italian (as in English) are formed from adjectives, by adding **-mente** to the feminine form of the adjective. Thus, for adjectives ending in **-o** [▶22a(i)] the formation is as follows:

Adjective	*Feminine*	*Adverb*	
lento	**lenta**	**lentamente**	slowly
onesto	**onesta**	**onestamente**	honestly
sincero	**sincera**	**sinceramente**	sincerely

• There are some exceptions to the above rule and they include:

violento	**violentemente**	violently
benevolo	**benevolmente**	benevolently
malevolo	**malevolmente**	malevolently
leggero	**leggermente**	lightly

• An adjective ending in **-e** [▶22a(i)] forms its adverb by adding **-mente**:

recente	**recentemente**	recently
breve	**brevemente**	briefly
cortese	**cortesemente**	politely

• Adjectives ending in **-le** and **-re** drop the final **-e** before adding **-mente**:

facile	**facilmente**	easily
normale	**normalmente**	normally
particolare	**particolarmente**	particularly
regolare	**regolarmente**	regularly

 The final **-e** is not dropped however when the **-le** and **-re** are preceded by another consonant:

folle	**follemente**	madly
acre	**acremente**	bitterly

• Some adverbs are formed from their adjectives in a completely irregular way:

buono	good	**bene**	well
cattivo	bad	**male**	badly

migliore	better	**meglio**	better

(ii)   *Alternatives to adverbs formed from adjectives*

•   Adjectives are used as adverbs in a range of fixed expressions:

abitare lontano/vicino	live far away/nearby
andare forte	go fast
costare caro	cost a lot of money (dearly)
lavorare sodo	work hard
mirare alto	aim high
parlare chiaro	speak clearly
parlare piano	speak quietly
picchiare sodo	hit hard
stare fermo	keep still
tagliare corto	cut short
tenere duro	stand fast
vestire leggero	dress lightly

•   In formal style, adjectives sometimes replace adverbs; they must then agree with the subject of the verb [➤22c(i)].

Si avviarono verso casa *lenti* e *silenziosi*.	They set off home *slowly* and *silently*.

•   There is a small number of adverbs that end in **-oni**:

bocconi	flat on one's face
carponi	on all fours
ciondoloni	dangling, hanging
dondoloni	idly
ginocchioni	on one's knees
a tastoni	gropingly

•   As the addition of **-mente** makes some adverbs rather long and clumsy, Italian often resorts to using an advervial phrase [➤26a(i)] using **con** or another suitable preposition + noun or **in un modo** (masculine), **in una maniera** (feminine) + adjective [➤22a].

La gente ha reagito *con calma, pazienza* e *in silenzio*.	
La gente ha reagito *in un modo calmo, paziente* e *silenzioso*.	The people reacted *calmly, patiently* and *silently*.
La gente ha reagito *in una maniera calma, paziente* e *silenziosa*.	

(iii) Other adverbs

Many of the most common adverbs, especially those answering the questions **Quando?** 'When?' and **Dove?** 'Where?', are not formed from adjectives. These are often short words such as **già** 'already', **fuori** 'outside', **giù** 'down', **dietro** 'behind' [➤27]. In many cases also, common words are used as adverbs, prepositions, adjectives, pronouns and/or conjunctions in different settings.

Abitiamo *vicino*.	We live *nearby*. (adverb)
Abitiamo *vicino alla* stazione.	We live *near* the station. (preposition)
La mia amica abita nella città *vicina*.	My friend lives in the *nearby* town. (adjective)
I nostri *vicini* sono molto gentili.	Our *neighbours* are very kind. (noun)
Ho fatto *poco* lavoro.	I've done *little* work. (adjective)
Ne ho fatto *poco*.	I've done *little*. (pronoun)
Ho finito *poco* fa.	I finished *a short while* ago. (adverb)

An adverb is an invariable part of speech. When the same word is used as an adjective then it must agree in gender and number with the noun it describes [➤22a(i)]. This point is illustrated by two of the examples above, i.e. **Abitiamo *vicino*** and **nella città *vicina***. In the first example **vicino** is an adverb and in the second example it functions as an adjective.

(iv) Comparison of adverbs

The comparative and superlative of adverbs in Italian are formed in much the same way as for adjectives [➤22f] by the use of **più..., il più..., meno..., il meno...**

Adverb	Comparative	Superlative
facilmente easily	**più facilmente** more easily **meno facilmente** less easily	**il più facilmente** most easily **il meno facilmente** least easily

Not all adverbs have a comparative and superlative form. Those that do are mainly adverbs of manner described under 26b(i) above, with the exception of adverbs ending in **-oni**, and a few adverbs of time and place such as **spesso** 'often', **tardi** 'late', **presto** 'early', **lontano** 'far', **vicino** 'near'.

Siete arrivati presto. – Sì ma siamo partiti *più presto* del previsto. Gli altri arriveranno *più tardi*. Come sapete, abitano *il più lontano* dal centro-città.	You have arrived early. – Yes but we set off *earlier* than expected. The others will arrive *later*. As you know, they live *furthest* from the town centre/center.

• As with adjectives, a small number of adverbs have irregular comparatives and superlatives:

Adverb	Comparative	Superlative	Absolute superlative (see (v) below)
bene well	**meglio** better	**il meglio** the best	**ottimamente/benissmo** very well
male badly	**peggio** worse	**il peggio** the worst	**pessimamente/malissimo** very badly
molto very, much	**più** more	**il più** the most	**moltissimo** very much
poco little	**meno** less	**il meno** the least	**pochissimo** very little

Quando il mio amico italiano parla con me al telefono capisco *poco*. Se comincia a parlare in inglese capisco *meno*, a dire il vero capisco *pochissimo*. È ancora *peggio* quando io cerco di dire qualcosa in italiano.	When my Italian friend speaks to me on the telephone I understand *little*. If he begins to speak in English I understand *less*, to tell the truth I understand *very little*. It's even *worse* when I try to say something in Italian.

| Però, se riesco a mettere insieme tre parole il mio amico mi fa sempre complimenti e dice che parlo *benissimo* ma vorrei parlare molto *meglio*. | However, if I manage to string three words together my friend always pays me compliments and says that I speak *very well* but I would like to speak much *better*. |

* Note the expression **il più/meno** + adverb + **possibile**:

| Abbiamo cercato di arrivare *il più presto possibile*. | We tried to arrive *as early as possible*. |

* Note the use of **di più/di meno** 'more/less, most/least' in the following type of construction:

| Dei due film questo mi è piaciuto *di più/di meno*. Quale film ti è piaciuto *di più/di meno*? | Of the two films/movies I liked this one more/less. Which film/movie did you like most/least? |

(v) The absolute superlative

This is simply an emphatic form of the adverb. It has two forms. Adverbs such as **spesso, tardi, presto, lontano** and **vicino** add **-issimo** after removing the final vowel – the absolute superlative of adjectives is formed in the same way [➤22f(v)]:

spesso	spessissimo	very often
tardi	tardissimo	very late
presto	prestissimo	very early
lontano	lontanissimo	very far
vicino	vicinissimo	very near

Adverbs ending in **-mente** form the absolute superlative by adding **-mente** to the feminine singular superlative of the corresponding adjective :

| facile | facilissima | **facilissimamente** very easily |

Note: This form of the absolute superlative is seldom used but the same meaning can be expressed by placing **molto** or **assai** 'very' before the adverb.

Abbiamo seguito _molto/assai_ facilmente tutte le direzioni.	We followed all the directions _very_ easily.

26c   Suffixes

There are a few adverbs whose meaning can be modified by suffixes:

bene	well
benino	quite well
benone	very well
male	badly
maluccio	not too well
poco	little
pochino	rather little
tardi	late
tardino	rather late

Stamattina mi sentivo _maluccio_ e sono andato in camera per sdraiarmi. Adesso mi sento _benone_.	This morning I was feeling _rather poorly_ and I went to my room to lie down. Now I feel _very well indeed_.
Non c'è da meravigliarsi dato che ieri sera hai mangiato _pochino_, hai bevuto mezzo litro di vino e sei andato _tardino_ a letto.	It's not surprising given that last night you ate _rather little_, you drank half a litre/liter of wine and you went to bed _rather late_.

[For position of adverbs➤27e.]

27 What adverbial expressions do

27a Negative expressions

(i) Making a verb negative

To make a verb negative **non** is placed immediately before it. It can only be separated from the verb by object pronouns [➤23b(ii)-(vi), 23c].

Non mangio la carne. **Non la mangio.**   I *don't eat* meat. I *don't eat it.*

(ii) Negative expressions

If any negative expression follows the verb in Italian, **non** must be placed before the verb. **Non**, however is *not required* if the negative expression comes first [➤27a(iv)], or it stands on its own without a verb [➤27a(vi)], or the verb is preceded by **senza** 'without' [➤27a(v)].

Most, though not all, negative expressions are adverbials, and it is convenient to list all of them here, since the above rule applies to them all.

no	no
non	not
non ... mai	never, not ever
non ... niente	nothing, not anything
non ... nulla	nothing, not anything
non ... affatto	not ... at all
non ... per niente	not ... at all
non ... mica	not ... at all
non ... più	no more, no longer, not any more, not any longer
non ... da nessuna parte	nowhere
non ... né ... né	neither ... nor
non ... neanche	not even
non ... nemmeno	not even
non ... neppure	not even

PREPOSITIONS AND ADVERBIAL EXPRESSIONS

non ... nessuno	nobody, not anybody
non ... nessuno	not ... any, no
non ... alcuno	not any, no

Note: **Niente** and **nessuno** are pronouns [➤23k(i)].
Alcuno and **nessuno** also function as determiners [➤21g(i)].

Quest'estate *non* vado *da nessuna parte*. *Non* ho *nessuna* voglia di uscire con questo caldo. I miei amici *non* capiscono *affatto* perché preferisco stare a casa. Abito a due passi dal mare ma *non* vado *neppure* a fare il bagno. Sono proprio pigro. *Non* faccio *niente*. Mi chiedono sempre di andare da qualche parte con loro la sera ma *non* vado *mai*. *Non* voglio andare *né* al cinema *né* in discoteca.	This summer I am not going anywhere. I have no wish to go out in this heat. My friends don't understand at all why I prefer to stay at home. I live a stone's throw from the sea but I don't even go for a swim. I am really lazy. I do nothing. They are always asking me to go somewhere with them in the evening but I never go. I don't want to go either to the cinema/movies or the disco.

• The position of the negative expression is the same with infinitives and imperatives, i.e **non** before and the second half of the negative expression after the verb:

Preferisco *non* fare *niente*.	I prefer to do *nothing*.
Non chiedergli *più*.	Do*n't* ask him *any more/again*.

(iii) Negatives in compound tenses

In compound tenses the negatives **mai, più, affatto, mica, neanche, nemmeno, neppure** can either precede or follow the past participle:

Quest'anno *non* ho *mai* fatto/*non* ho fatto *mai* il bagno nel mare.	This year I have *never* swum in the sea.
Dopo l'ultima volta, *non* mi hanno *più* chiesto/*non* mi hanno chiesto *più* di uscire con loro.	After the last time, they did*n't* ask me to go out with them *any more/again*.

• The negatives **niente, nulla, nessuno, per niente, da nessuna parte** come after the past participle:

Non sono andato *da nessuna parte* e *non* ho fatto *niente* di speciale.	I did*n't* go *anywhere* and I did *nothing* special.

In English it is possible to express a negative idea using a verb in different ways:

I went *nowhere*.	I did*n't* go *anywhere*.
I did *nothing*.	I did*n't* do *anything*.

These alternatives do not exist in Italian. In fact, in Italian it is perfectly correct in a number of cases to use two or more negatives in one sentence.

The following combinations are possible:

non ... mai da nessuna parte
non ... mai più
non ... mai nessuno
non ... mai niente
non ... più niente/nulla
non ... più nessuno

Non faccio *mai niente*.	I *never* do *anything*.
Non ho *più niente* da dire.	I have *nothing more* to say.
Durante il mese di luglio la mia famiglia *non* va *mai da nessuna parte*.	During the month of July, my family never goes anywhere.
Se continui a criticarmi, *non* farò *mai più niente*.	If you go on criticizing me, I shall *never* do *anything* again.
Quando abbiamo ospiti, mia sorella *non* dice *mai niente* a *nessuno*.	When we have guests, my sister *never* says *anything* to *anyone*.

(iv) *Negatives preceding the verb*

The negatives **nessuno** and **niente/nulla** can be the subject of a verb:

Nessuno ha telefonato.	*No one* rang.
Niente è successo.	*Nothing* has happened.

The negatives **mai, né ... né, neppure, nemmeno, neanche** can also precede the verb:

Né mia sorella *né* mio fratello vanno in vacanza quest'anno.	*Neither* my sister *nor* my brother is going on holiday/vacation this year. (note that the verb must be plural in Italian)
Mai in vita loro sono stati a casa nel mese di luglio.	*Never* in their life have they been at home in July.
Nemmeno una volta sono rimasti a casa durante questo periodo.	*Not even* once have they remained at home during this period.

 Non is omitted when the negative precedes the verb [27a(ii)].

(v)   *Senza* 'without'

Many of the negative expressions are used after **senza**, very often after an infinitive. **Non** is always omitted:

senza dire niente	without saying anything
senza vedere nessuno	without seeing anyone
senza mangiare più niente	without eating anything else
senza alcun dubbio	without any doubt

(vi)   *Negatives without a verb*

Many negative expressions can stand entirely on their own or with words other than verbs:

Che cosa hai imparato? – *Non* molto.	What have you learned? – *Not* much.
Hai detto qualcosa? – *No, niente*.	Did you say something? – *No, nothing*.
Ti hanno dato del lavoro scritto da fare a casa? – Un giorno sì e uno *no*.	Did they give you some written work to do at home? – Every other day.

Ti è piaciuto il posto?	Did you like the place? – *Not in*
– *Nient'affatto*.	*the least*.
Non ci vuoi tornare allora?	You don't want to go back there
– *Mai più*.	then. – *Never again*.
Neanch'io!	*Neither* do I!

Note also:

spero di *no*	I hope *not*
penso/credo di *no*	I think/believe *not*
vuoi uscire o *no*?	do you want to go out or *not*?

(vii)   *Non ... che* 'only'

Non ... che 'only' is used without the value of a negative:

Non **ho** *che* **un fratello.**	I have *only* one brother.

It is much more common, however, to use either **solo, sola-mente** or **soltanto** 'only' in place of **non ... che**.

Ho *solo* un fratello.	I have *only* one brother.

• Note the use of **non ... che** in the following type of con-struction with **fare** + **altro**:

Non **ha fatto** *altro che* **piovere.**	It has done *nothing but* rain.
Non **fai** *altro che* **fumare.**	You do *nothing but* smoke.

27b   Other adverbs and adverbial phrases

These answer various questions

(i)   *Quando?* 'When?': time [▶6d(vi)]

adesso/ora	now
al momento/in questo momento	at the present time
ancora	still, yet, again
a poco a poco	little by little
attualmente	at the present time
a volte	sometimes

qualche volta	sometimes
una volta	once
allora	then, at that time
a quel tempo	at that time
di buon'ora	early
di tanto in tanto	from time to time, occasionally
di quando in quando	from time to time
domani	tomorrow
dopodomani	the day after tomorrow
dopo	after, afterwards
d'ora in poi	from now on
finora	up to now, so far
fra poco	shortly
già	already
ieri	yesterday
ieri mattina	yesterday morning
ieri sera	yesterday evening, last night
l'altro ieri	the day before yesterday
improvvisamente	suddenly
ad un tratto	suddenly
tutt'ad un tratto	all of a sudden
infine	finally, in the end
intanto	meanwhile
nel frattempo	meanwhile
in passato	in the past
nel primo pomeriggio	in the early afternoon
mai	never, ever
oggi	today
oggi/questo pomeriggio	this afternoon
oggi a otto	in a week's time, a week today
ogni tanto	every now and again
ormai/oramai	by now, by then, by this time
per il momento	for the moment, for the present
poco fa	a short while ago
poi	then, next
presto	soon, early, quickly
prima	before, beforehand
prima o poi	sooner or later
proprio adesso	right now
raramente	rarely
recentemente/di recente	recently
ultimamente	lately, recently

sempre	always
quasi sempre	almost always
spesso	often
stamattina	this morning
stasera	this evening
stanotte	last night
subito	at once, immediately
tardi	late

Ci alziamo *sempre* molto *presto* anche se andiamo a letto *tardi*. *Stanotte* ho dormito poco perché ero preoccupato per mia figlia che ha perso *di recente* il suo posto di lavoro. Ha cercato *subito* un altro lavoro ma *finora* non ha trovato niente. *Attualmente*, c'è molta disoccupazione. *Prima*, c'era molto lavoro ma *poi*, *improvvisamente*, la situazione è peggiorata. Ci dispiace tanto per nostra figlia che si sposerà *fra poco*. *Prima o poi* ci sarà una ripresa economica ma *per il momento* dobbiamo tutti stringere la cinghia.

We *always* get up very *early* even if we go to bed *late*. *Last night* I didn't sleep much because I was worried about my daughter who *recently* lost her job. She *immediately* looked for another job but *up to now* she has found nothing. *At the present time*, there is a lot of unemployment. *Before*, there was lots of work but *then*, *suddenly*, the situation got worse. We feel so sorry for our daughter, who will be getting married *shortly*. *Sooner or later* there will be an economic recovery but *for the moment* we shall all have to tighten our belts.

(ii) **Come?** *'How?': manner, methods and means* [➤*6d(viii)*]

a fatica	with difficulty
(andare) a gonfie vele	(be) successful
a malincuore	reluctantly, unwillingly
a stento	barely, hardly, with difficulty
a tutto gas	at full speed, flat out
alla leggera	lightly, thoughtlessly
alla meglio	as best one can
(pagare) alla romana	(go) Dutch/halves
al passo	at walking pace
a rotta di collo	at breakneck speed
bene	well
abbastanza bene	quite well

(vedere qualcuno) di buon occhio	(look on someone) favourably/favorably
di male in peggio	from bad to worse
male	badly
per caso	by chance
in autobus	by bus
in pullman	by coach/bus
in treno	by train
in macchina	by car
in aereo	by plane
in bicicletta	by bicycle

Ho l'impressione che la situazione vada *di male in peggio*. L'anno scorso la ditta per la quale lavorava mia figlia andava *a gonfie vele*. Nel giro di pochi mesi tutto è cambiato. Mia figlia ha perso il suo lavoro e mentre prima stava *abbastanza bene* , adesso tira avanti *alla meglio*. Fa uno sforzo per prendere tutto *alla leggera* ma non è così facile.

I have a feeling that the situation is going *from bad to worse*. Last year the firm my daughter worked for was *successful*. In the space of a few months everything has changed. My daughter has lost her job and whereas before she was *quite well-off*, now she keeps going *as best she can*. She makes an effort to take everything *lightly* but it's not so easy.

(iii)   Dove? 'Where?': place [➤6d(vii)]

altrove	elsewhere
dappertutto	everywhere
da qualche parte	somewhere
da qualunque parte	anywhere
davanti	in front
dentro	in, inside
dietro	behind
di sopra	upstairs
di sotto	downstairs
fuori	outside
giù	down
indietro	behind
intorno	around
laggiù	down there
lassù	up there

lì/là	there
lontano	far away
qua e là	here and there
quaggiù	down here
quassù	up here
qui/qua	here
sopra	up, on, above
sotto	under, below
su	on, up
vicino	near, nearby

A mia figlia piace abitare *qui* e, anche se fosse possibile trovare lavoro *altrove*, non vorrebbe andare a vivere da *qualunque parte*. Siamo molto contenti che abiti *vicino*.	My daughter likes living *here* and, even if it were possible to find work *elsewhere*, she wouldn't want to go and live *anywhere*. We are pleased that she lives *nearby*.

• A number of these adverbs also function as prepositions [➤25c(viii)-(xi)].

(iv) *Quanto?* 'How much?': degree [➤6d(ix)]

abbastanza	enough, quite
altrettanto	as much
appena	hardly, scarcely, just
assai	very
meno	less
molto	a lot, much, a great deal
moltissimo	very much
parecchio	quite a lot
più	more
più o meno	more or less
piuttosto	rather
poco	little, not much
pochissimo	very little
pressappoco	approximately, roughly, about
quanto	how much
un poco/un po'	a little, a bit
sempre meno	less and less
sempre più	more and more
su per giù	more or less, roughly, about

tanto	so much
troppo	too much

È *piuttosto* difficile trovare lavoro in questa zona. Adesso che stiamo attraversando questa crisi economica c'è *sempre meno* lavoro. Quando lavorava, mia figlia guadagnava *parecchio*, se mi ricordo bene, *pressappoco* tre milioni di lire al mese, e il suo ragazzo guadagnava *altrettanto*.	It is *rather* difficult to find work in this area. Now that we are going through this economic crisis there is *less and less* work. When she was working, my daughter earned *quite a bit*, if my memory serves me right, *about* three million lire a month, and her boyfriend earned *just as much*.

(v)   *Perché?* 'Why?': reasons [➤6d(x)]

di conseguenza	consequently
perciò	therefore

La situazione attuale è *perciò* molto preoccupante.	The present situation is therefore very worrying.

(vi)   Adverbs of certainty and doubt

appunto	precisely
certo/certamente	certainly
davvero	really
esatto/esattamente	exactly
ovviamente	obviously
senz'altro	certainly
senza dubbio	undoubtedly
sì	yes
sicuro/sicuramente	certainly, surely
veramente	really
forse	perhaps
probabilmente	probably
quasi	almost

***Forse* mia figlia cambierà idea e andrà altrove in cerca di lavoro.**	*Perhaps* my daughter will change her mind and will go elsewhere in search of work.

> *Senz'altro* **troverà qualcosa. Qui** **è diventato** *quasi* **impossibile** **trovare un lavoro stabile.**
>
> She will *certainly* find something. Here it has become *almost* impossible to find a permanent job.

27c The position of adverbs in the sentence

(i) Verb + adjective/adverb

When an adverb modifies an adjective or another adverb, it is placed immediately in front of it as in English:

molto **importante**	*very* important
veramente **difficile**	*really* difficult
quasi **subito**	*almost* immediately

(ii) Verb + adverb

Adverbs that express *certainty* or *doubt* normally precede the verb:

> *Certamente*, **non sarà facile.** *Probabilmente*, **le faranno** **sapere qualcosa domani.**
>
> It will *certainly* not be easy. They will *probably* let her know something tomorrow.

- Many adverbs of time tend to come before the verb:

> *Stamattina* **ha scritto parecchie** **lettere.**
>
> This morning she wrote several letters.

However, it is not possible to give a hard-and-fast rule as adverbs are sometimes placed after the verb to create a different emphasis:

> *Domani* **andrà a parlare con** **qualcuno.** **Andrà** *domani* **a parlare con** **qualcuno.**
>
> *Tomorrow* she will go and speak to someone. She will go and speak to someone *tomorrow*.

In the first example **domani** simply indicates when the action will take place. The placing of **domani** after the verb in the second example stresses the point that the action will take place 'tomorrow' and not 'in two weeks' or 'a month' for example.

• Most adverbs, however, follow the verb they qualify:

Quando parlano *lentamente*, capisco *benissimo* ma se parlano *in fretta*, capisco *pochissimo*.	When they speak *slowly*, I understand *very well* but if they speak *quickly*, I understand *very little*.

(iii)   Compound tenses

In the case of compound tenses, the adverb usually follows the past participle:

Quando hanno parlato *lentamente* ho capito *benissimo*.	When they spoke *slowly* I understood *very well*.

However, some commonly used adverbs such as **già** 'already', **appena** 'just' and **mai** 'ever' are placed after the auxiliary:

Sono *appena* arrivati.	They have *just* arrived.
Abbiamo *già* mangiato.	We have *already* eaten.
Sei *mai* stato in Italia?	Have you *ever* been to Italy?

F
USING NUMBERS

Numerals

28a Counting: cardinal numbers

The cardinal numbers in Italian are:

1	uno (una)	22	ventidue
2	due	23	ventitré
3	tre	28	ventotto
4	quattro	30	trenta
5	cinque	31	trentuno
6	sei	38	trentotto
7	sette	40	quaranta
8	otto	50	cinquanta
9	nove	60	sessanta
10	dieci	70	settanta
11	undici	80	ottanta
12	dodici	90	novanta
13	tredici	100	cento
14	quattordici	101	centouno
15	quindici	200	duecento
16	sedici	300	trecento
17	diciassette	1.000	mille
18	diciotto	2.000	duemila
19	diciannove	10.000	diecimila
20	venti	100.000	centomila
21	ventuno		

1.000.000	un milione
1.000.000.000	un miliardo
1.000.000.000.000	un bilione

As can be seen from the above table, the cardinal numbers in Italian are fairly straightforward, though the following points should be borne in mind:

(A) Uno has a feminine form and it follows the rules of the indefinite article [▶21e] when it precedes a noun.

un libro	one book (or a book)
una rivista	one magazine (or a magazine)
uno studente	one student (or a student)

(B) Zero takes the plural **due zeri, tre zeri**

(C) The plural of **mille** is **mila**:

mille lire
duemila studenti

> **(D) Milione, bilione, miliardo** have plural forms (**milioni, bilioni, miliardi**) and require the preposition **di** before a following noun:

tre milioni di abitanti
cinque miliardi di dollari

> They do not require the **di** when followed by another number:

duemilionicinquecentomila lire

> Numbers such as the one above can be separated by **e**:

duemilioni e cinquecentomila lire.

> All other numbers are invariable:

quattro bambini, quattro bambine
duecento, trecento

> **(E)** When **uno** and **otto** are part of numbers above 20 then the final vowel of **venti, trenta,** etc. is omitted:

ventuno, trentotto, settantuno, novantotto, etc.

> **(F) Tre** has an accent with compound numbers:

ventitré, duecentotré, etc.

> **(G)** In Italian a full stop/period is used between thousands, and a comma to separate decimal points. The opposite applies in English [➤2b(vii)].

5.000	5,000
2,83	2.83

> **(H)** In spoken Italian it is quite common to use abbreviated forms, particularly to indicate the hundreds above a thousand:

settemila e tre = **settemila e trecento**

 This form could lead to confusion as **settemila e tre** can be interpreted as 7003 but if you hear this said at a market or in a shop, for example, then you can be sure that it means 7300.

28b Arranging in order: ordinal numbers

(i) The ordinal numbers - **primo** 'first',etc. - are adjectives
[►22] and must agree in gender and number with the
noun(s) they qualify. The most commonly used ordinal
numbers are:

primo	first
secondo	second
terzo	third
quarto	fourth
quinto	fifth
sesto	sixth
settimo	seventh
ottavo	eighth
nono	ninth
decimo	tenth

The remainder of the ordinal numbers are formed by removing
the final vowel of the cardinal number and adding **-esimo.**

undicesimo, dodicesimo, ventesimo, centesimo, millesimo, etc.

(ii) Ordinal numbers generally precede the noun except in the
case of monarchs and popes:

la prima volta	the first time
il secondo giorno	the second day
l'undicesimo secolo	the eleventh century

but

Enrico ottavo	Henry the Eighth
Pio nono	Pius the Ninth

Note: From the 'thirteenth' to the 'twentieth century' there is an alternative
form in Italian:

il Duecento/il tredicesimo secolo	the 13th century
il Trecento/il quattordicesimo secolo,	the 14th century
etc.	
il Novecento/il ventesimo secolo	the 20th century

The alternative form, written with a capital letter, is used particularly when referring to art, history, literature, etc. It is also
possible to use Roman numerals:

nel XIV secolo	in the 14th century

(iii) *Ordinal numbers can be written in two ways: I, II, or 1°, 1ª, 2°, 2ª, etc.*

 The ordinal number is only used with the first day of the month. Thereafter, cardinal numbers are used.

il primo agosto but **il 2 (due) agosto,** etc.

28c *Sharing out: fractions*

(i) *The most commonly used fractions are:*

un quarto	a quarter
tre quarti	three quarters
un terzo	a third
due terzi	two thirds
mezzo/la metà	half

(ii) *All other fractions are formed using ordinal numbers:*

un quinto	a/one fifth
tre quinti	three fifths

(iii) *'Half' as an adjective is **mezzo**, which agrees with the noun it refers to:*

mezzo litro di vino	half a litre/liter of wine
mezza bottiglia di rosso	half a bottle of red (wine)

Following a noun, the same rule applies and it is linked by **e**:

un'ora e mezza	an hour and a half
un litro e mezzo	a litre/liter and a half

'Half' as a noun is **la metà**:

Ho già speso la metà del mio stipendio.	I have already spent half my salary.
Sono riuscito a fare la metà del mio lavoro.	I have managed to do half my work.

(iv) *Where the fraction is followed by a noun, the two are linked by **di**:*

tre quarti della popolazione	three quarters of the population

un terzo di questo gruppo	a third of this group
un quinto del mio tempo libero	a fifth of my free time

28d *Grouping and estimating: collective numbers*

Italian has a few collective numbers which are useful for giving an approximate number. They are all joined to the following noun by **di**:

un paio	a couple, a pair
una decina	about ten
una dozzina	a dozen
una quindicina	about fifteen, about two weeks, a fortnight
una ventina	about twenty
una trentina	about thirty
un centinaio	about a hundred
centinaia	hundreds
un migliaio	about a thousand
migliaia	thousands
milioni	millions

Ieri c'erano *migliaia di* macchine in città. Per arrivare a casa ho impiegato *un paio di* ore, un viaggio che normalmente faccio in *una trentina di* minuti.	Yesterday there were *thousands of* cars in town. To get home it took me *a couple of* hours, a journey I normally do in *about thirty* minutes.

[To express approximation, see also 25c(vi).]

Telling the time

To ask the time, the standard questions are **Che ora è?** or **Che ore sono?**

As in English, there are two ways of giving the time: the conversational way and the one used for timetables of trains, buses, airlines, etc.

29a Time: the conversational style

È l'una.	It's one o'clock.
Sono le due.	It's two o'clock.
Sono le tre.	It's three o'clock, etc.
È l'una e cinque.	It's five past/after one.
Sono le due e dieci.	It's ten past/after two.
Sono le tre e un quarto..	It's a quarter past/after three.
Sono le tre e quindici.	It's three fifteen.
Sono le quattro e mezzo/mezza.	It's half past four.
Sono le quattro e trenta.	It's four thirty.
Sono le cinque meno un quarto..	It's a quarter to/before five.
Sono le quattro e quarantacinque.	It's four forty-five.
Sono le sette meno cinque.	It's five to/before seven.
Sono le sei e cinquantacinque.	It's six fifty-five.
È mezzogiorno.	It's midday.
È mezzanotte.	It's midnight.

• For **l'una** 'one o'clock' the verb is singular and the feminine form is used because **ora** is understood. For the remainder of the other hours (from two to twelve) the verb is plural and **le due,** etc. are feminine plural, **ore** being understood.

29b Time: the timetable style

When using this style the words such as **un quarto** and **mezzo** are discarded in favour of figures, given according to the 24-hour clock.

le nove e quindici	09:15
le diciassette e trenta	17:30

• At a particular time is **all'una, alle due** …

A che ora parte il treno? – *Alle* **quattordici e venti.**	At what time does the train leave? – *At* 14:20

- There is no Italian equivalent of 'a.m.' and 'p.m.' Where necessary, use **di/della mattina, di/del pomeriggio, di sera, di notte.**

Partiamo alle otto *della mattina* **e speriamo di arrivare alle due** *del pomeriggio.*	We are leaving at eight *a.m.* and we hope to arrive at two *p.m.*
L'ultima volta che abbiamo fatto lo stesso viaggio, siamo partiti alle dieci *di sera* **e siamo arrivati alle tre** *di notte.*	The last time we did the same journey, we left at ten *in the evening* and arrived at three *in the morning.*

- The following are useful:

Il negozio è chiuso *dalle* **12.30** *alle* **14.30.**	The shop is closed *from* 12:30 *to* 14:30.
La libreria è aperta *fino alle* **20.30.**	The bookshop is open *until* 8:30 p.m.
Arrivano *verso (circa)* **le nove.**	They are arriving *about* nine o'clock.
Devo essere a casa *per* **le dieci.**	I must be at home *by* nine.
È ora di **mangiare.**	*It's time to* eat.
Che ora *fai?*	What time *do you make it?*
Sono le due *passate.*	It's *gone* two o'clock.
Alle undici *precise.*	At eleven o'clock *sharp.*
Il mio orologio è *avanti di cinque minuti.*	My watch is *five minutes fast.*
Il mio orologio è *indietro di tre minuti.*	My watch is *three minutes slow.*
Ci vediamo *fra poco.*	We shall see each other *soon.*
Si sono trasferiti a Firenze due mesi *fa.*	They moved to Florence two months *ago.*

[For adverbs and adverbial phrases of time ➤27b(i).]

The calendar

Unless they start the sentence, days and months in Italian are written with a small letter [➤2a(ii)].

With the exception of **la domenica** 'Sunday', the days are masculine. The months of the year are all masculine.

30a   Days of the week

lunedì	Monday
martedì	Tuesday
mercoledì	Wednesday
giovedì	Thursday
venerdì	Friday
sabato	Saturday
domenica	Sunday

 'On Monday' is **lunedì**, 'on Mondays' is **il lunedì**.

Note also:

oggi	today
ieri	yesterday
l'altro ieri	the day before yesterday
domani	tomorrow
dopodomani	the day after tomorrow
sabato prossimo	next Saturday
lunedì scorso	last Monday
stamattina	this morning
oggi pomeriggio	this afternoon
stasera	this evening
stanotte	last night

Stanotte ho dormito male perché avevo mangiato troppo.	I slept badly last night because I had eaten too much.

30b   Months and seasons

gennaio	January
febbraio	February
marzo	March
aprile	April
maggio	May
giugno	June
luglio	July
agosto	August
settembre	September
ottobre	October
novembre	November
dicembre	December
la primavera	spring
l'estate	summer
l'autunno	autumn/fall
l'inverno	winter
nel mese di gennaio/a gennaio/	
in gennaio	in January
all'inizio di/ai primi di febbraio	at the beginning of February
a metà (di) luglio	in the middle of July
alla fine di agosto	at the end of August

'In spring', 'in autumn/fall', etc. is **in primavera** and **in autunno** but with 'summer' and 'winter' **di** is also possible and is used to indicate an habitual action.

D'estate vado al mare ma	In summer I go to the seaside but
d'inverno vado a sciare	in winter I go skiing.

30c   Dates

The ordinal number **il primo** [▶28b(i)] is used for the first day of each month and the cardinal numbers [▶28a] for all the other days. Sometimes **di** 'of' follows the number but it is not essential. When writing a date in a letter heading, the definite article is omitted.

il primo (di) marzo	March 1st/1 March
but	
il due aprile	April 2nd/2 April
il ventun novembre	November 21st/21 November

il trentuno ottobre   October 31st/31 October

These would normally be written **il 1° marzo, il 2 aprile, il 21 novembre, il 31 ottobre**. Note that **ventuno** and **trentuno** tend to drop the **o** with months beginning with a consonant.

Note **l'otto maggio (l'8 maggio)** and **l'undici settembre (l'11 settembre)**, as both numbers begin with a vowel.

'On' a date is expressed by simply using the definite article.

Quando arrivano? – *Il* **nove giugno.**	When are they arriving? – *On* June 9th.

• Some useful expressions to note:

Che data è oggi? – È il 15 dicembre.	What is the date today? – It is the fifteenth of December.
Quanti ne abbiamo (del mese)? – Ne abbiamo cinque.	What day is it today? – It's the fifth.
Che giorno è oggi? – È mercoledì.	What day of the week is it today? – It's Wednesday.
In che giorno siete liberi?	On what day are you free?

30d   *Years*

Years are expressed using the cardinal numbers preceded by the definite article.

il 1990 (millenovecentonovanta)   1990
il 1996 è un anno bisestile   1996 is a leap year

To express 'in', use **in** + the definite article (**nel**).

In che anno sei nato? – Sono nato *nel* **1962 (millenovecentosessantadue).**	In what year were you born? – I was born *in* 1962.

When the complete date is written out, the article is omitted before the year.

Sono nato il 14 marzo, 1945.	I was born on March 14th/March 14, 1945.

Years are frequently shortened in everyday speech:

Ho cominciato ad imparare l'italiano nel '79 (settantanove).	I started to learn Italian in '79.

Note also the way of expressing decades:

Mi è sempre piaciuta la musica degli anni '60 (sessanta).	I have always liked the music of the 60s.

30e *Age*

Age is expressed in Italian using the verb **avere** + number + **anni**:

Mia sorella ha diciassette anni.	My sister is seventeen.

Anni would normally be omitted in response to the question 'How old are you?'

Quanti anni hai? Sedici (or **ne ho sedici**).	How old are you? Sixteen (or I am sixteen).

[For the use of **ne** to replace a noun ➤23f.]

Note the following expressions to convey approximate age:

Il mio collega ha *una trentina di anni*.	My colleague is *around thirty*.
Mia zia è *sulla sessantina*.	My aunt is *about sixty*.
Mio cognato è *sui quarant'anni*.	My brother-in-law is *about forty*.

• Note also:

un dodicenne	a twelve year old boy
una ventenne	a twenty year old girl

 This form can only be used with the numbers from eleven upwards. Remove the final vowel of the cardinal number and add **-enne**.

G
INDEX

Index

N.B.   Cross references are to chapters and paragraphs

O

P